PAUPERS AND POOR RELIEF
in New York City and Its Rural Environs, 1700–1830

PAUPERS AND POOR RELIEF

in New York City and Its Rural
Environs, 1700–1830

Robert E. Cray, Jr.

TEMPLE UNIVERSITY PRESS
Philadelphia

Temple University Press, Philadelphia 19122
Copyright © 1988 by Temple University. All rights reserved
Published 1988
Printed in the United States of America

LIBRARY OF CONGRESS CATALOGING-IN-PUBLICATION DATA

Cray, Robert E.
Paupers and poor relief.

Bibliography: p.
Includes index.
1. Urban poor—New York (N.Y.)—History—18th century. 2. Urban poor—New York (N.Y.)—History—19th century. 3. Public welfare—New York, (N.Y.)—History—18th century. 4. Public welfare—New York (N.Y.)—History—19th century. 5. New York (N.Y.)—Social conditions. I. Title.
HV4046.N6C7   1988   362.5'8'097471   87-26693
ISBN 0-87722-542-7

The paper used in this publication meets the minimum requirements of American National Standard for Information Sciences—Permanence of Paper for Printed Library Materials, ANSI Z39.48-1984

To my parents
ROBERT E. CRAY, SR.
and
EILEEN A. CRAY

Contents

	List of Tables	ix
	Acknowledgments	xi
	Introduction	3
I	Land of Promise: Economic and Social Portrait of Early New York	8
II	The Evolving System of Poor Relief, 1700–1750	35
III	The System Under Siege: Restructuring Public Welfare, 1750–1790	65
IV	The Almshouse Triumphant?: The Response of the City and Countryside to the Poor, 1790–1830	100
V	Paupers and Wanderers: The Identity of the Rural Poor, 1800–1830	136
VI	This Confusion of Dialects: The Dependent Poor of Manhattan, 1800–1830	168

Conclusion	196
Appendices	201
Notes	203
Selected Bibliography	247
Index	263

List of Tables

1	Poor Rates for the Parish of Rye, 1724–1776	52
2	Gender of Keepers and Paupers in Eighteenth-Century Rye, East Chester, Hempstead, Huntington, and Brookhaven	59
3	Percentage and Occupation of Non-County Recruits, Queens, Suffolk, and Westchester, 1759	89
4	Geographic Origins of Non-County Recruits, Queens, Suffolk, and Westchester, 1759	89
5	Poor Tax and Public Dependents of Hempstead, 1751–1773	93
6	A General Account of Electors in New York City, 1796	104
7	Poor Rates for Selected Towns, 1806–1809	124
8	Public Dependents in Queens, Suffolk, and Westchester, 1822–1823	139
9	Public Dependents in Queens, Suffolk, and Westchester, 1825	141
10	Growth of Population and Number of Public Dependents, Queens and Suffolk, 1825–1835	143
11	Percentage and Number of Foreign Nationals, 1821	172
12	The Foreign and Domestic Poor of Manhattan's Almshouse, 1800–1830	173

13	Irish Inmates in Manhattan's Almshouse, 1805–1830	174
14	British and German Inmates in Manhattan's Almshouse, 1805–1830	178
15	The Domestic Poor in Manhattan's Almshouse, 1800–1830	181
16	Household Status and Race of the Transported Poor, New York City, 1808–1811	185
17	Place of Origin of the Transported Poor, New York City, 1808–1811	186
18	Sex Ratio of Whites and Blacks in New York City, 1813	189

Acknowledgments

Many people helped in the study and publication of this work. The willingness of individuals to read and criticize countless versions and drafts of this manuscript attests to the generosity of spirit in the history profession. Naturally, I take full responsibility for any errors that may have gone unnoticed. I would first like to thank several faculty members from the State University of New York, Stony Brook, for their assistance over the years. Jackson T. Main proved a model graduate advisor, offering constructive criticism and steadfast support. I owe much to him. Wilbur R. Miller, who first introduced me to the new social history, played an important role during the evolution of this study. Ned Landsman taught me to ask questions about the nature of my research that I would not have asked, and he provided me with a keen appreciation for the written word. A SUNY Intercampus Graduate Fellowship to New York University allowed me to test out early ideas about my work; it also enabled me to profit from the comments of Carl Prince, Daniel Walkowitz, and Patricia U. Bonomi. A year as a visiting assistant professor at the University of Puget Sound provided me with a congenial academic environment as well as travel money to present a paper on an aspect of my work. I would like to thank Terry Cooney and the rest of the history department.

    Curators, archivists, and librarians generously aided me. Anyone studying New York City history can appreciate the helpful staff at the New York Historical Society. So, too, I benefited from the people at the Municipal Archives of the City of New York, the New York Public Library, the Ward Melville Library at Stony Brook, and the Handley Collection at the Smithtown Pubic Library. Local historians and town clerks at Huntington, Hempstead, Bedford, and Brookhaven gave me access to records. I would also like to thank the editors of the University Press of Virginia, *Slavery and Abolition,* and their publishers, Frank Cass and Co., Ltd., for allowing me to reproduce previously published material.

Additional assistance of one sort or another was furnished at the later stages of this work. George E. Webb graciously volunteered to read and criticize the manuscript, for which I am thankful. Few people have had a more considerate colleague. Patrick Reagan played no direct role in this study but offered good company as we pondered the ironies of academic life. The editors at Temple University Press and the manuscript referees helped tremendously with their thoughtful comments and professional expertise. Janet M. Francendese and Doris B. Braendel polished the manuscript, while Thomas P. Slaughter offered a valuable critique along with another, anonymous, referee. Personal friends provided solace and support also. William S. Jugus gave me a place to stay and a cheery welcome in Virginia during my auto treks between Tennessee and New York. Kerry Cadden convinced me to be optimistic, as did her parents, John and Phyllis. Paul Chase and Janet Weigman were always there. Mary Rose Lamb remained a loyal and true friend, supportive of my work during trying times. And my parents—to whom this book is dedicated—deserve the greatest thanks of all.

PAUPERS AND POOR RELIEF
in New York City and Its Rural Environs, 1700–1830

Introduction

America is often revered as a land of plenty. Perhaps no single image has so marked the American character, symbolizing the people and their way of life. For countless waves of immigrants, past and present, America has meant a new beginning; here the poverty of Europe, Asia, and Latin America would be left behind. The notion of a better life first appears in the promotional tracts of seventeenth-century colonies, where proprietors and investors alike spoke glowingly about the abundance of resources. Subsequent accounts from the eighteenth century, notably Crevecoeur's *Letters from an American Farmer,* echoed the theme of plenty, detailing the solid comforts of the American yeomanry. By the early nineteenth century the opening of the trans-Mississippi West reconfirmed the optimism of earlier chroniclers, unleashing a century of boosterism. And in truth such accounts, however embellished, have a basis in fact; America did possess a rich, verdant environment. Large tracts of fertile land complemented forests teeming with game, and fish proved so plentiful along the coast and in the interior lakes and streams that they could be caught with ease. Equally significant, the land was often inexpensive to acquire—once the native Americans had been removed. A farmer could stake a claim, plow the soil, raise a crop, and become relatively self-sufficient with the assistance of neighbors and the occasional merchant. For many, America was indeed the "best poor man's country."[1]

This roseate portrait, however, contrasts sharply with the darker side of American society, in which scarcity and poverty sometimes figured prominently. To destitute Americans the notion of abundance was an illusion, especially when they required public assistance to maintain themselves. Anyone who was aged or young, impaired, sick, or crippled, or unemployed, and without other resources, saw a different America from the one Crevecoeur described; it was an America of dependence. Although destitute persons were always a minority, they still proved numerous enough during the eighteenth and early nineteenth centuries to create concern among the citizenry, who sought some efficient means to provide for them. In an age of minimal government and low taxes, public welfare expenditures often represented the most costly item in the city or town budget. As such, it stimulated people to consider carefully the types of relief provided. Poor relief could come in many forms—at home, among neighbors, with town-appointed keepers, and inside institutions. Of course, the quality of such assistance varied, as might the philosophy behind it. Civil officials had to balance a sense of compassion with a sense of economy, favoring one more than the other depending upon the region and period. Poor relief was an integral and changing aspect of early American society, and poverty was a very real issue for local municipalities.[2]

Poverty and poor relief have not gone unnoticed by historians of early America. During the past few decades an impressive amount of literature has emerged, describing more precisely not only the extent of poverty but the response of society toward its indigent members. The resulting wave of scholarly treatises has documented a society where economic inequality and social stratification were notable features; works by Gary Nash, James Henretta, and Edward Pessen have led the way in this regard.[3] Substantial work has also revealed a society determined to revamp public welfare. Perhaps the most significant account remains David J. Rothman's *The Discovery of the Asylum*, which helped to establish the intellectual contours of the debate on the nature of poor relief. Sweeping aside the dull, legalistic treatments authored by social welfare experts during the 1930s and 1940s, Rothman developed a bold thesis to explain the origins of institutional relief. Briefly stated, his view was that poverty was a relatively minor problem for much of the eighteenth century, with poor relief remaining an informal system based primarily upon home assistance. The few existing almshouses, according to Rothman, were little more than extensions of the home environment; their philosophy and operation reflected a familial ethos that had little actual resemblance to an institutional viewpoint per se. The early nineteenth century, however, witnessed a widespread adoption of the almshouse—a response to the growing, if still small, number of dependent persons and a belief that such persons posed a threat to the society. Americans began to perceive poor people less as victims and more as outcasts, a class of people whose various moral failings, such as intemperance, gambling, and indolence, had led to their destitute condition. The best way to assist these folks was inside an almshouse. Here they would be removed from the temptations of the world and possibly rehabilitated. Consequently, the almshouse itself became a more formal institution, governed by strict rules and punishments. By the Age of Jackson the almshouse had emerged as the cornerstone of the public welfare system in city and countryside.[4]

This particular interpretation has not gone unquestioned. Such historians as Gary Nash and John K. Alexander have explored more closely the eighteenth-century response; they discovered, for instance, that the almshouse was not necessarily the home-like building that Rothman depicted. Urban officials often treated eighteenth-century poor people little differently from their nineteenth-century counterparts, expecting them to work at various tasks to defray the cost of maintenance.[5] But these historians, by and large, have restricted their investigations to urban areas, leaving untouched the countryside, where most Americans resided. Despite work by Douglas L. Jones on the rural poor of eighteen-century Massachusetts, we still lack a clear picture of village welfare practices. Historians interested in community studies treat poor relief as one aspect of village life, seldom offering much information; and Rothman insists that rural welfare remained centered upon household relief until the 1820s, when the almshouse materialized.[6]

Further questions persist over the evolutionary development of public welfare during the eighteenth and nineteenth centuries. How exactly did it evolve? Did welfare follow a straightforward course from home relief to institutional relief, or was it characterized by constant policy shifts between traditional and newer methods? If the latter, what circumstances compelled city and village to adopt different methods? Was it, as Rothman has claimed, an effort to promote social stability on the part of a concerned citizenry? Or did economics play a role? Again, the answers are uncertain.

Historians have also not illuminated the local dynamics of urban and rural life that were mainly responsible for the changing mechanisms of public welfare. Implicit in the works of Rothman and others is an image of destitute persons as hapless victims ensnared by the manipulative policies of civil officials. Ideological currents, in turn, guided the actions of the authorities. Yet public welfare was more than an intellectual arena for the theories of reformers; it also represented a system of relationships between the community and its poor citizens. The actual method of assistance had its genesis from within local communities, urban and rural, rather than in the minds of social reformers. This was especially true in village society. Although urban citizens responded to the plight of residents, it was the rural freeholders who took a more active part in establishing new means of supporting their poor neighbors. The town meeting served as a forum for discussion, with any proposed welfare alterations requiring the consent of the villagers. Local concerns, then, supplanted ideological currents in the matters of assistance.

And what of poor people themselves? So much attention has been directed toward the method of poor relief that the danger exists we might forget about the people who found themselves needing such assistance. While many destitute persons were powerless to alter their immediate economic circumstances, some could change location, moving with relative ease through both urban and rural environments. This mobility strongly contradicts assumptions about their helplessness. In fact, a substantial body of literature reveals that the inarticulate folks were often defiant of authority and quick to protest injustices. If some were too old or feeble to argue, others disobeyed rules, defied officials, and subverted poor relief methods to meet their own needs. Michael Katz has demonstrated this for poor Americans of the nineteenth century. What needs to be done is to place this spirit of resistance into the context of earlier methods of poor relief, to realize that poor people also had a response to poor relief.[7]

This book attempts to explore these various aspects by employing a regional approach to poverty and poor relief. New York City and the nearby countryside of Queens, Suffolk, and Westchester counties between 1700 and 1830 offer an appropriate setting; it was during this period that Manhattan rose to prominence as a commercial center, eventually drawing the countryside into its economic orbit. Although these environments were increasingly connected by networks of trade, they possessed distinct economies—commercial as opposed to agrarian—along with different degrees of social cohesiveness. The crowded, ethnically diverse seaport had a different character from the more homogeneous farming communities, yet city and countryside had one concern in common—the poor. Like so many seaports,

Manhattan attracted migrants and immigrants, some of whom were penniless or too ill to work. Then, too, periodic epidemics and depressions sent many clamoring for relief. By 1817 perhaps as many as one-seventh of the population received some form of assistance.[8] The countryside could fall prey to natural disasters that might reduce crop yields, while economic catastrophe might reduce prices for surplus crops. The continued maturation of rural society—that is, the growing population and the limited supply of arable land—made the threshold between comfort and subsistence wider for some. In Long Island and Westchester the townsfolk relied upon several methods of assistance, resorting to home relief, pauper auctions, and poor farms; sometimes they alternated among all three in a short period of time.

This study also tries to say something about poor people themselves. After all, they were the people for whom the system had been designed. Poor relief records from city and countryside, despite an evident class bias, do allow for a greater understanding of poor persons as individuals. Not only can we observe their desperate condition, but we can also say something about the type of people who required assistance and their response to welfare. Because New York City and its rural environs was a multi-racial, multi-ethnic society, we can see how different poor folk survived. This is an important point. In a nation that even today champions a belief in self-made individuals, that delights in a rags to riches success story, it helps to understand something about those individuals who did not prosper.

CHAPTER I

Land of Promise: Economic and Social Portrait of Early New York

*I*n 1692 Charles Lodwick wrote to his uncle, Francis Lodwick, a member of the Royal Society, and enclosed an account of New York. Apologizing for the delay—it had been four years since he agreed to furnish a description of Manhattan—Lodwick resolutely set out to honor the commitment. Although a newcomer to the city, Lodwick had involved himself quickly in political affairs, first as a supporter and later as an opponent of Jacob Leisler and his failed rebellion. He knew some of the leading citizens and had made the acquaintance of the "gravest sages," men who provided him with information about the city. Consequently, his enclosed narrative is rich in detail and offers an insider's view of the land and the people. Lodwick stressed the benefits of a fair climate and abundant resources. Weather and soil, he said, combined to supply "plenty of all sorts of provisions needful for ye support of mankind." Fruit trees did well despite the sharp frosts of winter that made apricots, for example, "very rare." The bounty of the sea proved no less plentiful, for fish could be taken in great quantities and provided "excellent food." Admittedly, the cattle weighed less than in Europe and the horses too often ran wild, but these problems, thought Lodwick, could be corrected. Only the inhabitants drew much criticism from the author; too many people from different nations not only gave Manhattan an unusually diverse population but also constituted "the chiefest unhappiness." But this criticism, which might have reflected Lodwick's own disgust over ethnic divisions in the wake of Leisler's rebellion, could not obscure the potential richness of the land. At one point in the narrative Lodwick mused, "Doubtless this country has gold or silver." Such thoughts, if fanciful, are understandable considering New York's natural resources. This was a land of opportunity.[1]

Such praise was not reserved for New York City alone. To the east of Manhattan was Long Island—appropriately named for its long, narrow land mass that extended over one hundred miles. Daniel Denton, a resident and magistrate of Jamaica, Long Island, had published an account of the province of New York in 1670 that in some ways surpassed Lodwick's description of Manhattan. Long Island received special mention. Denton was almost lyrical in detailing the fruitfulness of the Island, where "grapes, great and small, Huckleberries and Cranberries, Plums of various sorts, Raspberries and Strawberries," abounded and flourished. The strawberries, in fact, were so abundant according to Denton that the fields and woods appeared to be "dyed red" every June. Like Manhattan, the Island offered opportunities for those willing to reap them. It provided stands of fine timber and rivers stocked with fish. As for livestock, there existed "no place in the north of America better" than Long Island with its "precious meadows and marshes." Farmers could also expect to raise "all sorts of English grains," besides such crops as "Tobacco, Hemp, Flax, Pumpkins, Melons, etc." For those interested in commercial enterprises, Denton recommended whaling; in fact, many Long Islanders on the south shore already employed small boats "to make a trade" in this business to their "no small benefit." The large school of seals with their "excellent oil" provided similar possibilities to any "skillful man" with an eye for profits. Clearly, this was no ordinary land, and Denton in describing the entire province remarked "that if there be any terrestrial happiness to be had by people of all ranks, especially of any inferior rank, it must certainly be here."[2]

Similar sentiments were expressed, albeit more cautiously, for Westchester county. Located north of Manhattan and across the Sound from Long Island, the county had no Lodwick or Denton to praise its potential. Indeed, the most telling account of early Westchester came not from a resident but from a wayfarer, Sarah Knight. In 1704 she traveled from her home in Boston to New York City and then returned to Boston, passing through such settlements as New Rochelle, East Chester, and Mamaroneck. Perhaps more comfortable with the urban environment of the Puritan metropolis, Knight found the rustic atmosphere of the county occasionally depressing, especially the primitive accommodations with their crude furnishings. East Chester, for example, Knight considered "a very miserable poor place," in part because of her difficulty in securing shelter and then having to spend the night, sick, in an uncomfortable bed. Nevertheless, she also found much to praise in Westchester. The town of New Rochelle illustrated the economic potential of the county. When passing through the settlement, Knight noted with evident approval the "good handsome houses" in addition to the "three fine taverns." More important, the town possessed "an abundance of land well fined and cleared," which so impressed her that she would have been happy to settle there. At nearby Mamaroneck, Knight observed a "neat, though little place, with a navigable river before it," as well as several "good buildings," evident signs of prosperity. Here was proof that despite its occasional drawbacks the county could furnish a solid existence for some.[3]

These three accounts provide a brief glimpse of New York City and its rural environs to the north and east during the late seventeenth and early eighteenth centuries. If not always flattering or totally accurate, they do reveal a generally prosperous region that allowed many of the inhabitants a decent livelihood. Natural resources proved abundant. Plant and animal life flourished. Of course, there existed varying degrees of comfort among the settlers, as Knight's comments about East Chester reveal, but southern New York would seem to have had more to praise than to condemn.

The island of Manhattan at first glance appears little different from its neighbors to the north and east. Like them, the island's geography had been shaped and molded by glaciers, which transformed the landscape, depositing soil and rocks in their wake while carving out ridges and valleys. The effects of this could be seen in the middle of Manhattan, where rocky and hilly terrain dominated. Along the northern and southern portions more level land was evident. Over time the environment evolved into a mixture of fields, woods, and marshes, much of it quite lush. The smell of wildflowers drifted across the island in spring. Such a description might also be applied to various parts of Long Island and Westchester, but Manhattan had one great distinction: the tiny island possessed a sheltered, deep-water harbor, one of the finest in North America. Vessels that passed through the narrows, which separated Long Island from Staten Island, entered a huge bay that offered a safe anchorage from storms. Once in the bay ships could travel either north up the Hudson River into the interior or east along the East River into Long Island Sound. Manhattan, then, was well positioned, surrounded by water yet near to land, an excellent site for a settlement.[4]

The Dutch were the first Europeans to exploit the region. In 1609 Henry Hudson, an Englishman employed by the Dutch East Indies Company, entered the harbor and sailed up along the river that now bears his name, searching for a passage to the Indies. Unsuccessful in his quest, Hudson returned to his sponsors with news of his voyage. His employers, however, did little in the following years to develop the land, for they preferred to invest in Asian markets. A few small trading posts marked the extent of the Dutch East Indies Company's presence in the region. The Dutch West Indies Company, which acquired control of the area in 1621, embarked on a more ambitious policy. They decided to settle Manhattan and use it as a base of operation for the fur trade. By 1626 company officials had purchased the island from the Indians and established the town of New Amsterdam, which was located on the southeastern tip of Manhattan.

The settlement at first consisted of a fort, a countinghouse, and thirty bark-covered houses; several farms were scattered along the East River by 1628. Into the town came a flow of the beaver pelts so much in demand by fashion-conscious Europeans. Although the colony never matched the expectations of the company, the town matured into a commercial center, populated by an astonishing array of people. When Isaac Jogues, the French missionary, visited Manhattan in 1643, he described a community in the incipient stages of urban development; three large ships in the harbor testified to the commercial tone of the town, as did the artisans who practiced their trades alongside the fort. More amazing was the degree of ethnic diversity. Father Jogues reported that eighteen languages could be heard—a remarkable total for a city of fewer than one thousand residents. Not surprisingly, these individuals adhered to a number of religious faiths, for along with Dutch Calvinists could be seen Puritans, Lutherans, Catholics, Jews, and Huguenots; some belonged to no particular church, much to the dismay of Dutch religious authorities. Perhaps no other town in mainland North American could boast such a pluralistic community.[5]

Life in early Manhattan had its drawbacks. The town possessed a ramshackle appearance in places, guarded by a fort in various stages of disrepair and serviced by a meetinghouse that was occasionally little better. Settlers complained about inept officials and the lack of social services. Indian attacks, moreover, sometimes threatened the town, forcing the residents to take refuge behind the protective palisades of Wall Street. Even the harbor lacked a wharf to facilitate shipping. Much of the difficulty could be attributed to the particular character of the Dutch colony; it was, after all, a company-sponsored settlement, which had been designed as a commercial outpost rather than a full-fledged community. The residents, some of them employees of the Company, found themselves in an awkward situation, plagued by innumerable restrictions and too few actual rights. They desired greater autonomy. The Company was more interested in recouping its investments. Tensions arose between the two parties. Only with the arrival in 1647 of the new governor, Peter Stuyvesant, did conditions change for the better. A loyal officer of the Dutch West Indies Company, Stuyvesant was a military man with a penchant for getting things done. Even the inhabitants, who chafed under the Governor's autocratic style of management, considered him an energetic, if harsh, leader. Stuyvesant negotitated treaties, passed fire ordinances, built a wharf, and refurbished the meetinghouse. The Company, meanwhile, granted the settlers a greater share of political power, allowing them to elect local officials in 1652. Stuyvesant continued to dominate affairs, but the settlers at least had the framework of a local government. By 1664 Manhattan was a prosperous, reasonably ordered community of perhaps fifteen hundred inhabitants.[6]

Beyond Manhattan, Dutch authority extended outward in varying degrees. The villagers along the banks of the Hudson River up to Fort Orange were within the Company's sphere of influence, as were those on Staten Island and the west coast of Long Island, later Brooklyn. There existed a strong Dutch presence in most of these places; even the English settlers in such western Long Island towns as Flatbush and Gravesend accepted Dutch rule. Further south in the Delaware Bay area the Dutch also succeeded in impressing their authority upon the Swedes, who had earlier formed a colony there. Yet limits existed to Dutch influence. Further east on Long Island and north of Manhattan in what would become Westchester few Dutch settlers appeared. Most of the territory remained inhabited by the Indians. Thus, it was an easy matter for migrating New Englanders to push into the region, sometimes in defiance of Dutch claims.[7]

New England expansion was most evident on the eastern end of Long Island. By boat it was but a short trip across the Sound to the north fork or by way of the ocean to the south fork of the Island. Settlers here were well beyond the reach of the Dutch. Eager for farms, small groups of individuals along with their families settled along the coast during the 1640s, bargained with the Indians for the land, and distributed small parcels among themselves. By this means the settlements of East Hampton, Southampton, and Southold developed—virtual replicas of New England covenant communities with their strong communal and religious emphases. They would be followed shortly by yet other settlements, founded by groups of like-minded people, who established the towns of Brookhaven and Huntington during the 1650s. Within all these communities Puritan ministers shepherded the settlers, preaching the word of God on the Sabbath and inviting the faithful to partake of the Lord's Supper. The town meetings handled the everyday affairs of the secular world, electing officials, dispensing land, and levying taxes.[8] For the first few years the townsfolk concentrated on taming the land, which required cutting trees and cultivating fields. Indian troubles were few. Despite occasional incidents, the two cultures managed to coexist, in part because the native population declined rapidly due to disease. Politically, these settlements remained under the jurisdiction of Connecticut.[9]

Further west, however, migrating New Englanders had to contend with the Dutch, who claimed jurisdiction over the territory just west of present-day Suffolk. In what would become Queens county the settlements of Oyster Bay, Hempstead, Flushing, Newtown, and Jamaica appeared in the 1640s and 1650s. These communities—with the exception of Oyster Bay—acknowledged Dutch authority; even so, they remained relatively autonomous when it came to local affairs. The town meetings were usually the main forum of government, as on eastern Long Island, dealing with the demands of the settlers in regard to land distribution. Although the majority of the residents were Calvinists, either Presbyterians or Independents, small numbers of Quakers found the region a refuge—something that would seldom occur in eastern Long Island. Indeed, town officials in Flushing struck a blow for religious freedom in 1654, when they refused to obey Dutch laws against harboring Quakers, claiming it was contrary to the law of God. The Dutch were not amused; they fined the town officials for their disobedience.[10] More serious from the Dutch perspective was the reluctance of the English to prevent outward displays of nationalism. The raising of the English standard in 1653 in both Hempstead and Flushing, without any resistance from the populace, illustrated just how precarious the Dutch hold was upon these communities.[11]

Conflicts of a different sort flared up between the two ethnic groups in Westchester. Under the terms of the Treaty of Hartford, which had been signed in 1650 to resolve boundary disputes between Connecticut and New Netherland, Westchester stayed under Dutch control. A few Dutch settlers resided in the extreme southern portion (now the Bronx), but much of the territory remained undeveloped, inhabited by Indians. Despite the treaty, Thomas Pell, a former confidant of Charles I and now a resident of Fairfield, Connecticut, purchased nearly all of southeastern Westchester in 1653 from the Indians. He then proceeded to sell parcels to New Englanders. Almost immediately, the Dutch protested the enterprise, sending an official in 1655 to warn the "squatters" off the land. They met him at gunpoint. The Dutch authorities were furious. Not only had a settlement been established contrary to the treaty, but the English were sheltering criminals and negotiating with the Indians, whom the Dutch had been recently fighting. The Dutch then dispatched an armed detail in 1656. The show of force worked. The settlers petitioned to remain there under the authority of New Netherland, much like the English residents of western Long Island. But other New Englanders were less easily daunted; Pell pressed his claims upon the region, insisting upon his ownership of the property. Such disputes would stay unresolved until the English conquest of New Netherlands in 1664.[12]

The process of expansion continued apace after the English acquisition of the province, henceforth called New York. Under the rule of James, Duke of York, his lieutenants, and subsequent royal governors, southern New York entered a new period of development and consolidation. Settlers from Europe and New England entered the region; local populations increased. Southern New York also acquired an administrative identity, for by 1683 the counties of Queens, Suffolk, and Westchester had been created. New York City and the village of Harlem comprised Manhattan county.[13] Within these counties overall growth varied: some became more heavily populated than others, in part because of migration, in part because of natural increase. Much of Westchester was wilderness during the seventeenth century, unoccupied by white settlers except along the coastal regions of Long Island Sound and the Hudson River. Long Island, on the other hand, apparently possessed some heavily settled regions, which prompted Governor Thomas Dongan in 1687 to report: "The people increase so fast that they complain for want of land and may remove from thence into neighboring province."[14] Other areas of the Island were more lightly settled. New York City was not only the largest town, but the most densely populated, since the great majority of residents inhabited the southern portion of Manhattan, which received a steady swarm of newcomers.

Under English rule the rural countryside of southern New York witnessed the creation of various manors. In an effort to promote settlement and to consolidate their own political authority such governors as Richard Nicolls, Thomas Dongan, and Benjamin Fletcher granted land patents with particular privileges to several individuals. Aside from having title to thousands of acres, manor lords could recruit tenants, arrange leases, and collect rents; several had considerable political autonomy, which freed them from paying taxes to neighboring towns; and all commanded a degree of power and respect. Westchester contained the largest manors in southern New York: Philipsburgh and Van Cortland manors located in the western and northern portions of the county comprised over 92,000 and 86,000 acres respectively. Other manors in southern Westchester, which included Pelham, Scarsdale, and Fordham, were less impressive in size, often no more than a few thousand acres. Long Island manors were few and small, perhaps the most prominent being the 3,000-acre Lloyd estate north of Huntington. Yet, whatever the variation in the size of the estates, relatively few people chose to become tenants. Probably no more than one-third of Westchester's population ever resided on a manor, while Long Island's tenant population was even less. Lloyd manor, for instance, never contained more than a few tenants.[15]

The townships, then, dominated the political and social landscape of Westchester and Long Island despite the existence of the manors. During the latter part of the seventeenth century settlers founded few new towns in Queens and Suffolk; Smithfield (later Smithtown) was one exception, inhabited by members of the same family. Instead, individuals concentrated on acquiring new tracts of land within the towns, pushing outward from the center of the settlement. New land purchases and new land divisions became commonplace activities for the townsfolk. Occasionally, settlers who were discouraged with prospects in one town moved onward to another settlement. The Queens county town of Jamaica drew in people from Hempstead, Flushing, Oyster Bay, and Kings county, and residents from there also left to go to New Jersey and Orange county.[16] In general, most people preferred to occupy land along or near the coast, where the soil proved more fertile. The interior portions of the Island distinguished by the Hempstead Plains—a long grassy strip in Queens devoid of trees—and the pine forests of Suffolk deterred settlers. In Westchester, by comparison, several new towns appeared after 1664, as the largely unsettled areas along the eastern coast bordering the Sound beckoned to New Englanders. With the overthrow of the Dutch the way was cleared for settlers from neighboring Connecticut to establish such towns as Rye and East Chester—covenant communities similar to those on Long Island. French Huguenots, moreover, formed the town of New Rochelle, having purchased a tract by the Sound near Mamaroneck in 1689 from Pell. Still other settlers, although hindered by the manor grants, eventually traveled into the interior portions of the county, starting the settlements of Bedford and White Plains.[17]

The size and profile of these rural settlements differed. Early census records are few and probably less than accurate, while tax lists furnish only a crude sort of estimate as to the number of inhabitants; nevertheless, sufficient information exists for some villages. In Westchester the 1698 census for the towns of East Chester, New Rochelle, and Mamaroneck listed 44, 43, and 15 adult males respectively. The town of Rye had 112 freeholders in 1683. The entire county in 1698 had 1,063 inhabitants, of whom 146 were black and presumably slaves.[18] More detailed information is available for Queens and Suffolk. The town of Southampton in 1698 contained 389 "Male Christians" and 349 "Female Christians," adults and children, along with 40 black males and 43 black females. In ad-

LAND OF PROMISE 17

dition, an unusually zealous census taker enumerated the Indian population, despite their being "scattered to and fro" across the town; he found 50 adult men and estimated that there were approximately 100 women and children. On the western end of the Island in Flushing an "Exact List" of all the inhabitants of the town for that same year showed 530 whites and 113 blacks. The great majority of whites lived together as families; only a few single men resided alone. The 1698 census listed 3,366 white inhabitants and 199 black inhabitants for Queens and 2,119 whites and 558 blacks for Suffolk.[19]

Numbers tell only part of the story. As already mentioned, the ethnic character of the population reveals a strong New England strain; most of the townsfolk had come from Massachusetts and Connecticut. But there were also Dutch, French, and Africans inhabiting the countryside. The degree of diversity varied from county to county, town to town. Suffolk county was easily the most homogeneous with its New England migrants, although blacks and Indians lived among them in a clearly defined subordinate position. Queens contained a more diverse population. The town of Flushing, for example, had English, French, and Dutch residents as well as African slaves; Jamaica and Newtown were Anglo-Dutch communities. In Westchester, however, despite a pluralistic population, individual towns were often inhabited by one particular European group rather than two or more. Thus, Rye was a New England-like community, and New Rochelle remained French. The manor of Philipsburgh and sections of southern Westchester were mainly Dutch.[20]

Ethnicity and religion often went hand in hand in the rural countryside. New Englanders, by and large, were Calvinists, either Independents (Congregationalists) or Presbyterians. Their meetinghouses dotted the three counties, with the greatest number being found at Suffolk. Most of the Dutch were associated with the Dutch Reformed Church, which existed in Queens and Westchester. The Reverend John Miller, the Anglican chaplain to the British army in Manhattan, noted in 1695 the strength of the Calvinist sects across the countryside. In that year he compiled a provincial census of each county's religious affiliation. Suffolk, of course, was solidly Calvinist, inhabited by "Dissenters for the most part," with a meetinghouse in almost every town and seven dissenting ministers. Queens had meetinghouses in Jamaica, Hempstead, and Flushing to serve the English and Dutch populations, most of whom were Calvinists. Miller did not mention Newtown, but the town had a Congregational and Dutch Reformed meetinghouse around by the turn of the century. Similarly, Westchester remained a largely Calvinist domain, populated, in Miller's words, by "English and dissenters, few Dutch."[21] Fordham and Philipsburgh had Dutch Reformed churches, while Rye, Bedford, and East Chester had Puritan congregations. Despite the Ministry Act of 1693, which had established the Church of England in Queens and Westchester, the Anglicans were a tiny minority, lacking both clerics and adherents. Indeed, attempts to place Anglican ministers in the two counties sometimes met with resistance from many of the residents. The Anglican rector of Rye wrote to his superiors in 1708 that one of the justices had warned him against preaching; furthermore, the Puritans had informed the few Anglican parishioners that "they [the Puritans] will not suffer the house of the lord to be defiled with idolatrous worship and superstitious ceremony."[22]

Nevertheless, Dutch Reformed and English Calvinist sects did not monopolize the countryside. Quakers had been active since the earliest decades of settlement in Queens and Westchester, while a few could even be found in Suffolk, much to the dismay of the Puritans there. The followers of George Fox were especially strong throughout Queens, attracting adherents in Flushing, Oyster Bay, and Newtown. When Thomas Story, a Quaker itinerant, held a meeting in the village of Westbury in Hempstead town in 1702, he reported "many hundred of Friends and abundance of other people here." Westchester also had some Quakers, but probably fewer than Queens.[23] Even the Anglicans, despite opposition, assembled a small body of worshippers. Anglicans chapels, often former Calvinist meetinghouses, could be found in Hempstead, Jamaica, Westchester, and Rye during the early 1700s. By 1710 the Huguenots of New Rochelle conformed to the Church of England. In addition, scattered numbers of Baptists and Lutherans lived in Queens and Westchester. Calvinist sects, while clearly in the majority, had some competition from other denominations, particularly in Westchester and Queens, which featured a more religiously pluralistic environment than homogeneous Suffolk. And, of course, there were the unchurched, that is, people with no particular religious affiliation, who often lived too far away from any meetinghouse to attend services. The Reverend Mr. Miller, perhaps unjustly, condemned the entire province for "wickedness and irreligion," and Caleb Heathcote, manor lord of Scarsdale, considered Westchester in the 1690s to be one of the "most rude and heathenish country that I ever saw."[24]

Manhattan's evolution under English rule took a different course from that of the countryside. Here there was no frontier to tame or new townships to create; rather, city growth became a process of building upon the already existing Dutch structure. This meant a transition to English forms of government. In deference to the Dutch population, the English conquerers moved slowly and cautiously, unwilling to alienate the inhabitants, upon whose support they depended. Dutch individuals retained positions of authority and kept control of their property. They were also allowed to practice their religion. Even so, certain alterations proved inevitable, as new legal codes—a blend of Anglo-Dutch statutes—were enacted. The format of government changed also. By 1684 Manhattan had a municipal government with a mayor, a recorder, aldermen, and assistants—the last two being elected by the citizens of the various wards of the city. These individuals comprised the Common Council. This governing body transacted all the necessary business of the city; it drafted legislation, heard petitions, acted as a court, and enforced the law. For most New Yorkers, then, the Common Council functioned as a kind of urban counterpart to the town meeting, with the aldermen and assistants representing the people. Although the Dominion of New England absorbed New York City into its administrative structure by 1688, and although Leisler's Rebellion produced a chaotic state of affairs, the Common Council resumed its normal activities by 1691 and remained the locus of local government for Manhattanites.[25]

The urban evolution of Manhattan after 1664 was no less evident. Physically, the city expanded its borders, edging outward past the protective barrier of Wall Street, which had been the traditional boundary of the municipality. New streets and lanes appeared. By 1699, moreover, Wall Street lost its distinctive fortification, symbolizing, in effect, the opening of territory to the north.[26] Yet movement in that direction remained modest during the seventeenth and early eighteenth centuries, for city authorities preferred to lease rather than sell urban real estate. Houses, tenements, shops, taverns, and warehouses crowded into the southern tip of Manhattan, giving the city a congested appearance. In 1678 Manhattan had

343 houses, and by 1696 there were 937. Even so, people scrambled to find housing; there never seemed to be enough. One official in 1701 bemoaned the lack of accommodations, writing to his superiors in London that "I have eight in family and know not yet where to fix them, houses are so scarce and dear, and lodgings worst in this place."[27]

Crowded conditions did not prevent certain modest improvements in the quality of urban life: what Carl T. Bridenbaugh has termed the "Awakening of Civic Consciousness" was very much in evidence for Manhattan at this time. The streets of the city were paved in the center so water could run off into the soil along the sides. Sidewalks were non-existent, but brick pathways could be found. In 1697 the Common Council decreed that every seventh householder should place a candle and lantern in front of his or her dwelling, with the other six householders to pay a share of the expenses. And by this time the city nightwatch patrolled the streets.[28]

By 1698 New York City contained 4,937 inhabitants, making it the second largest city in the British North American colonies, behind Boston and ahead of Philadelphia. As always, New York City was the largest and most diverse settlement in the province, inhabited by several ethnic and racial groups. The Dutch, of course, represented the largest single group, even though immigration from the Netherlands had almost completely halted. A steady flow of Dutch farmers' sons from the countryside reinforced the Dutch presence, and the number of British arrivals was small, for most preferred to live elsewhere. In 1687 Governor Dongan complained about the scarcity of British migrants, noting "for these last seven years past there has not come into this province twenty English, Scotch, or Irish families."[29] Nevertheless, the Dutch found their majority status threatened all the same. French Huguenots, who fled Catholic France in the 1680s and 1690s, found Manhattan an attractive environment where they could practice their religion unmolested by the authorities. In fact, English officials welcomed them warmly, allowing the Huguenots to receive the freedom of the city. According to one estimate by Governor Fletcher in 1696, French Huguenots comprised one-quarter of the city's population. By 1700 even the English, despite the scarcity of migrants, were probably as numerous as the French, if not more so. New Englanders arrived in Manhattan, lured by the prospect of trade opportunities, and British soldiers from the city garrison supplemented their numbers. Then there were small numbers of Jews, who perhaps formed between 1 and 2 percent of the population. Some found the city an excellent place for business.[30]

Manhattan was also a biracial environment. Blacks had comprised a significant proportion of the population under Dutch rule, forming perhaps a quarter of the inhabitants in 1664. Joyce Goodfriend in her study of New York City indicates that there were 300 black slaves and 75 free blacks at the time of the Dutch surrender. During the next few decades the ratio of blacks to whites declined only slightly; indeed, Manhattan flourished as a slave-trading center, which guaranteed a steady influx of bondspeople from Africa and the West Indies. Well-to-do merchants, shopkeepers, and artisans found them indispensable. By 1698 the black population stood at around 14 percent, and almost 35 percent of the white population owned one or more slaves.[31]

Ethnic and racial diversity worked against having a unified community. Lodwick's complaints about "too great a mixture of nations" in Manhattan illustrates the sorts of tensions that prevented any meaningful consensus, a consensus that was usually characteristic of towns settled primarily by one ethnic group. As Thomas Archdeacon has argued, Leisler's Rebellion was prompted in part by ethnic disputes among the Anglo-Dutch populace. If some Dutch inhabitants embraced English ways and sought English spouses, many others preferred to remain true to the old ways, clinging tenaciously to their language and religion. Such people often lived apart from the English. Throughout Manhattan could be found certain streets where the Dutch predominated—ethnic enclaves that perhaps served to reinforce their sense of identity. Here at least the English could be kept at bay. Jews were a group apart also. No matter where they might reside, their religion made them distinct from the rest of society. The French, on the other hand, after a short period of time, began to assimilate into the English population; many of them married English spouses while others embraced the Church of England. The French, generally, could be counted upon to side with the English against the Dutch. The other major group, black Africans, although dispersed throughout the city and living in the households of the English, French, and Dutch citizens, were legally and socially subordinate to the white population. Their lowly status, however, did not prevent them from displaying their discontent, setting fires, stealing goods, and running away dramatized the black reaction to bondage. Ethnic divisions among the European population were quickly forgotten during any rumored slave rebellion, for that was the one thing that served to unite Manhattan's otherwise divided white population.[32]

As might be expected, religion was often a badge of ethnicity in Manhattan, which meant the city was home to a large number of sects. Governor Thomas Dongan reported in 1687 that

> New York has first a chaplain belonging to the Fort of the Church of England; secondly a Dutch Calvinist; thirdly a French Calvinist; fourthly a Dutch Lutheran—there be not many of the Church of England; few Roman Catholics; abundance of Quaker preachers men and women especially: singing Quakers, ranting Quakers, Sabbatarians, Anti-Sabbatarians, some Anabaptists, some Independents, some Jews: in short of all sort of opinion there are some, and the most part of none at all.[33]

Not all these denominations possessed a house of worship, for some had to meet in private dwellings due to prejudice or too few numbers. The Presbyterians lacked a meetinghouse until after 1700, and Catholics and Quakers met privately in the homes of adherents. Manhattan's Jewish population confronted a similar situation for a time after Edmund Andros in 1685 prohibited the practice of their religion, although they already had their own burial ground. Yet Manhattan did possess several meetinghouses and churches. The Dutch Calvinists, who were the largest sect, with an estimated 450 families, held services at a new church they had constructed in 1693, complete with brick steeple and coats of arms adorning the windows. By the first decade of the eighteenth century the Lutherans and French Huguenots could attend their own services in separate structures. Even the Anglicans, with their relatively few members, had the imposing edifice of Trinity Church. The 175-foot steeple was one of the highest points in Manhattan, proclaiming in a symbolic sense the establishment of the Church of England in New York City.[34]

New York City at the turn of the century possessed an expanding economy. Despite competition from Boston and Philadelphia, Manhattan continued to evolve into a major North Atlantic shipping center; the sheltered harbor, always a major asset, became even more valuable in 1675 with the construction of a stone dock along the coastal areas. Internal improvements were complemented by special economic privileges bestowed upon the city by political officials. Not only did Manhattan serve as the port for the Hudson River trade of fur and grain, but it also controlled the export of all products from the province by 1678. Manhattan's position was enhanced further in 1684, when the city became the port of entry for the province; now all overseas shipping had to enter there. Trade and commerce powered the urban economy. Governor Fletcher in 1691 went so far as to claim that Manhattan had "nothing to support it but trade."[35]

Hyperbole aside, Fletcher was still on target. Trade was an essential ingredient of the Manhattan economy, and to facilitate trade a fleet of ships proved necessary. At first Manhattan's merchant ships were few in number, for Andros in 1678 reported only five small ships and a ketch as belonging to New York. By 1687, however, Dongan mentioned to his superiors that Manhattan had nine or ten three-masted vessels, two or three ketches, and twenty sloops. Shipping increased even more rapidly over the next few years: over 100 vessels of varying size could be seen in the harbor by 1696; several years later the number increased to 120. Foreign vessels, too, entered Manhattan; ships from New England, Europe, and the West Indies anchored at the port, providing New York with a steady flow of business regardless of the season.[36]

Domestic and foreign ships, whatever their ownership or destination, represented a crucial component of the urban economy. They took on the produce of the colony, chiefly flour, cattle, and pelts, while unloading the commodities of distant and nearby lands. Thus, the seaport community at times resembled a vast marketplace, filled with all sorts of merchandise on display. City markets, shops, and warehouses bulged with goods; rum, wine, sugar, fabrics, and slaves were just a few of the commodities offered for sale. Added to this was the supply of provisions from the nearby countryside to feed the urban residents. The flow of business, that is, the buying and selling, dominated much of city life. The ever-observant Sarah Knight in 1704 noted that New Yorkers had "venues very frequently" and that high profits were common. The return on merchandise also fascinated the Reverend John Miller, who reported in 1695 that English-made goods could yield profits of over 100 percent. Alcoholic refreshment often sealed such transactions. Indeed, many buyers, after being liberally treated with "good liquor," raised prices (and hence profit margins) even higher in spirited bidding, more than repaying the retailers for their generosity.[37]

In their pursuit of profits Manhattanites were seldom fastidious; anything was fair game. Merchants kept close watch on any opportunity that might yield a decent return, even if it meant disobeying the law. Thus, it should come as no great surprise to find that piracy played an integral role in the urban economy. During the 1690s pirates received a warm welcome not only from members of the merchant community but from the civil authorities, in particular, Governor Fletcher, who furnished them with immunity from prosecution. In return, he demanded a share of the booty. The Governor and several merchants also employed pirates as privateers. Once commissioned, these freebooters could set sail for the West Indies, looting Spanish ships of gold or silver. Other pirates preferred the Indian Ocean near Madagascar, where ships carrying gold, spices, and jewels from the Red Sea proved enticing targets; Captain William Kidd, a Manhattan resident, was but one of several sea rovers who favored this route. Returning to New York City and protected by the Governor, pirates could then sell their plunder and repay their backers, many of whom were merchants. Stolen goods, in turn, fetched a high price in the market. Equally important, pirates needed to be refitted, equipped, and entertained while in port, and they were willing to spend liberal amounts of money. Gold and silver coins, perhaps as much as £100,000 per year, provided the specie-scarce economy with a desperately needed circulating medium. Little wonder that officials and merchants alike condoned the presence of pirates; they were a necessary spur to the local economy.[38]

Piracy, however, had faded from sight in Manhattan by 1700. The new governor, Lord Bellomont, the corrupt Fletcher's successor, proved determined to halt the trade connections between the merchant community and the pirates. Naval ships stationed off Sandy Hook guarded the approach to the harbor and deterred pirates from entering. And stricter licensing procedures made it more difficult for mechants to engage in such illicit trade.[39]

The loss of this business, although a blow to some members of the business community, failed to harm the urban economy seriously. This was due in part to the nearly continuous state of war that existed between England and France, which provided merchants with valuable contracts from the British government. Long a major flour-exporting center, Manhattan enjoyed the added advantage in King William's War (1689-1697) and Queen Anne's War (1702-1713) of victualing the English military. This generated substantial profits for the economy. Not only merchants but sailors, artisans, and laborers could benefit from this trade. Of course, drawbacks existed in supplying the armed forces, for enemy vessels regarded the city's merchant fleet as fair game. Although Manhattan's fleet suffered little during the 1690s, by the early 1700s the French navy had destroyed a large portion of the city's shipping; perhaps as much as a quarter of the fleet was lost in 1704 due to French depredations. To make matters worse competition from cheaper Boston carriers also drew business away from the port. Fortunately, an additional influx of English money during the war years revitalized the port.[40]

This business-oriented environment contrasted sharply with the rural economy of Queens, Suffolk, and Westchester. Agriculture was the major enterprise. With few exceptions the vast majority of settlers remained true to the seasonal rhythms of an agrarian society: in the spring the farmer plowed his fields in order to plant his seed; by summer he saw his crops standing tall in the fields and his orchards laden with fruit; and by the fall he was ready to harvest this bounty. When the cold winds of winter swept across the Hudson River and Long Island Sound the farmer, his wife, and his children performed other chores, sawing wood, tending livestock, and mending fences, while awaiting the return of another planting season.[41] Artisans, too, were tied into the agrarian economy, tending small plots of land. As the Reverend Thomas Standard of Westchester town in 1729 reported about his parishioners: "Their employment is husbandry, even innkeepers, shopkeepers, smiths, and shoemakers not excepted." The same was no doubt true for Long Island. Most farmers probably exchanged needed crops and supplies with each other, for few, if any, were totally self-sufficient, as Bettye Pruitt has shown for colonial Massachusetts. If urban merchants and artisans worried about profits and employment, country farmers concentrated their attention upon the land and its bounty.[42]

The type of farming also differed within the three counties. Although most farmers planted the same crops by the same methods, some might depend more upon raising cattle or sheep than grain. The town of Hempstead had a huge area set aside for grazing—the aforementioned Hempstead Plains, where livestock roamed freely—and the town of East Hampton, judging from an assessment list in 1683, possessed much of its actual wealth in livestock rather than in crops. Indeed, it appears that Long Island farmers were far more interested in animal husbandry than were those of Westchester. This is easily seen from the amount of livestock owned by the respective residents of Westchester town and Newtown in 1675. Over 60 percent of the townsfolk listed in the assessment rolls of Newtown for that year engaged in sheep farming; by contrast, only 33 percent of the Westchester residents did so. Most likely the more fertile pastures of the Island, which Daniel Denton had praised in 1670, explain the distinction.[43]

Commercial activity existed among some of the rural populace, in particular the great manor lords, who often evinced considerable business acumen. Frederick Philipse is a case in point. A Dutchman by birth, he had advanced steadily upward every since his arrival in the province in the 1650s, marrying a rich widow and engaging in trade. As the proprietor of Philipse manor he and his descendants did more than rely on the rent of tenents, for they shipped flour from their estate on the banks of the Hudson down to the city. Location and considerable capital furnished them with their opportunities. Similarly, the manor lord Lloyds displayed a flair for trade, using family connections throughout New England to their advantage. In 1715, for example, they sent 370 bushels of winter wheat to Boston.[44] Nor was commercial activity confined to the great landlords; small farmers, too, could take advantage of their proximity to the city. Farmers in southern Westchester traveled with their produce over a toll bridge across the Harlem River as early as 1693 to city markets, while settlers from Newtown could take ship to Manhattan—the ferry from Brooklyn, for instance. Long Island wheat commanded a price of more than three shillings per bushel in the city. Trade of a different sort even went on between Manhattan and Huntington in 1697, when the vestry of Trinity Church instructed one of their members "to purchase all the oyster shell lime here." Apparently, Huntington's oyster shells had something of a reputation among city buyers.[45]

Commercial activity did not always flow from the rural hinterland to the city; a considerable trade existed between the east end of Long Island and New England. Cultural ties and geographic proximity drew these two regions together economically despite the constant complaints of royal governors, who sought to prohibit trade between these two parties. Eastern Long Island was also the center of a flourishing whaling industry during the latter part of the seventeenth century. Residents of Southampton and East Hampton stood watch by shore, ready to launch their boats at the sight of the great leviathans. Long Island Indians aided in these enterprises; many of them signed contracts to serve as whale boat men in return for such goods as clothes, gunpowder, and shot. Southampton especially reaped the benefits of the whale oil trade, and for a time in the 1680s it was not only a major port but the third largest settlement in New York next to New York City and Albany.[46]

Even so, commercial activity, while present in the countryside, was nevertheless limited in scope. With the exception of the manor lords, who possessed ample reserves of capital and well-established trading connections, most farmers remained relatively immune from the workings of the marketplace, content to sell a small surplus at best. A lack of roads deterred farmers from sending crops or cattle to market, as did sheer distance from the urban seaport. Even people close to Manhattan sometimes found access to the city difficult. In 1706 the governor, Edward Hyde, Lord Cornbury, complained to the Lords of Trade that council members from Long Island were under "great difficulty" in coming to Manhattan, often requiring four to six weeks. Those in Westchester had the same problem, according to the Governor.[47] Not surprisingly, trade was also limited in many cases. Perhaps the clearest proof of this comes from the pen of the Reverend James Wetmore, Anglican rector of the parish of Rye. Writing in 1728, Wetmore observed that the early settlers had seldom engaged in trade: "I can't find if they raised much of anything for the market but what they trafficked in was chiefly wood and cattle." Only the occasional bushel of wheat, moreover, found its way to the city from Rye according to Wetmore.[48] Other commercial endeavors reveal similar limitations. Whaling activity on eastern Long Island, although significant, remained an erratic enterprise, dependent upon the supply of whales. Indeed, the whale oil trade declined substantially during the early 1700s, perhaps forcing more people to rely upon farming.[49] The market, then, had a decidedly minor impact upon rural society of the seventeenth century.

No portrait of the urban-rural economy would be complete without an assessment of the regional social structure. Access to wealth varied within the city and its rural environs, as did the social distinctions of the different classes. In addition, the amount of wealth controlled by the richest inhabitants might reveal a stratified or egalitarian social structure depending upon the particular settlement. Even in the late seventeenth century there was some degree of inequality—leading merchants, manor lords, professionals, and civil officials occupied a different sphere from most of their neighbors—yet overall the distinctions among the different classes were modest by European standards. Southern New York was still a relatively young society, and parts of Westchester in 1700 remained little more than a frontier. Social mobility was more the norm than the exception here. In Manhattan, the ranks of the well-to-do individuals were constantly being supplemented, as newcomers to the city reaped the opportunities of the expanding seaport economy. The countryside, if less dynamic economically, saw a steady progression into the land-owning ranks by the inhabitants. Class differences existed, yet they could not obscure the overwhelming middle-class character of seventeenth-century New York.

Of crucial importance to New York City's emerging social structure was the influx of immigrants. The arrival of English, French, and Jewish merchants and entrepreneurs not only provided Manhattan with a more diverse ethnic population, but prompted alterations in the traditional wealth-holding patterns. This was quite evident among the merchant elite. Prior to the English conquest of 1664 Dutch merchants had controlled much of the city's wealth, exploiting the fur and flour trades while importing consumer goods. With the arrival of other Europeans and the severance of political links with the Netherlands, some Dutch merchants found themselves hard-pressed to maintain their traditional dominance. English, French, and Jewish merchants could rely upon contacts in England and the West Indies for credit and market information. The Dutch often lacked such connections. Consequently, the newcomers forged ahead, taking over a greater share of the trade, while many Dutch merchants lagged behind. A few of the more capable and farsighted Dutch traders preserved their positions: Jacobus Van Cortland sent ships to England and communicated regularly with London businessmen; Abraham De Peyster apparently benefited commercially from close political ties with Governor Bellomont.

But as Thomas Archdeacon has revealed, many were unable to follow the path charted by their more successful fellows. City tax lists furnish proof of this phenomenon. At first, the Dutch held their own, for the 1677 tax list reveals a preponderance of Dutch surnames among the wealthiest classes, although a "significant minority" of English were also listed. Yet by 1703 the English and French combined to outnumber the Dutch merchants and control a larger share of the import/export trade.[50]

Additional evidence of this shift in power can be seen in the rise of several recent arrivals to Manhattan during the latter half of the seventeenth century, as recounted by Archdeacon. Such men prospered handsomely by means of political power, business expertise, and marital alliances. One example is John Lawrence. An early inhabitant of Long Island, Lawrence had been a patentee in the towns of Hempstead and Flushing before the English conquest of the province. His talents blossomed once he moved to Manhattan: he owned a house and store along the river front, which provided a commercially strategic site for business; in addition, he served two terms as mayor in 1671 and 1691. Another successful immigrant, Thomas Delavall, was a captain in the English army that had seized the city. He changed careers, engaged in "merchant pursuits," and purchased several estates—one of which was Barn Island, located in Hell's Gate. Delavall served as mayor also. George Heathcote had been a merchant ship captain. Upon his arrival in Manhattan in 1678, Heathcote purchased the seat of a Dutch merchant on the west side of Pearl Street, where he dealt in a large quantity of goods and exploited the riches of the West Indies trade. A fourth success story, William Dervall, was a Boston merchant prior to coming to New York. Shortly after the English conquest, he established a store in partnership with his brother; later he solidified his position by marrying Delavall's daughter and inheriting Barn Island. By 1676 his total estate was valued at £3,000.[51]

Among French and Jewish merchants the path to comfort and security took the form of ethnic and religious ties. Many French Huguenots traded with their country until the revocation of the Edict of Nantes in 1685 deprived them of this outlet; afterward, they drew upon their experience in the maritime trade, as Jon Butler has revealed. Others made use of French Huguenots in London. Such prominent French merchants as Stephen DeLancy, John Pelletreu, and Isaac Deschamp were the economic equals of wealthy English and Dutch merchants, and many of these Frenchmen could be found residing in the more affluent neighborhoods of the city. Jewish merchants, too, did well in forging ties with their fellows in London; some such as Isaac Rodriques belonged, in Archdeacon's words, "to the highest commercial bracket."[52]

Visitors to the city presented a more comprehensive portrait of the ethnic wealth. Judging from some accounts the Dutch residents, although perhaps declining in terms of overall wealth, often appeared to be quite well off, or were at least believed to be so. Benjamin Bullivant, a Boston physician, considered Dutch residents in 1697 plainly attired for the most part despite their middle-class background: "I cannot say I saw any of ye Dutch that were favorably well dressed, though rich enough to wear what they pleased, they are a parsimonious people . . . which makes them unusually well-mannered and good pay masters." John Miller echoed Bullivant's description. Looking at the entire province he found the Dutch to be "rich and sparing," while the English appeared "neither very rich nor too great husbands." The French, thought Miller, were poor. Sarah Knight said little about ethnicity and wealth per se, but she did note differences in female attire. Knight found the English "very fashionable in their dress"; by comparison, Dutch women favored a different, presumably unfashionable, style. Their status and wealth were visible in other ways than clothes, however. Knight noted that Dutch women usually wore "jewels of a large size and many in number" in or along their ears, and their fingers were "hoop't with rings, some with large stones in them of many coulers."[53]

Ethnic differences aside, wealth was becoming more concentrated among the richest taxpayers of Manhattan. Tax lists provide our best indication of the degree of economic stratification. Under the Dutch, Manhattan had been an economically segmented society, for the highest tax assessment of between three and four florins was levied against slightly less than 10 percent of the populace.[54] With the establishment of English rule and the influx of migrants the urban social structure continued to reflect a noticeable concentration of wealth: the wealthiest 10 percent of the taxpayers controlled 45 percent of the assessed wealth in 1695, whereas the bottom 50 percent had only 10 percent. These wealth-holding ratios are similar to those in other colonial seaports: in 1687 the top 10 percent of the taxpayers in Boston had 42 percent of the total assessed wealth, and the bottom 50 percent were only slightly better off than their New York counterparts, with 12 percent. Another Manhattan tax list for 1703 shows little change. While the upper 10 percent now held 47 percent of the assessed wealth, the bottom half of the taxpayers retained their 10 percent share.[55]

This cursory analysis of the urban social structure illustrates that Manhattan's obvious economic advantages did not always translate into economic equality. A small pecentage of well-to-do people possessed a significant amount of the city's wealth, while a majority of the taxpayers owned a very modest amount indeed. Even so, these percentages tell only a part of the story; they fail to reveal the relative lack of poverty that characterized early Manhattan. Working-class folk may have held an insignificant share of the wealth, yet they managed to create a life of subsistence, if not plenty. Laborers, artisans, sailors, and carters could expect high wages in comparison to their European rivals, and the evolving economy provided an ever-growing number of jobs. Gary Nash has noted that seaport towns such as New York during the 1690s provided people with ample resources, in particular, food, clothing, and shelter. Perhaps the best evidence of this can be found in the public welfare rolls: in 1700 only thirty-five people required charity, and most of these were either elderly, orphaned, widowed, or impaired, in short, people unable to care for themselves. The city fathers, for their part, handled the matter casually, renting a house in 1700 for the lodging of destitute persons instead of constructing an actual almshouse. Poverty, although present, was a decidedly minor problem in the seventeenth-century metropolis.[56]

The rural social structure on the whole presented a more egalitarian appearance than that of Manhattan. Excluding the manor lords, who were a tiny group anyway, most settlers were in roughly the same economic position, neither wealthy nor poor. In the villages there were few great merchants to monopolize wealth and no great number of landless laborers unable to support themselves. Few towns in the seventeenth century bothered to record the occupational profile of their inhabitants, but we do know that East Hampton in 1687 had two merchants and thirty-five servants; the rest of the white male inhabitants, presumably, were farmers or sons of farmers.[57] More important, individual towns generally saw to it that land was evenly distributed, with no one settler receiving a disproportionate amount of real estate. When the proprietors of East Chester founded their community in 1664, they decreed in their covenant "that none exceed the quantity of fifteen acres until all have that quantity [and] that every man have that meadow that is most convenient to him." In Jamaica each man in 1656 received a six-acre house lot, a ten-acre tract for crops, and twenty acres of meadow land.[58] Other towns resorted to similar devices of land distribution. By such means a rough equality could be achieved at least among the first planters. Nor was ownership restricted to the first residents; newcomers, too, might receive a parcel of land, which placed them on an equal footing with their neighbors. And when the children of the proprietors came of age they might expect an additional grant of land from the town.[59]

Of course, landownership, if widespread, was never universal, and the quantity of land held by the residents in time could range from between two and three acres to fifty or more. People could and did buy additional parcels, sometimes directly from the Indians; others purchased extra land from neighbors. Young men just starting out might be little more than landless laborers, awaiting the day when they could acquire sufficient funds for a farm. How often did such people acquire land? We have no direct information for Long Island or Westchester, but in nearby Connecticut a substantial percentage of young men could expect to become property holders, especially those who were the sons of already established farmers. While a third or so of all adult men were landless, many of these people would achieve the position of farmers; even some apprentices could rise upward and acquire property. Such conditions may well have existed in the rural countryside of New York, a countryside that in many ways resembled Connecticut geographically and socially.[60]

The pattern of landownership on Long Island and Westchester may best be deduced from the assessment lists of the 1670s and 1680s. Admittedly, as Jackson T. Main and others have shown, such lists remain far from accurate, often distorting the actual degree of wealth—a point Robert Ritchie has noted for Long Island.[61] Yet they are valuable if only because of the lack of probate records for the seventeenth century. In the town of East Chester, already mentioned for its egalitarian philosophy, only three of twenty people in a 1675 assessment list owned neither land nor meadow; most of those persons listed had between ten and twenty acres, while no individual held more than thirty acres total. In the neighboring town of Westchester only one person out of forty possessed neither pasture nor arable land. On Long Island the percentage of landless taxable inhabitants seems to have been higher: Ritchie has discovered that 15 percent of the adult men were propertyless. This percentage, however, varied from town to town, for Brookhaven had five landless taxpayers among fifty-two listed, and in Smithtown all seven taxpayers held property. Long Island towns also had some people with considerably more land than others, which might reflect the slightly greater age of these settlements compared to those in Westchester county. In Brookhaven, Richard Floyd possessed 94 acres compared to 36 for Joseph Longbottom and John Tooker, Sr., the next largest landowners. Similarly, in Flushing, Charles Bridge had 110 acres compared to 48 for his closest rival.[62]

As for the percentage of wealth controlled by the more well-to-do element, the countryside once again reveals an egalitarian social structure. To be sure, such men as Richard Floyd might stand out from their neighbors as first among equals, but generally speaking most rural communities saw no great concentration of wealth in the hands of a few. The tax lists reveal this fact with great clarity. Consider the town of Huntington. Founded in 1653, the town was perhaps representative of many other communities—a village of small farmers with no great landowners. In 1683 the top 10 percent of the taxpayers owned 20 percent of the assessed wealth. This percentage, moreover, was very much in keeping with that of other towns: in Westchester town the top 10 percent controlled 23 percent of the total wealth. Indeed, Ritchie has found that on Long Island as a whole the wealthiest tenth of the populace held only a little over 21 percent. Variations did exist—eastern Long Island villages had slightly less open social structures—but the overall picture was one of rough equality. Even in 1696 a tax list for Southampton shows the top 10 percent being credited with 22.5 percent, hardly an unequal distribution of wealth. These figures only add weight to Denton's statement about happiness existing for all ranks of men.[63]

Perhaps the final word on New York's generally prosperous environment should come from Governor Bellomont. Taking up his official duties in 1698, the new governor had a busy agenda before him, reforming the abuses of his predecessor, Benjamin Fletcher, and attempting to enforce imperial edicts. He also wished to revamp the public welfare system. Consequently, Bellomont proposed a bill in 1699 to erect public workhouses that could "employ the poor and also vagabonds." The members of the Assembly did not take his proposal seriously. As Bellomont remarked: "They smiled at it because indeed here is no such thing as a beggar in this town or country; and I believe there is not another populace anywhere in the king's domain that is in this turn."[64]

CHAPTER II

The Evolving System of Poor Relief, 1700-1750

*T*he smiles that greeted Governor Bellomont's proposal for the construction of workhouses provide a telling commentary upon the nature of poverty and poor relief in seventeenth-century New York. Unlike England, where paupers and poorhouses were common sights, New York City and its neighboring countryside did not have to contend with a large impoverished lower class or an elaborate system of relief. The great majority of residents were neither rich nor poor; most were able to support themselves and seldom in need of assistance. Nor were transient paupers from outside the province a threat; ever-wary officials kept a close watch upon all newcomers, especially those who appeared destitute. As Governor Dongan noted in 1687, "No vagrants, beggars, nor idle persons are suffered to live here."[1] Poverty when it did materialize among local residents was easily handled. City and town officials provided food, clothing, and medicine to the indigent person, either at home or in the lodgings of friends and neighbors. Churches, too, furnished alms for members in need. Institutional relief of the type Bellomont suggested was virtually non-existent, since charity centered upon the household. Indeed, poor relief was a casual, almost informal operation; it required but small amounts of money and little effort to assist those unable to support themselves. A land that afforded opportunity for many was a land that required only a rudimentary system of public welfare.

This roseate image, however, began to crumble during the first decades of the eighteenth century. Poor people, though remaining a tiny minority, nevertheless increased in number, placing a greater strain upon the welfare system. Traditional means of assisting them sometimes proved inadequate; new measures were adopted. Nowhere was this more evident than in Manhattan. During the 1690s the city fathers had relied upon outdoor relief, that is, assistance within the home; by 1750, outdoor relief, although still employed, was now complemented by institutional relief. Not only did the city resort to an almshouse, but it attempted to put poor people to work—a sharp contrast indeed from the preceeding century. And yet, while the city restructured its welfare program, the rural counties of Queens, Suffolk, and Westchester stayed wedded to the traditions of the past. Poverty, if perhaps more apparent, seldom troubled rural villagers, who continued to assist poor members of the community at home. Attempts to devise new strategies of poor relief were almost non-existent. Thus, villagers treated the poor as they had always done, as neighbors rather than as outcasts.[2]

Long before poverty merited serious concern civil authorities had enacted laws for the welfare and maintenance of poor persons. In effect, such ordinances provided the guidelines for the dispensing of alms. English settlers and their descendants employed many of the laws and statutes of the mother country in the New World, often relying upon the Elizebethan Poor Law of 1601 as a rough model. New York was no exception. The conquest of the province in 1664 left the English free to impose their own standards upon existing Dutch laws; nevertheless, the English did not interfere at first with Dutch modes of assistance. For a time poor relief in Manhattan was managed by the deacons of the Dutch Reformed Church, although civil officials apparently monitored and oversaw their charitable activities. In the English villages the Duke's Laws of 1665 established the office of overseer to tend the poor. It was not until 1683 that the first major colonywide law for "maintaining the poor and preventing vagabonds" passed. This statute was the cornerstone of all subsequent colonial poor laws. The treasurers and overseers of each municipality, county, and town had the responsibility of seeing that local poor persons—the legal inhabitants of the town—were assisted and that "vagabonds and idle persons . . . from other parts" were expelled. Newcomers wishing to settle in the province who lacked a visible estate or skills had to put up security to prevent themselves from becoming a drain upon the community. After two years they could become residents. Those without funds or skills were subject to removal. This legislation, then, was more preventive than remedial, seeking to distinguish among poor persons upon the basis of residency.[3]

If colonial poor laws proved relatively rigid on matters of residency, they did possess a degree of flexibility. The colonial legislature enacted new laws or rescinded particular features of old laws as circumstances warranted. Consequently, the Act of 1683 underwent revision in 1691, 1695, and 1701 in order to facilitate the collection of the poor tax. The administrative aspects of public charity were further amended in 1693, when Benjamin Fletcher established the Church of England in the counties of Manhattan, Queens, Westchester, and Richmond. This Ministry Act stipulated that the vestrymen and churchwardens of the parishes, together with the justices of the peace, levy taxes for the maintenance of both the minister and the poor inhabitants. Although the freeholders of the parish elected the vestrymen and churchwardens, ensuring that non-Anglicans could serve in these parishes, the law placed the operation of charity within an ecclesiastical setting as in England. Even so, the power of the churchwardens and vestrymen was far from absolute in Manhattan, since the mayor and the aldermen maintained authority over them. In Suffolk, by comparison, local town officers continued to be responsible for poor relief, remaining outside this ecclesiastical framework. And throughout the province such religious groups as the Dutch Calvinists, Lutherans, Quakers, and Jews provided assistance to their fellows. A dual system of public and private charity existed.[4]

During the seventeenth century urban officials seemingly had little trouble in caring for destitute members of the community. To be sure, fiscal questions sometimes arose over the collection and spending of the poor tax, but on the whole the system worked. In the 1680s the aldermen determined the needs of poor persons in their respective wards, assisted on occasion by the constables. Disbursements of money were made as needed. In 1688, for instance, Francis Rambut furnished £2-9-6 to his destitute constituents, while Jonathan Kipp provided his with £6-1-9. Total poor relief expenditures for the year stood at a little over £22—hardly a large outlay.[5] Whether city officials checked closely to see if impoverished persons satisfied the legal requirement for public welfare is less clear;

yet a resolution in 1695 from the Common Council did instruct the authorities to "examine what poor there is that are fit objects of charity," implying that some may have been denied assistance. Certainly the small size of the city at the time—under five thousand residents—made possible a degree of vigilance. Relief, when granted, occurred in the home or some other suitable lodging. Thus, Captain Collier, "an object of charity" in 1691, had three shillings, six pence per week paid by the city to his landlord, who apparently tended the Captain. That same year the Widow Barbarry's landlady received three shillings a week for her services, and Arthur Strangwich's wife became the recipient of an identical sum of money for tending her husband. The total number of paupers, not surprisingly, was low during the seventeenth century: Steven Ross in his study of early urban poverty and poor relief counted only seven individuals on relief between 1691 and 1694. Given the relative lack of poverty in seventeenth-century Manhattan there was no pressing need for elaborate mechanisms of welfare. Home relief proved sufficient for all.[6]

Public welfare remained a modest operation for several reasons. Manhattan's growing economy fueled by piracy and overseas trade enabled many people, even working-class folk, to earn a satisfactory livelihood, hence avoiding much need for assistance. Indeed, people who required relief were generally those unable to sustain themselves. Orphans and impaired, sick, and elderly persons comprised the majority of such cases. Another reason why public welfare aided so few persons probably reflects the importance of private charity, most of it church-centered. Although the degree and extent of such charity is difficult to determine, it clearly helped to keep some people off public welfare. The Dutch Reformed Church, which served the largest segment of the population, had a long tradition of assisting destitute members. Collections in their churches handled by the deacons promised a steady flow of funds. The fact that relatively few people with Dutch surnames appeared on the early extant poor relief lists confirms indirectly the importance of private benevolence. Other denominations, too, looked after their own. Quakers relied upon the meeting—the gathering of the Friends—to supply assistance to impoverished members, and the Jewish community did likewise through their synagogues. In 1728 Shearith Israel, the first Jewish synagogue in Manhattan, supplied over £30 in assistance to needy co-religionists.[7] Perhaps the best evidence of the importance of private charity can be seen in regard to the French Huguenots. Many of them, as the Reverend John Miller had noted, were poor in comparison to the English and Dutch populace, yet few French Calvinists ever required public support. The French church regularly supplied destitute members during the 1690s, and as late as 1715 only one Huguenot required institutional relief. Not until the decline of the church in the 1720s do we start to see a number of Huguenots appearing on the welfare rolls.[8]

There were also other forms of private charity. Colonial ministers implored congregations to assist the needy, shelter the homeless, and care for the sick. Poverty was not a sin even if some indigent persons appeared less worthy of assistance than others, and the notion of Christian charity may have motivated people to leave bequests in wills, as happened in 1697, when William Baker gave the city £40 to aid the destitute. Quite possibly, people like Baker did more than leave legacies; they might have aided the poor privately when alive. Admittedly, we have no direct proof of such actions for this period, but we do know that in 1693 a request for funds to ransom Christian captives from Moslem pirates netted over £374 from the residents of the province. New York City inhabitants led the way with £245. Such generosity may well have paralleled private acts of benevolence to needy persons—benevolence that enabled such people to avoid public charity.[9]

A less charitable means of keeping destitute persons off public welfare involved scrutinizing individual requests for assistance. As mentioned earlier, city officials—first aldermen and then churchwardens and vestrymen—examined who should be assisted. Two types of indigent persons were commonly denied charity—the non-resident poor and the "undeserving" poor. The former, who ran afoul of New York's residency laws, were transported from the province; the latter, whom officials considered vagrants and beggars, might be punished through hard labor. There are several instances of paupers being relocated. Kenneth Scott, who examined the years from 1693 to 1747, found twenty-five families or persons expelled from Manhattan to such locations as New Jersey, Pennsylvania, Long Island, and New England. Of these, John Wilkes went to Philadelphia in 1721, and Thomas Davis ended in New Jersey in 1740. William Humbleton, a "dangerous vagabond," was simply expelled from the city in 1721 without any particular destination noted.[10] To provide the city with an additional defense against destitute non-residents another poor law passed the Assembly in 1721; its purpose was to "prevent vagrants and idle persons from being a charge and expense to any of the counties, cities, towns, manors, or precincts within this province." Residents who entertained strangers in their homes for more than three days had to report them to the local authorities. The citizenry, in effect, had now become an arm of the civil officials, yet another weapon to prevent migratory paupers from entering Manhattan unnoticed.[11]

Private charity, however, could only go so far to assist needy persons, and poor non-residents may have become more difficult to distinguish with the growth of the urban populace. People lacking any church affiliation or a sympathetic neighbor had nowhere else to turn but the city fathers. And non-resident paupers who did manage to enter the city might conceivably have ended on the welfare rolls, if they were too sick to be removed. Indeed, despite the best of efforts, urban officals could do little to stem the constant arrival of immigrants, many of them poor. The fact that artisans from the nearby countryside regularly entered Manhattan, practiced their trades, and avoided paying taxes illustrates the inability of officials to enforce settlement laws effectively.[12]

Perhaps not surprisingly, poor relief itself took on greater urgency, particularly as charitable expenditures rose. The poor tax went to £156 in 1697; during the next few months, from November 1697 to April 1698, it reached £250. The reasons for this became evident in 1702 with the passage of a new poor law. Urban officials could now raise taxes since the "numbers and necessity of the poor were much increased."[13] Again, by 1713 the churchwardens complained about insufficient funds being available for indigent people, "who are in great want and a miserable condition and must inevitably perish unless some speedy method be taken for their support." The following year the poor tax had increased to £438—the highest rate yet recorded. Along with higher taxes also came a willingness on the part of the city fathers to rely upon different welfare systems, namely, an almshouse. By February 15, 1700, the city government purchased Colonel Abraham De Peyster's house on Broad Street to be used as both a poorhouse and a house of correction.[14]

Reliance upon an almshouse would seem to indicate a harsher attitude toward poor people; it certainly suggests that civil officials sought a more economical means of lodging them. Placing destitute folk in a separate shelter under the care of a single keeper would be less expensive than lodging them among several keepers throughout the city. So, too, institutional relief of this sort implies that some poor people were now isolated from the greater community. Yet appearances in this regard must be treated carefully. The almshouse, while indeed marking a shift in policy, remained a sanctuary of last resort for a tiny minority of the urban poor, generally the most serious cases. If Christian Hanneke need to be maintained in the poorhouse in 1712, Grace Pangborne received relief at home in 1714, as did the majority of applicants for assistance. Steven Ross, who offers us the most detailed analysis of the urban poor, found under 10 percent were sent to the building from 1712 to 1735. The others stayed in private lodgings. Even life within the almshouse, despite its dual function as a charitable and correctional facility, was not really onerous for the inmates. It would appear that the structure was less an actual institution with well-defined rules and more an extension of the household. No rules for running the house have survived—if indeed they ever existed—and little effort was made to set the residents to work. Perhaps the building should not even be considered an almshouse, if by that we mean an institution designed to rehabilitate and organize the lives of its inmates.[15] City officials themselves appear to have been of two minds concerning its role: although they described it as a poorhouse, efforts to construct an actual poorhouse, that is, one specifically designed for the purpose, failed in 1714. Increased poor taxes the previous year apparently were insufficient to motivate the city to change its policy further. The rented quarters would suffice.[16]

A more significant sign of changing policy toward poor individuals involved the custom of badging. Lacking a formal almshouse, which would have served to segregate the dependent poor from the general community, the Common Council devised a plan to distinguish some destitute persons from the rest of the populace. In 1707 the Council ordered the churchwardens in charge of the indigent to "put a badge upon the clothes of such poor as cloathed by the City with the word: N. Y. in blue or red cloth at their discretion." Badging poor people in this fashion was hardly new; it had been the standard practice in England during the seventeenth century. The procedure publicly marked some persons as recipients of alms and rendered them distinct from other needy folk and from society in general. The badge might well be seen as an emblem of shame or at least a reminder that some destitute persons, like criminals and other outcasts, were branded, albeit less harshly. Badging also served an important administrative function, for it enabled officials to keep track of persons on public welfare—an essential consideration in a city that sought to distinguish among the different types of paupers. Individuals so marked could then be more easily relieved without an elaborate inquiry into their residential status. The actual extent of this practice remains unclear, yet subsequent accounts in the 1720s reminded officials about badging. And by 1732 the Common Council told the churchwardens they "could not relieve or support any poor . . . but such as shall wear a badge publicly on the sleeve of the right shoulder." Paupers refusing to do so lost any hope of assistance.[17]

Neither poorhouse nor badges quite prepared the city for the arrival of the Palatine German refugees of 1710. Originally, some 2,800 of these peasant farmers (newly arrived in England) had agreed to go to America, where they would obtain farms and process naval stores upon the New York frontier. The British government would pay their expenses over, and the Palatines would then work off the debts. Trouble started from the beginning. The sea voyage claimed the lives of 470 Palatines, while it left many of the others too weak or sick to go any further once they sighted Manhattan. Now the city fathers became alarmed. Immigrants, of course, arrived frequently in the seaport city, but to have approximately 2,300 people, many of them ill, together in a city of less than 6,000 inhabitants could create a crisis. Of particular concern was the threat of disease. Like other seaports, Manhattan had to guard against disease victims starting an epidemic among their own inhabitants; in fact, even the rumor of disease might be enough to stop farmers from victualing the city. Then there was the matter of lodgings. With its eight hundred or so houses and one poorhouse the city was clearly not up to the task.[18]

Moving quickly, the urban authorities prohibited the vessels from unloading their passengers in Manhattan. They then made ready Nutten (now Governor's) Island at the mouth of the Hudson River for the Palatines' reception, sending carpenters to build temporary houses and hospitals. Tents were employed also. During the summer the Palatines recuperated from their ordeal. Although the city fathers provided shelter and medical assistance for the immigrants, we cannot be certain about the quality of such aid. One account from Peter Romers, probably a carpenter, related the construction of 250 coffins, which translates into a 12 percent mortality rate.[19] Even with the reduction of numbers, assisting such a large group of people was a formidable task—so much so that Governor Robert Hunter, who had conceived the plan for bringing the Palatines over, issued an order to apprentice the children. Although the apprenticeship system involved the training of young children in a trade or calling, it could be employed by civil officials as a tool of public welfare. Orphans and the children of poor parents might be placed in other households, in effect keeping them off public charity. The city fathers, too, could hardly object to Hunter's order, for there was always a market for apprentices. What neither party anticipated was the reaction of the Palatines. Parents too ill to protest and perhaps daunted by the language barrier saw their children sent not only to households in the city but to Westchester, Long Island, and Rhode Island. Eight-four children were thus dispersed. Physical separation was made doubly painful by the geographic distances that divided parents from offspring; many parents never saw their children again. Indeed, the memory of the event lingered long among the Palatines, for they recorded this as one of their grievances before the governor in 1720:

> About the same time took the said Governor, without and against their consent, many children from them, and bound them to several of the inhabitants of that province till they should arrive at the age of twenty-one years; particularly two sons from Captain Weisner . . . by which means they were deprived of the comfort of their children's company and education, as well as the assistance and support they might in a small time have reasonably expected from them.[20]

For city welfare officials the memory of the affair faded quickly. Aside from a small number of remaining Palatines, who occasionally appeared on the city welfare lists, there was little trace of them after 1711. The crisis had been weathered; no sign of disease materialized. Segments of the urban populace also profited by the acquisition of the Palatine apprentices, who could serve as domestic or artisanal help. William Bradford, the colony printer, took on John Peter Zenger, while James Elemes became the master of Christine Angle and Mary Robinson did likewise for Anna Maria Angle, the sister of Christine. In total, New York City residents acquired forty-one apprentices.[21] The city welfare officials, in turn, were saved the expense of maintaining them.

No welfare crisis of this sort confronted the city for the next two decades. Poverty remained the lot of some residents, but at no time did their numbers dictate any drastic action or policy alteration; rather, welfare officials relied upon the methods already in use. Indigent persons, normally, received aid at home with only a tiny minority being lodged in the poorhouse. Despite reminders from the Common Council about badging and occasional upsurges in the poor tax, public charity was easily managed. In part, this situation reflected the general economic well-being of the city. So long as business profited and so long as work proved plentiful, Manhattan and its lower classes were able to take care of themselves.

The situation, however, did not last, for by the close of the 1720s the city entered another period of rising poor rates. For much of the decade the rates hovered at between £400 and £500, yet by 1728 they crested above £500 and in 1730 they reached £555. Four years later the figure stood at £649.[22] These numbers boded ill for the city, for they reflected the depressed state of the Manhattan economy. Over the course of the late seventeenth and early eighteenth centuries Manhattan had become firmly integrated into the Atlantic economy. Ships and goods left the seaport city for the West Indies, Europe, and Africa; lumber, fur, flour, and cattle found ready markets overseas. Naturally, the economy benefited and grew to reflect Manhattan's commercial might. Merchants made profits. Workers secured employment. Then in the 1720s the economy began to alternate between periods of prosperity and depression; by 1729, it plunged downward. For the next few years into the middle 1730s New Yorkers saw their shipping decrease and their workers lose jobs. Forlorn reports harped upon the serious state of affairs, noting the exodus of artisans from Manhattan to more prosperous Philadelphia. Rents declined and houses stood empty—clear signs of depression. The causes of this downturn, if not precisely known, can perhaps be ascribed to several developments. Gary Nash, for one, has noted that Manhattan's nearby economic rival, Philadelphia, was in a position to steal traditional New York City markets in the West Indies as the result of the Quaker city's higher-quality flour and beef. Changes in shipping regulations as well as the city's lack of an adequate currency may be other reasons for the depression. So, too, the absence of war meant a decline in military contracts, which Manhattan often depended upon.[23]

As the economy reeled and the poor rates rose, urban citizens viewed their destitute neighbors in a more critical light. A newspaper account in 1734 complained about the "many beggarly people daily suffered to wander about the streets," citing this as a reason for an almshouse. City political factions saw the need to revamp public welfare, too. With the election of the Morrisite candidates in 1734 came a call for a new almshouse. Nor was a declining economy the only reason for such an institution: Steven Ross has argued that periodic epidemics incurred by the urban populace made the idea of a separate building for ill and poor persons appealing. Just as street beggars could be removed from the public eye, so could disease victims. These various factors, then, led to the construction of an almshouse by 1735, and the next year the first inmates were admitted.[24]

This new structure symbolized an important shift from the policies of the past. Unlike the earlier poorhouse, this building had been constructed especially for the poor; it served as a combination almshouse, workhouse, house of correction, and hospital that lodged not only elderly, maimed, and truly needy persons, but those whom city officials viewed as lazy, disorderly, and corrupt. The keeper of the building cared for the "deserving" poor and corrected the "incorrigible," which included "disorderly persons, parents of bastard children, beggars, servants running away or otherwise misbehaving themselves, trespassers, rogues, and vagabonds." Any of the incorrigible who refused to labor faced a "moderate whipping." Various rooms in the house further reflected, in theory at least, the division between these different categories of paupers: living and working quarters were kept separate, and the basement was divided into three sections, with the eastward room reserved for inmates at forced labor, the middle room serving as a general storage facility, and the western room incarcerating the "unruly."[25] Once admitted into the building both deserving and non-deserving persons lived in a structured environment. Upon entering, they were supplied by the city with clothes "marked with the first letters of their names." Various rules told the inmates how to behave: bedtime was set at 9:00 in the summer and at 7:00 in the winter; no person could smoke in bed; and those who refused to attend the Wednesday or Friday prayer sessions went without one daily meal. Other restraints were effected also. City officials prohibited the inmates from asking "for money or drink directly or indirectly from any who came to view the poorhouse." And those who left the facility without permission could face disciplinary action, as happened to Elisabeth Smith, who was warned about leaving the premises on May 16, 1738, under threat of punishment.[26]

From another perspective the almshouse symbolized in effect the changing character of the urban environment. Why city officials chose such a device—apart from the economic reasons—reveals something about the evolution of urban society upon the island of Manhattan. New York City possessed little of the social cohesiveness that so often characterized rural villages established by covenants; in fact, the social codes that governed rural communities, with their emphasis on harmony, order, and the subordination of the individual to the dictates of the village had disintegrated in New York City even in the seventeenth century. Discord between the Dutch and English populations prevented the city from attaining more than a superficial degree of unity, while the continued arrival of immigrants added to the ethnic diversity. Then there was the transformation of the city's social environment. The clustering of the population along the southern portion of Manhattan had resulted in semi-distinct residential districts as early as the 1730s. The six wards of the city contained varying proportions of artisans, merchants, farmers, and mariners, further subdivided along lines of wealth and ethnicity. Economic necessity and cultural groupings propelled these residential divisions as individuals settled in areas most conducive to their business or among their own ethnic group. This process of geographic dispersion by city residents probably weakened the social cohesion of the city further, in effect creating many small villages of people. This consequence in turn provided an incentive for institutional relief.[27]

Into the building came nineteen individuals during its first year of operation. This may well be significant, for it represents a dramatic decrease from the normal number of people on relief, which had totaled between sixty-eight and twenty-eight during the 1720s and 1730s. Quite possibly, some poor persons simply refused to enter the two-story stone structure. For individuals accustomed to assistance in private dwellings the transition to institutional relief might have been too difficult to accept, hence the drop in recipients. After all, the almshouse was not merely a place of refuge; it was also designed as a correctional facility of sorts for the unruly poor. Living among such people was perhaps impossible to accept for some. The alternative, presumably, meant some form of private charity, although in certain instances poor people still received relief at home.[28] Inadequate records make it hard to know precisely what occurred. Steven Ross suggests that institutional relief, while clearly more popular, handled only a minority of those in need; by contrast, Stephen Wiberly argues that between 1737 and 1747 New York City had all but eliminated outdoor relief.

Whatever the truth of the matter, city welfare officials could congratulate themselves on accomplishing an important goal, for poor relief expenditures dropped after the opening of the establishment. The reasons for this are several. The almshouse provided an economy of scale that the boarding out of poor people among urban residents could not match. So, too, inmates in the facility were expected to labor, which meant carding wool, picking oakum, and raising garden crops. The renumeration from such activities remained low, but it might have minimized some expenses such as food costs. And the fact that the almshouse perhaps deterred some from public welfare was a factor in alleviating expenses. Indeed, during the 1740s city officials maintained a surplus in the poor funds.[29]

Given these various developments, can we say anything about the identity of the urban poor and their response to poor relief? Extant poor relief records often detail little about poor people per se, except to note their names and sometimes their reasons for needing relief. One such list of dependent poor people for 1713 has two adult males, twelve adult females, and two male orphans. Their conditions are not always ascertainable. The circumstances of Effie, "a blind woman," and Sarah, "an old maid," who was probably quite elderly, need little comment; the same is true of the two boys. The others were perhaps sick, injured, crippled, or simply unable to care for themselves.[30] Perhaps the best analysis of who these people were comes from Steven Ross, whose data show women outnumbering men both in the almshouse and among those on home relief—148 to 91 in the poorhouse and 38 to 29 at home between 1691 and 1748. Among the children, 47 boarded out and 62 entered the almshouse. Of interest is the reason why such people required relief, and not surprisingly injury, sickness, and old age ranked as prominent causes for assistance. Unemployment, by contrast, was rarely a reason for needing support.[31]

Regarding the response of poor persons to poor relief there is even less information. Here we face the difficulty of inferring from official records the actions and motivations of people who left few traces of themselves and their attitudes. Nevertheless, it would appear that some paupers did evince a reaction to some aspects of poor relief. Considering the corpus of literature dealing with the response of inarticulate people to naval impressment, taxes, and food prices, it would be odd indeed if destitute persons—as the recipients of charity in an evolving welfare system—failed to react in some way. Even in the seventeenth century poor people did not shy away from making their wants known: the Palatines had demonstrated their discontent with the system when they protested the massive apprenticing of their children, and in 1689 the Common Council noted how some of the city's welfare recipients "have made complaint to the Mayor . . . that they are not maintained."[32] The almshouse inspired yet other reactions. Admittedly, no angry mobs placed themselves before its doors or threatened to burn it down; but several of the inmates at least knew how to use the facility to their own advantage. Despite prohibitions against leaving the house, some paupers did exactly that, timing their departure in accordance with the warmer weather. As the city fathers ruefully noted in 1738:

> Whereas several of the poor who are relieved in the poorhouse as objects of charity have of late (when well cloathed at the public charge) made a practice of absenting themselves from the said poorhouse and selling or making away with their clothing in the summertime and returning to the said poorhouse on the approaching winter almost naked to the great expense and charge of the parish, for other clothing to defend them from the inclemancy of the weather and preserve them from perishing by cold.[33]

Not everyone sought to sever their ties with the institution. Many of the inmates had no place else to turn. Circumstances of one sort or another compelled them to seek assistance in the structure rather than among friends, neighbors, and co-religionists—if indeed they had any. Old people without families and orphans had little choice. Thus, Edward Brenen, the public whipper, and his wife Mary entered the house, being "sickly, weak, and ancient, not able to labor and objects of charity."[34] Newcomers to the city, in particular immigrants from overseas, were likely candidates if ill. And for injured and impaired persons the almshouse was possibly the only available refuge they could find. The degree and quality of assistance such persons received remains difficult to discern; certainly, city authorities believed in treating deserving poor people justly and kindly, motivated by Christian benevolence. Stephen Wiberly in his study of urban poor relief even indicates that sick poor persons were better cared for in the almshouse than at home, for they could draw upon the assistance and sympathy of other inmates as well as visits by the almshouse doctor. Yet even deserving poor people, as several vestrymen made clear, had to obey the "good and wholesome orders and rules" in order to maintain "decorum." Whatever the quality of the care it was expected that those of "bashful, modest, humble, and patient temper" be "encouraged and comforted," while the "troublesome and discontented" be "severely checked." In addition, there existed the close proximity of the different classes of poor to one another in the house. Until the construction of an addition in 1747, the vestrymen noted, "there were not apartments sufficient for the comfort of the sick, the repose of the ancient, and keeping a due and proper distance between offenders sent here for correction and such as were real objects of compassion and charity." Additional room, however, did not totally resolve the situation, for officials expressed concern over the deserving poor persons being too close to those "factious, disobedient, stubborn, and incorrigible people." How much they affected their deserving neighbors cannot be determined. Most likely, some of the indigent residents found the almshouse experience unpleasant, with its regulations and boisterous inmates, a far cry from home relief.[35]

This portrait of the New York City almshouse contradicts David Rothman's description of the poorhouse as an institution similar to a "large household" without a "distinctive architecture and special administrative procedures," a place where the keeper and the residents mingled together and "lived as free of discipline and organization as any member of a normal household."[36] Although this description may reflect the philosophy behind the first poorhouse—a private dwelling with no evidence of rules—it bears scant resemblance to the purpose of the second poorhouse. The new structure sought not only to assist its indigent residents, but to rehabilitate them via strict rules and harsh punishments. The city fathers may not have been totally successful in these endeavors—witness the case of the wandering poor—yet they were nonetheless intent on establishing a set structure for the administration of public charity that had been lacking in previous years. In a sense the municipal almshouse illustrates well the double-edged sword of public welfare, whereby relief and assistance were increasingly dependent upon obedience.

The cares and woes of the city largely escaped the countryside of Long Island and Westchester during the late seventeenth and early eighteenth centuries. Vagrants were not unknown, but neither were they present in large numbers; sick, crippled, and elderly persons appeared, but posed less trouble than they did in the city. As a result, a village seldom possessed any real need to employ a separate building for its destitute citizens; they were simply too few in number. Sporadic accounts before 1750 further support this argument, showing only a few needy people in the villages dependent upon charity, either in Long Island or Westchester. This is especially evident for the seventeenth century. In general, towns might have only one or two destitute persons to support a year, if indeed they had that many. In 1687 Huntington had only one apparent potential pauper, John Finch, who, being "deprived in some measure of his intellect . . . and much given to extravagant courses of drinking strong drink," was liable "to come to want and the town liked to be burdened by him." However, Finch was probably never a public charge, for town officials had attached his estate by legal warrant. This meant they could use the proceeds from his property to support him. Other towns were less fortunate. In 1697, for example, the town of East Hampton "ordered by a major vote that the trustees should oppose the receiving of Sarah Whitehair as an inhabitant," disqualifying her from relief under the residency statutes of the poor law. They still ended up treating her, paying Whitehair's medical expenses and sending her to doctors in Oyster Bay and Flatbush. In 1700 she and Martha Stanerd were the only dependent persons being supported, at a cost of under one pound. Much the same appears to have been true for Queens and Westchester, where paupers proved few or non-existent.[37]

Later records for the eighteenth century reveal only a gradual increase in the number of needy persons. The parish of Hempstead, which included not only Hempstead but Oyster Bay, totaled six paupers in 1739, five in 1740, and six in 1741. In portions of Westchester there were even fewer paupers. The vestry and churchwardens of Rye parish served several towns such as Bedford, Mamaroneck, and North Castle, yet in 1738 apparently only two people required assistance, Maragaret Stringham and Ned Rogers. And the latter needed support for only four weeks. In 1725 Brookhaven officials cared for one sick family and looked after a "Negro wench."[38] Of course, the number of people listed in such accounts may well be understated, since people on relief were not always mentioned by name. A gift of firewood or food from the town or parish might go unnoticed, treated as a general part of the poor fund rather than a separate entry. Yet the poor rates themselves indicate that poverty was rarely a costly burden: the parish of Westchester, which also encompassed the town of East Chester, raised £29 for the poor in 1707 and £33 in 1720; this proved considerably less than the £50 stipend collected for the support of the Anglican minister. In the neighboring parish of Rye the vestrymen spent an average of £7-10-0 per year on poor relief in the 1720s. The following decade poor relief rates rose to £50 per year; but this occurred because two years, 1743 and 1748, had rates of £100 and £78 respectively, whereas the middle years averaged only £25 (see Table 1). Such high rates would probably imply outbreaks of sickness, with resulting high costs, rather than an actual increase in the number of truly poor people, that is, people permanently dependent. Individual paupers required varying amounts of money, depending upon the severity and duration of their condition. The Hempstead paupers between 1739 and 1741 normally cost between £4 and £6 a year, although one person was as high as £9 and another as low as £1. In any event, poverty was seldom a serious social problem requiring large sums of money or a restructured welfare system.[39]

Under these circumstances most villages could easily provide for the existing class of paupers at the discretion of local officials: if a poor widow fell ill, the town paid her doctor bills; when a child was orphaned, a family could be found to raise him or her, often as an apprentice; and if a wandering beggar arrived sick and penniless in a village, the town would provide for him until he was well enough to be returned to his last legal residence. Individuals unable to support themselves were normally given aid in their homes or sent to live among other members of the community. Indeed, the latter method of relief sometimes involved an unusual degree of participation among the villagers, since several members of the town might board a destitute person. In 1740 the churchwardens and vestrymen of Rye placed Margaret Stringham, a poor lame woman, with Samuel Hilt for nine weeks and Christopher

Table 1
Poor Rates for the Parish of Rye, 1724-1776

Year	Cost (in £'s)*	Year	Cost (in £'s)*	Year	Cost (in £'s)*	Year	Cost (in £'s)*
1724	5	1738	7	1751	60	1764†	194
1725	8	1739	27	1752	80	1765†	160
1726	8	1740	12	1753†	91	1766†	150
1727	10	1741	60	1754†	91	1767†	210
1728	—	1742	30	1755†	51	1768†	325
1729	8	1743	100	1756	52	1769†	200
1730	8	1744	30	1757†	52	1770	—
1731	—	1745	20	1758†	74	1771	300
1732	47	1746	25	1759†	97	1772	250
1733	5	1747	50	1760†	186	1773	250
1734	—	1748	78	1761†	84	1774	200
1735	8	1749	30	1762†	90	1775	150
1736†	12	1750	54	1763†	245	1776	220
1737†	8						

*All figures are expressed in current money and rounded off to the nearest whole number.

†These years also contain money paid to individuals who rang the church bell and swept the meetinghouse floors, which amounts to no more than a few extra pounds.

Source: Figures found in Proceedings of the Vestry and Churchwardens of the Parish of Rye, 1710-1795, Microfilm Collection, SUNY-Stony Brook.

Isinghart and Catherine Knowlton for seven weeks each. Similarly, in the town of Southold in 1707, John Rogers, who had been recently crippled, was passed around from villager to villager: Henry Tuthill received seven shillings, six pence for carting him from Oysterponds; Sarah Coryn, a widow, received nine shillings for "entertainment charges"; Thomas Tuthill received five pounds, eight shillings, and nine pence for boarding him and paying his doctor bills; and Ann Caryne received eight shillings for housing him. The list of people associated with the unfortunate Rogers included more than a half-dozen individuals performing various tasks. Tending the needy, then, was clearly a community responsibility, a moral obligation instead of a social chore.[40]

The social network of obligation among family members in many rural communities also formed a safety-valve mechanism that prevented towns from becoming overrun with dependents. Family ties not only served as an important means of support for family members, but undoubtedly minimized the need for poorhouses in colonial villages. Provisions in various wills usually ensured some degree of support, however slight, to a wife and children. Widows could expect a third or more of the estate, real and personal; sometimes they even held the estate until the children came of age. Occasionally, specific instructions accompanied the will regarding the maintenance of family members. When Jacob Schellinx of East Hampton wrote his will in 1712, he left the estate to his wife, but made provisions for his executors to guarantee that she would "live in the house and be well maintained during her life." In 1738, Thomas Bunce of Huntington, a widower, took special pains to see that his children looked after their sister, Deborah, since she was "very small in stature and not likely to be able to do laborous work." Bunce, in fact, charged his son Nathaniel with supporting her if she should ever "come to want." In other instances the town could reach agreements with family members to support destitute or impaired relatives. David Edows in 1731 agreed to provide for his younger brother, now insane; in return, the trustees and justices of Brookhaven gave the elder Edows his brother's personal and real estate.[41]

The operation of poor relief in the countryside for much of the eighteenth century reflects a largely paternalistic policy, whereby indigent persons received assistance from their neighbors, friends, and relatives. Inhabitants of small rural villages usually possessed strong ties, often attended the same church, and generally shared similar ideas. Above all, they recognized the need for harmony and consensus in their public affairs regarding the levying of taxes, the drawing of boundaries, or the relief of their poor neighbors. Although the settlers of Westchester, Queens, and Suffolk condemned idle and disorderly behavior, they also recognized that deserving poor persons were a distinct element in society needing assistance and not criticism.[42]

Private charity played a role in the countryside also. Much of this centered upon the churches, which customarily provided for distressed members of the congregation. The Quakers and Dutch Calvinists both saw to the needs of their fellows, and since both sects were well represented in Queens and Westchester they must have lessened public welfare expenditures considerably. Much of this charity went unrecorded because it was private; churchmen simply distributed the money as needed. We do know, however, that the Dutch Reformed Church for the manor of Philipsburgh had £94 in the poor fund in 1706, and that expenditures for poor relief and other church-related expenses ranged between £100 and £300 in the 1720s. The Dutch Reformed congregation of Jamaica had an alms chest from which to distribute funds. One entry for June 25, 1720, reveals thirteen shillings given to needy persons; later years saw amounts ranging from under one shilling to over one pound. Sometimes ministers even assisted persons who did not belong to their parish, motivated by feelings of compassion. The Reverend Mr. Bartow, an Anglican minister, apparently made regular collections for the poor in his church at Westchester. A "distressed woman," who passed through the parish after losing her husband and nine children to an Indian attack, received eleven shillings and six pence in 1708; the next week yet another poor man had an offering raised for him.[43] Not all private charity was church-centered. Benevolent individuals desiring to aid the less fortunate might earmark funds in wills, as happened in 1661, when a Flushing resident left the balance of his estate for poor relief. The destitute population of Southampton received a £5 legacy in 1699. In both instances the towns could use the money to defray public welfare expenses.[44]

Individuals might be compelled by the towns to render private assistance under particular circumstances. If no family connections existed for a dependent individual, towns might recognize the presence of a moral obligation between such persons and their former employers. Instances of this sort may have been rare, but in 1742 Huntington officials had James Rogers post bond for £200 pledging the support of James Chappel, a laborer previously employed by the Rogers family:

> And notwithstanding the said Chappel's labor and industry for twenty years past or more he has not been so careful as to lay up any money or other estate whereby to support himself when old and sick or otherwise disabled from labor and it being very reasonably that those that have had his labor in health and strength should support and maintain him when old age, sickness, or lameness shall come upon him.[45]

Although few towns perhaps went to such lengths, all rural villages could transport non-resident poor persons, sending them to their last legal settlement. Rural communities had an advantage over Manhattan in this regard: it was far easier for them to spot potential dependents and bar the newcomers from entering the community than it was for the city. People wishing to acquire land had to be admitted as inhabitants, that is, receive the approval of the town officials or the freeholders. In this fashion such men as Samuel Hoit in 1671 and Richard Barrett in 1677 became legal residents of East Chester. Towns such as Jamaica enforced local ordinances against the admission of strangers, declaring that "no habitant in the town . . . shall receive any stranger or foreigner in his house that may in any ways be chargeable to the Town without acquainting the Commissioners." East Hampton in 1698 held a town meeting to prevent potential dependents as well as persons of ill fame from becoming inhabitants; all such strangers still in the town after one week were to be "warned out." Once warned, such persons had no legal claim for assistance.[46] These preventive measures did not always erect a protective cordon around rural villages, for the occasional transient or public dependent appeared. The aforementioned John Rogers, who had been tended by several Southold residents in 1707, was one such individual. In that year Southold sent Rogers into neighboring Brookhaven on September 25, considering him an inhabitant of that town; two days later Brookhaven officials returned him to Southold for precisely the same reason. Over the next two years the villagers argued about Rogers's legal residency. Finally, by 1709, Brookhaven had relented, accepted him as an inhabitant, and compensated Southold for maintaining him. Other paupers caused less trouble: they were speedily transported. In 1732 Rye transported Rebecca White from the parish, and in 1749 Smithtown removed two vagrants from their village, while Huntington sent off one.[47]

Rural villages were not necessarily callous in their handling of such paupers. To be sure, no official welcomed these people or relished tending them, but some sense of compassion did exist toward non-resident paupers. Most such persons, typically, were removed only when well enough to travel. Rebecca White, though transported, had been lodged for an indeterminant period of time in the parish. In the town of Brookhaven the local authorities in 1742 provided for "Old Richard," although he was a non-resident, declaring: "It is not intended or to be understood that we take said Richard as our poor [but in charity] as a poor of North Castle in

Westchester county till we can be further advice[d]." The same year that the Rye vestrymen transported White, they also agreed to allow Thomas Flowolling, an older man of "indigent circumstances," to be maintained by his sons in their home at Hempstead. More remarkably, they permitted Flowolling to return to Rye "whenever he pleases and shall want further help which he shall be permitted to ask for and receive to all contents and purposes as though he had not removed out of the parish of Rye."[48]

Despite the dearth of public dependents and the use of forced removal, rural villages and parishes had in place an administrative system for assisting poor people. Queens and Westchester, as mentioned, relied upon a parish system, with vestrymen, churchwardens, and justices to handle the needy residents, and Suffolk depended upon justices and local town officials. Revenue for poor relief came from the county taxes, set by representatives from the various towns who met to decide the rates. Once the rates had been allocated for the parish or town, it became the task of the various officials to distribute assistance. This could take the form of food, clothing, firewood, or medicine; other times it involved paying sums of money to the people who tended the poor.[49]

In general, the system as established appeared to function adequately, although there were difficulties at times in Queens and Westchester because of the parish system. Non-Anglicans resented maintaining an Anglican minister, who was supported along with the poor; this, in turn, may explain why tax revenues failed to arrive. The villages of Bedford and Scarsdale, both in the parish of Rye, fell behind in the parish rate in 1730, and earlier in 1721 only one-half of the sum raised for the minister and the poor in the preceeding year had been collected.[50] Similar problems surfaced in Queens. The Anglican rector of Hempstead observed firsthand the unwillingness of the inhabitants to raise the necessary revenues, noting in the 1720s "the strange convulsion of his parish [Poyer of Jamaica] upon the constables collecting his taxes. I have the neighboring parish inhabited by men of the same temptuous kidney in a great measure. . . . They are a people of unhappy, turbulent spirits."[51] There were even hints of internal corruption in Hempstead. In 1719 one of the justices was accused of "eating and drinking up the poor's money." Yet these incidents, if reflective of the degree of religious animosity between churchmen and non-churchmen, became less frequent over time. The Church of

England in Queens and Westchester grew in number and strength, attracting more inhabitants. Towns paid their taxes, too. And at no time does there appear to have been any problem in supporting poor people; the available records make no mention of this. Suffolk, of course, remained untroubled in regard to poor relief rates. Town relief of poor persons was also perhaps easier there. Unlike the parish system, where several towns had to present petitions for reimbursement to a central town, Suffolk communities handled these matters on the local level within the individual settlement. Only in rare cases was the county itself involved.[52]

Of crucial importance to rural poor relief officers was their reliance upon the citizenry. A lack of formal welfare institutions made the participation of the freeholders essential, especially when it came to "boarding out" poor people. As we have seen, several or more persons might assist one destitute person for a varying length of time. Towns could place paupers with a keeper or guardian for several weeks, several months, or an entire year. Yet our knowledge about the keepers of needy persons remains vague. Who precisely were they? What relationship did they have to their charges beside the obvious one of serving as a kind of paid guardian, and how were they selected for this task? Our ability to raise these sorts of questions—and to hint at what needs to be answered—testifies to our lack of knowledge regarding those people who assisted and boarded their poor neighbors. At present, the historical literature on poor relief offers few clues, except to note that keepers had a role to play in tending the needy. Steven Ross, for one, speculates that the urban guardians of poor persons sought the responsibility in order to procure an additional income from the city. This argument is strengthened by the fact that a few keepers eventually needed public assistance themselves. But he is almost alone in examining the issue, and no study of rural poor relief supplies more than a cursory analysis. In many respects, the people tending rural poor persons have remained as invisible to the historian as the inarticulate paupers they assisted.[53]

Local records from rural villages throughout the eighteenth century illuminate the role of the keepers toward people. Apart from furnishing a quantitative framework that details the number and gender of both keepers and paupers, such documents provide qualitative insights suitable for advancing theories about the mechanism of rural charity—theories that hitherto have not been raised.

It becomes possible to construct a crude demographic profile of the keepers, ascertaining whether there were more men than women, or if relatively affluent keepers rather than marginally poor ones predominated. The records also give a glimpse, though hardly more than that, of the reasons why people assumed the duty of supporting poor persons. In order to present a more comprehensive picture, material from beyond 1750 has been included.

Examining the keepers and the destitute population in terms of overall numbers reveals different patterns among the several townships. The ratio of keepers to paupers ranged from nearly one to one in Brookhaven, where thirty-nine keepers handled thirty-five dependents between 1739 and 1777; or it might attain a ratio of nearly two to one, as happened in the parish of Rye between 1732 and 1776, when seventy keepers sheltered forty-three paupers (see Table 2).[54] These proportions, however, convey a slightly distorted picture, since total numbers fail to show how some keepers might over time board or assist more than one pauper, while others aided only one. Thus, Justice Kissam of Hempstead parish tended Betts Brook's young child in 1763, William Francis and his wife in 1764, and a Mr. Tice and his wife in 1769. Dependent poor persons could also live with several keepers: Richard Hulse of Brookhaven boarded with four different persons during the 1750s. While some paupers might spend several weeks or more in a single household, others could be exchanged quite frequently. Margaret Stringham of Rye was not alone, for Daniel Councel of Southold experienced similar treatment. In 1702 Councel spent three weeks with Captain Horton, three months with William Whitehare, and three separate six-week periods with the Widow Mary Young, Benjamin Moore, and the late Captain Horton's executors. Frequent moves of this sort reflected the sense of community, the sense of cohesiveness, that personified early rural villages.[55]

Over time, paupers apparently remained with keepers on a quarterly or yearly basis. This was especially the case by the middle and later portions of the eighteenth century, when yearly contracts became commonplace. The Hempstead vestry records, which are unusually complete, show the overwhelming majority of poor persons boarded out on a yearly basis. Annual contracts were increasingly common in Rye, too. It was not unusual to see a pauper residing for the entire year with the same keeper, and on occasion special provisions or deals arose between the parish officials and the keep-

Table 2
Gender of Keepers and Paupers in Eighteenth-Century Rye, East Chester, Hempstead, Huntington, and Brookhaven

Community	Men (%)	Women (%)	Children (%)	N
Brookhaven				
Keepers	77	23	—	39
Paupers	34	31	34	35
East Chester				
Keepers	81	19	—	16
Paupers	50	42	8	12
Hempstead				
Keepers	87	13	—	150
Paupers	26	35	39	119
Huntington				
Keepers	68	32	—	50
Paupers	26	42	32	38
Rye				
Keepers	81	19	—	70
Paupers	37	42	21	43

Source: Proceedings of the Vestry and Churchwardens of the Parish of Rye, 1710-1795, Microfilm Collection, SUNY-Stony Brook; *Records of the Town of East Chester, New York*, vol. 6 (New York: East Chester Historical Society, 1964), vol. 6; Hempstead Town Records, MS vol. 5, 1709-1843, Town Clerk's Office, Hempstead, N.Y.; Town Accounts Folder, HHO; *Records of the Town of Brookhaven*, bk. C: *1687-1789* (New York: Derrydale Press, 1931). The figures for Rye are from the years 1732-1776; for East Chester from 1788-1796; for Hempstead from 1739-1773; for Huntington from 1729-1786; and for Brookhaven from 1739-1777.

ers. In 1765, for example, the vestry agreed with John Varnell to keep the Widow McCloon and her daughter for £20 a year, adding that in case of "extraordinary sickness . . . the said Varnell to give notice to one or both of the churchwardens for such further support." In 1745 the town of Huntington made an "agreement" with James Chichester to support Sarah Chichester for a one-year period of time.[56]

The actual mechanism by which officials selected keepers remains rather uncertain; the records can only reveal so much directly. In regard to rural keepers David Rothman has concluded that local welfare officials "made their decisions on purely pragmatic grounds," attempting in effect to match a destitute person with an appropriate keeper. This meant placing dependent poor people among relatives and friends. Yet what about those instances where the poor person had no close relatives or acquaintances? Although the exact process may never be known, it does appear likely that bargaining between the authorities and potential keepers figured prominently in deciding who would assist whom. For example, the town of Brookhaven instructed two individuals in 1746 to "go inquire at what price . . . they can have the child of Dorothy Smith maintained at the cheapest rate as a Christian child ought to be maintained." The following year the town fathers told Richard Floyd to "agree with some person who he shall think proper to keep Mary Smith, . . . the charge to [be] paid of Parish." Other towns seem to have followed an almost identical policy by the middle of the eighteenth century. The vestrymen and churchwardens of Hempstead could rely upon occasional competition between potential keepers for the same pauper. In 1767 they placed a female pauper in the Widow Langdon's home at the rate of nine pounds per year, but the officials also added that "in case John Hageman will keep her for eight pounds a year she is to go there." Perhaps because of such competition the vestry sent this particular pauper to another keeper the following year for six pounds a year. Indeed, in 1763 the vestry even complained about keepers seeking too extravagant prices for their services. Bargaining, apparently, assumed an important role in the boarding-out system.[57]

Sometimes bargaining was unnecessary or impossible. The local elite of the community, that is, the economically affluent and politically active, might shoulder the task of tending the poor, perhaps if no other keepers could be found. The vestrymen of Rye and Hempstead relied upon the charitable feelings of the well-to-do. In 1756 the Hempstead vestry ordered Justice Allyn to aid Henry Underwood; one year later in 1757 Justice Thorne received a similar command to support "blind wench Nan." In Rye Justice Samuel Purdy, a member of a locally prominent family, also kept indigent persons, such as Francis Parker in 1750 for five shillings a week. Most likely, civil officials tended destitute persons because no one else volunteered to take them, or because other potential keepers wanted too high a price for their services. Such persons, moreover, might have been selected because of the quality of the care they bestowed; locally prominent people might have possessed larger homes as well as a servant or slave to assist them.[58]

In other instances the choice of where to send a poor person resolved itself. Persons suddenly confronted with a pauper at their doorstep too weak to be removed became thrust into the role of guardians; their best hope in such circumstances was that the village or parish would compensate them adequately for their efforts. In 1790 Benjamin Drake of East Chester aided John Clark, "a wayfaring man," who presumably just appeared at his house. Jonathan Haight of Rye was paid by the parish in 1738 for the "nursing and burial" of an unnamed pauper. An anonymous freeholder of Huntington became a keeper by default in 1773 when a "mustee called Vanc" arrived at his house "with a small child and fell sick." The evidence is quite sketchy, but it would seem that the keepers of such paupers seldom reappeared in the poor relief records. The unforseen events that virtually forces them to attend the indigent person were unlikely to be repeated; nor were such persons eager to volunteer their services again.[59]

Social considerations as much as economic circumstances and happenstance might have compelled village officials to turn on occasion to female guardians. The identification of women with the home, and their acknowledged role as mothers, nurses, and midwives, made them ideally suited in the eyes of local officials to assist the ill and disabled people. Admittedly, it is difficult to separate social and economic factors in this regard—in fact, they may at times have coincided—for some women clearly desired the stipend. The Widow Thurston of Hempstead demanded greater sums of money for sheltering an indigent female in 1762, and she earned fifteen shillings in 1773 for digging two pauper graves. Others, perhaps, were motivated by like concerns.[60] Even so, village authorities found women, especially widows, quite useful in the boarding out of poor persons. Sarah Purdy combined the roles of midwife and mother when she attended Susannah Tomkins during her "lying in" in 1757 and boarded Patrick Holiday's son in 1762. In Huntington the Widows Wilkes and Arthur sheltered Silas Hand's child in 1777 and 1779, respectively. And in Hempstead, fourteen widows out of a total of twenty women aided the less fortunate, the majority of whom were children or other adult women. Rural widows normally found themselves caring for young children or older women rather than adult men; in fact, out of twenty-four widows identified as guardians of the poor, only five sheltered adult men. Town officials apparently believed that widows were better with small children, for whom they could furnish the place of a mother, or with adult women, for whom they could serve as a companion. Even married women received some credit for their efforts: the Rye vestry paid two pounds to Thomas Dewose but cited his wife's efforts in tending one Gimberton in 1747; and Brookhaven town officials furnished the stipend directly to Mary Slatterly, wife of Joseph, for the keeping of Joseph Grey, a child, in 1754. Despite the economic jockeying that so often influenced the selection of a guardian, rural authorities were not unmindful of the advantages offered by women.[61]

However chosen, keepers were clearly not a homogeneous social group. The individuals sheltering destitute persons were drawn from various classes, reflecting in part the different factors at work in the selection process. Although tax lists, which provide a rough notion of economic ranking, are lacking for many rural communities, the Brookhaven lists for 1741 and 1749 illustrate the status of the keepers during the 1730s, 1740s, and 1750s. Tracing the names of the keepers via these lists reveals a wide assortment of people over time who tended the needy; everyone from the marginally poor of the village to the local elite participated. Definite extremes of wealth existed among such keepers as the Widow Moger, who paid out a scant two and one-half pence in 1741, and Captain Robert Robinson, who paid out one pound, two shillings, and three pence in 1749. Yet the vast majority of people boarding poor persons seem to have been of middling economic status, neither rich nor poor. Seventeen keepers out of a total of twenty-five ranked in the broad middle of the tax lists, between the upper 10 percent and the bottom 20 percent of all taxpayers. While three keepers, two women and one man, belonged in the lowest assessed class of taxpayers, four persons, three men and one woman, ranked among the top 10 percent. Seven keepers failed to appear on the tax lists; perhaps they were not present in the community those two years, living in another household, or were too destitute to be rated. Certainly, someone like Phebe Mulatto, who received thirteen shillings for nursing Sarah Gray in 1735, lived in modest circumstances compared to Henry Woodhull, member of a prominent Brookhaven family, who sheltered Jane Samons in 1757. Whatever the actual status of the unknown keepers it seems reasonable to suggest that a majority of them in Brookhaven were individuals of middling circumstances.[62]

A lack of corresponding evidence prevents the same sort of detailed analysis from being applied to other towns. Nevertheless, incomplete records illustrate that several keepers from Westchester at least belonged to the solid yeoman class of the county, if not the most well-to-do element. In Rye such keepers of the poor as Christopher Isinghart, Thomas Veal, and Archibald Telford appeared in the county freeholders' list in 1763, a document that recorded only the wealthiest 20 to 25 percent of the white, male taxpayers. At least eleven keepers from a total of seventy were located on the list, suggesting an upper-class role in assisting needy persons. The fact that local justices served as guardians in Queens indicated a similar pattern of participation there.[63]

As for the recipients of this assistance, we have even less information about them. Unlike the keepers, who may occasionally surface in tax lists or other documents, dependent poor persons often had uncertain ties to the community—too destitute to be rated and too shadowy to attract much attention except when petitioning for assistance. Rural poor people for much of the eighteenth century exist merely as names on a ledger. And quite often we have no sense as to why they even required aid. Take the case of Tom Jones of Hempstead. From 1753 to 1771 he received support in the homes of several keepers, yet we possess no indication as to the cause of his poverty. Only the sobriquet of "poor Tom" has survived along with a notation that he could no longer support himself. The Widow Hurst of Brookhaven required support in 1739, but whether because of old age, illness, physical impairment, or all three cannot be determined. Sometimes the records do provide detail. The inhabitants of Bedford described Phebe Chambers in 1731 to the Rye vestry as an "ancient woman," who was also "very poor" and an "object of charity." John Rogers of Southold (or Brookhaven) was lame. And James Burtis of Hempstead was a young man "almost blind and not capable of getting his living." Children, of course, require little or no comment, for their age made them unable to support themselves, whether ill or well, illegitimate or legitimate, orphaned or not. If well, they could always be apprenticed off to a master.[64]

In terms of gender and age the records culled from the five towns in Table 2 provide a crude portrait of some of their poor residents. Women and children combined always equaled or outnumbered men, although the latter might be more numerous than women, as proved true in East Chester and Brookhaven. Are such proportions necessarily surprising? This is difficult to say. David Rothman has noted that parishes in Virginia showed more men than women on relief, which contradicts the findings for Huntington, Hempstead, and Rye. He notes, however, that men commonly outlived women, reflecting the impact of childbirth upon women, and he speculates that women might have been aided more often by means of private charity. Alan Watson in his examination of eighteenth-century rural poor relief in North Carolina reveals that men comprised 40 percent of the public dependents in St. Paul and St. John's parishes, while women formed 30 percent, children 20 percent, and women with children 10 percent. In Manhattan, as we have already seen, there were more women than men in both institutional and home relief. Disparities of this sort, if they tell us anything, suggest that more work needs to be done on the identity of the rural poor. Nor can we really say much regarding the response of rural poor people to poor relief at this time: the boarding-out system seemingly sparked little protest—or at least none that has survived—and the absence of institutions and badges might also explain their silence. A system that generally worked to meet the needs of the indigent population created little response.[65]

Whatever the identity or the response of rural poor people we do know that dependency of one sort or another could afflict persons regardless of class. No one was immune to injury, illness, or old age—the kinds of things that made it difficult for people to work. Nevertheless, the effect of a broken leg or collarbone upon a substantial farmer with an extensive family network was small in comparison to an injury upon a landless laborer without friends or relatives. While the well-to-do yeoman might fret, he was in little danger of economic ruin; the despair of the propertyless laborer was presumably greater. As for the females, those married to a well-off farmer or artisan might depend upon relatives or they might even operate the farm or business themselves, if their spouse died. Single women or widows might be less fortunate if they lacked family or resources. The life history of dependent poor people, that is, the stages by which they required relief, often remains unclear. To be sure, a sudden injury or illness might prompt a request for assistance, but what about their condition prior to this? The life cycle, it seems, might have played a role here, for as individuals matured their ability to labor might decline and perhaps their need for charity increased. Normally, young men starting out could expect to increase their wealth and become property holders in their twenties, thirties, and forties. Then they would commonly be worth less as they dispensed their holdings and property among their children. Something of this sort might have occurred among the less prosperous elements of society.[66]

One rather poignant example of this is William Bonnis, whose disputed legal residency reached the Suffolk courts in 1770. The dispute prompted the court to chart briefly his life history and provide a chronicle of his activities over the past few decades. Like many persons of humble origin, Bonnis changed residences several times, yet never moved long distances. At the age of twenty he left Smithtown, his birthplace, moved to Huntington for one year "whilst he served out," and later purchased several parcels of land in his new home. The former servant turned property holder was a good citizen who paid his taxes for the minister and the parsonage lot. Bonnis then sold his property and moved to Oyster Bay. Here he "bought a small house and piece of ground" valued at £58, resided upon it for two years, and then built a "small house" upon the commons, where he remained for some time and had eight children. This land, too, was taxed. So far, it would seem that Bonnis possessed a modest economic standing in the community, perhaps as a small farmer or landed laborer; certainly, he had improved upon his position as a servant. Then for reasons that are never explained Bonnis left Oyster Bay and returned to Huntington, here he labored "from house to house for the freeholders" over the next twelve years. Now that he was older and perhaps unable to support himself, the town of Huntington decided to check upon his legal residency. Whether other public dependents followed this path is hard to say, although Douglas Jones has noted the existence of a class of strolling poor persons in Massachusetts during the middle of the eighteenth century. Perhaps in this regard Bonnis may well have typified the condition of other rural poor folk.[67]

Looking at poverty and poor relief in early New York City and its rural environs reveals both similarities and contrasts. On the one hand, poverty, if defined by the inability to support oneself, had a universal application irrespective of environment; neither city nor countryside possessed safeguards against extreme old age, severe illness, physical injury, or mental handicap; each was an evident reason for assistance. So, too, city and countryside had to contend with a stream of non-residents, who might in time become destitute; and urban and rural officials both attempted to remove such individuals as the occasion demanded. Yet certain crucial distinctions do emerge. Rural towns often possessed a greater degree of cohesiveness and unity, which enabled them to police against outsiders; by contrast, the seaport city witnessed a steady number of arrivals, who could not be easily removed. This was particularly true of foreign immigrants. Family and religious ties are important considerations, too. Kinship networks in Manhattan due to the constant arrival of newcomers were probably weaker than in many areas of the countryside, where parents, children, and grandchildren occupied farms in the same village or county. Similarly, despite Manhattan's several churches, many persons may have been unattached to any denomination, hence requiring public assistance in times of need. Rural villagers no doubt had a closer identification with their churches; indeed, some towns had only one church, and it served as the focal point of the community. As a result, the city was more likely than the countryside to have larger numbers of public dependents.

The increased number of poor people, their mounting expenses, and the evolution of the urban environment into little communities prompted the establishment of the almshouse. Public charity thus took on a more formalized appearance, and the poorhouse provided not only for the relief of destitute persons but for their rehabilitation and occasional correction. This was a far cry from earlier forms of urban relief. In another sense, poor people were now more isolated from the general populace, confined in a building and bound by rules regarding their everyday activities; dependent poor people might contest these developments, but they could not do away with them. In the countryside, however, the boarding-out system remained the cornerstone of public welfare—a system that allowed indigent persons to be tended in private dwellings. This arrangement also made it possible for different members of the community to participate as keepers. No separation between dependent poor persons and the community appeared. Indeed, the rural community as a whole was actively involved in the system of poor relief.

CHAPTER III
The System Under Siege: Restructuring Public Welfare, 1750-1790

*I*n 1757 the town of Huntington named its trustees to the new office of overseer of the poor. Their appointment came ten years after the colonial assembly of New York had passed "An Act for the Relief of the Poor in Suffolk County," which instructed each of the county's towns to elect such overseers, and twenty-two years after New York City had finished construction of its municipal almshouse.[1] Such tardiness on the part of Huntington was not surprising: semi-autonomous rural villages on Manhattan's outskirts experienced few of the concerns of the city in caring for its poor residents and therefore possessed little incentive to change already existing practices, even when commanded to do so by the legislature. Unlike the city, with its noticeable number of impoverished persons in the first half of the eighteenth century, rural communities across New York rarely contained more than a few needy individuals. Those that did exist were normally boarded out among the freeholders or given direct payments of money, food, clothes, or firewood for a specific period.

This method of handling poor people came under increasing scrutiny during the Revolutionary period. The informal attitudes of the past toward poor members of the community gave way in the face of growing concern on the part of town residents, as political, social, and economic upheavals engulfed large portions of New York. New conditions demanded new methods, and several towns began to emulate the city by aiding and segregating its poor citizens. The external dynamic of the American Revolution, that is, the presence of armies and refugees, along with the internal dynamics of village society, encouraged a more formalized approach to rural poverty—an approach that depended upon both almshouses and pauper auctions. New methods of assisting needy persons lessened the distinction between urban and rural poor relief. The departure from previous practices of public welfare heralded the beginning of a new social ethos whereby many of a community's destitute residents were viewed less as neighbors and more as outcasts; indeed, compassion over the plight of indigent persons was invariably mixed with concern over the cost of their upkeep. The countryside of Queens, Suffolk, and Westchester was starting to resemble Manhattan in its treatment of the poor.

In Manhattan, meanwhile, the public welfare system continued to rely upon both institutional and home relief. Into the municipal almshouse came the elderly, impaired, sick, and orphaned members of the community along with unruly and incorrigible individuals, whom the city fathers attempted to correct. Less serious cases of poverty involving unemployed people normally received assistance at home.[2] Although the framework of urban welfare underwent few substantial alterations, there remained the usual administrative details to contend with: paupers had to be clothed, fed, doctored, and sheltered; keepers or wardens had to be hired. And, of course, there was the policy, not always successful, of maintaining order within the almshouse, as officials sought to police and rehabilitate poor people by devising codes of conduct. Enforcing such policies of public welfare could be difficult given the changes within urban society, for periods of prosperity and depression produced fluctuating numbers of destitute people requiring support. Immigrants, too, arrived in Manhattan and sometimes needed aid. The removal of poor persons from the city during the Revolution and the subsequent occupation of Manhattan by the British created a strain upon the public welfare system. Ad hoc programs of charity had to be put into operation. At war's end the city fathers had to grapple with restoring order and aiding the poor.

New York City at mid-century was a bustling seaport community dominating the southern tip of Manhattan. Long an important center of commerce, the city witnessed prosperous times for much of the 1740s and 1750s as shipping increased and revived from the depression years of the 1730s. The streets and avenues that stretched past the mansions of the wealthy and the tenements of the needy bore the footprints of artisans and shopkeepers, lawyers and merchants, carters and laborers, all of whom played a role in the commercial life of Manhattan. Visitors to the city commented favorably on its overall appearance in the 1740s, noting the "spacious and well-built roads," many of which were paved and lined with trees; or they acknowledged the "stir and frequency upon the streets, more populace than Philadelphia," along with the great amount of shipping in the harbor. Later visitors in the 1760s and 1770s depicted a similar portrait, praising the appearance of the city, the extensive amount of trade, and the generally prosperous condition of the citizenry. In fact, the highly commercial economy often benefited worker and merchant alike, providing employment for the former and profits for the latter.[3]

Yet the city could be a cruel mistress to some. Peter Kalm, the Swedish traveler, noted the presence of a poorer class of citizens in Manhattan during the relatively prosperous 1740s "who lived all year long upon nothing but oysters and a little bread." Unlike the artisans and small shopkeepers, whose fortunes rose and ebbed with the conditions of the economy, these oyster-eating citizens apparently remained untouched by the general prosperity of others. For them, the shellfisheries along the coast provided a marginal subsistence; the *Independent Reflector* acknowledged this fact several years later in 1753, when it wrote that clams were the "daily food of the poor."[4] Who, however, were these poor people? Why were they supporting themselves on a diet of shellfish instead of the meat and poultry fare of their more well-to-do neighbors? Newspaper articles furnish little help in this regard since the word "poor" could be applied indiscriminately to members of the working class, those without regular employment, or common street beggars. Indeed, one newspaper account from 1744 claimed that the cheap price of provisions ensured that anyone willing to work would never be in want, save for the "lazy, drunken wretches not fit subjects for the almshouse."[5] Such a description of needy persons ignores people with physical and mental disabilities: a one-legged sailor or a slightly retarded adult probably had few opportunities to obtain regular employment and may have had to rely almost entirely upon the shellfisheries; anyone strong enough to use a rake or shovel could dig for clams, oysters, or mussels. Others may have depended upon fishing. These food sources, in fact, were probably important to laborers, carters, fishermen, and sailors—people who sometimes found themselves during the winter with little or no work and high-priced provisions. What savings they once possessed might be quickly spent, making the shellfisheries a necessary recourse.[6]

How well did the public welfare system function after the establishment of a municipal almshouse in the middle of the eighteenth century? Almshouse records, regrettably, no longer remain to answer this question with precision, yet other sources do illuminate to some extent the machinations of the system and the people it aided. In 1747 the vestrymen of Manhattan—officials who dealt with poor relief—issued a pamphlet "to show the duty and power of the vestrymen of the City of New York." Designed as a "standard" for future vestrymen to draw upon, it was filled with advice regarding the duties of these officials. The ideal vestrymen, according to the authors, were men of middling circumstances who lived most of the time in their respective wards. Persons of "mean circumstances" as well as men with a "multiplicity of business" were unsuitable, since they were too likely to be in a "hurry to be gone." Those of "Proud and haughty Temper," on the other hand, deterred poor individuals from applying for assistance. As the vestrymen noted:

> If a man necessities obliges him to apply to such a man for help he finds so much difficulty and ceremony to come at him and when in his presence, a stern look, which is natural to those men and perhaps a surely answer cuts him to the heart that he chooses rather to perish under his trouble than apply a second time.[7]

These individuals not only deterred some poor people from asking for alms, but gave "disgust" to their fellow vestrymen and may have prevented some of them from offering their own proposal "for the advantage of the poor." It was left to men of middle-class background to run the system effectively—or so thought the authors of the pamphlet.[8]

As public welfare officers the vestrymen had to attend to numerous administrative details. This might mean signing warrants from the churchwardens, who procured "common necessaries" for the almshouse; it could also entail "particular orders" for when an "object of charity" requested asssistance from the aldermen. Of paramount importance to the vestrymen, however, were regular monthly visits to the almshouse to observe the operation of the facility and the condition of the inmates. Constant visits enabled the vestrymen to determine "what was wanting for conveniency and benefit of the poor." Thus, children, if healthy, should be bonded out as apprentices, with the vestrymen keeping a close watch upon their masters; sick and helpless persons and "others in better health" should do some work; and aged and decrepit persons were to be well cared for. Then there was the matter of discharging the inmates. Apparently, the vestrymen decided when poor persons could be sent away from the building "once able to maintain themselves." And regular monthly visits would in theory prevent able-bodied poor people from remaining on the dole. These visits, moreover, allowed the vestrymen to note the behavior and ability of the keeper—the man who ran the institution on a daily basis, residing in the structure with his charges. When the keeper needed to be admonished, the vestrymen had to do it discreetly in private, for a public reprimand in front of the inmates might undermine his authority and "produce much disorder and confusion."[9]

The actual operation of the almshouse was subject to various difficulties whatever the intentions and advice of the vestrymen. Official guidelines might not always be followed, as we have noted with the wandering poor, and circumstances of one sort or another might require attention. Consider the normal task of adequately sheltering people who entered the facility: room had to be made and quarters prepared. The building itself required constant upkeep and repair. Although erected in 1735, the almshouse needed an addition by 1746 in order to better segregate the different kinds of paupers. Over the next few years attempts to maintain the structure and improve it continued. For example, the city fathers ordered the old wooden partitions or walls that divided the almshouse into separate rooms to be replaced with lath and plaster in 1747. Several years later, in 1750, the almshouse dining area, the overhead room, and the entryway of the building underwent an identical treatment. Every few years, other kinds of improvements and simple upkeep took place: the city set aside a separate room for weaving in 1753, and it put iron gates in place for the workhouse by 1757. If both of these developments tell us something about the prevailing philosophy behind the structure, that is, the emphasis on work and incarceration, other instances reflect a degree of consideration for residents themselves. New vaults (privies) were constructed for the almshouse inmates by 1752 and for the workhouse residents by 1761, which perhaps allowed for the better separation of the two distinct classes of paupers. New stoves and a washhouse appeared in 1767 and 1769, respectively. And in 1766 new windows and a coat of paint graced the apartments of the facility. Between 1747 and 1770 repair work or improvements were being performed a little less than every two years.[10]

Almshouse keepers were yet another essential element pertaining to the operation of the system. Their duties included tending the deserving poor inmates—that is, the sick, elderly, and maimed inmates—while employing those who could work in spinning yarn and picking oakum. Keepers also kept watch upon the unruly inmates sent to the House of Correction for punishment. We know little as to why people assumed the office, but financial considerations may have been a factor for some: the office came with a £30 yearly stipend plus room and board; moreover, the keepers could depend upon various kinds of additional income, as when masters sent servants or slaves to the house for punishment. The keeper received one shilling apiece for admitting disobedient servants or slaves, one shilling, six pence for their correction by the city whipper, and another shilling for discharging them. Alexander Forbes in 1764 openly complained to the Common Council about the "many perquisites he has lost occasioned by the said House of Correction being without any whipper for a considerable time." The city reimbursed him. Extra funds were possible, too. John Sebring, the first keeper, was reimbursed by the city for turning up the ground, planting seed, and other expenses "about the garden," receiving £3-7-1 for his efforts.[11]

Applicants for the position seem to have viewed it as a potentially lucrative job, which may explain why Tobias Van Zandt in 1769 petitioned to become a keeper at the then current salary of £40, "or as cheap as any other person whatsoever." Such persons were not necessarily greedy; it is quite possible that several of them were only marginally better off than their charges. John Sebring, for one, appears to have been an unsuccessful businessman, whose efforts to build a wharf and storehouse on city property incurred the wrath of the Common Council. The Council refused to compensate him or recognize his right to conduct business upon it during the 1720s.

After his death in 1739, the city authorities permitted his widow, perhaps because she was destitute, to remain on as keeper until the following year. Frederick Sebring, who held the post between 1747 and 1750, was reduced to the level of one of his charges along with his wife during his last year in office. That year a serious illness afflicted them both, leaving him almost totally blind and his wife near death; they remained in one of the "best apartments" of the building while another keeper took their position.[12]

Did the keepers perform their jobs well? Here again, the records seldom provide us with sufficient information, although it does appear that some of these officers were older, more mature individuals. This can be deduced from their limited terms of office or the occasional remark in the available records. Both Sebrings served for only a few years, and Captain Jacobus Kiersteed had been in office for a little over three years when in 1758 the Common Council declared him "much indisposed and unable to execute the said office of overseer of said house." Still, there is no direct evidence that old age interfered with their duties without attracting the attention of the vestrymen and aldermen. And if a keeper did prove inept he could be swiftly discharged, as happened in 1755 to Robert Provoost, who had failed in "the duty of his office."[13]

As urban welfare officials supervised the system and tended the poor they could not fail to notice the increasing demands placed upon them. The problems that had led to the construction of the municipal almshouse showed no sign of abating after 1750, despite efforts by officials to put paupers to work and to transport non-residents.[14] Immigration into Manhattan was something urban officials had little control over. Short of sending indigent foreigners to Europe, which did occasionally happen, the city was often powerless to do much in the matter except to assist the immigrant poor folks. Laws designed to prevent the dumping of destitute foreigners were difficult to enforce, especially when crafty ship captains landed their passengers just outside city limits. The laxity of officials in ferreting out such paupers was also called to attention by William Livingston, editor of the *Independent Reflector,* who wrote in 1752:

> Thus armed with legal authority we might be effectively guarded against any but home bred poverty and indolance would all our magistrates exert an equal activity in the execution of their public

duties. But alas! far from feeling the happy effects of the influence of these laws, one would naturally imagine, that either thro' antiquity or neglect, they are grown dispicable in our eyes, and have entirely lost their original authority.[15]

Equally daunting was the continued maturation of the urban economy and its impact upon public welfare. It would be incorrect to say that Manhattan's economy became capitalist during the 1750s and 1760s—it had, in effect, been so even during the seventeenth century—but some of the labor practices that characterized the early period declined. For instance, artisans and laborers now had more freedom to change jobs, which reflected the growth of a wage labor system on a per diem rather than monthly or yearly basis. Greater horizontal mobility between jobs eradicated ties between workers and their employers, and undoubtedly it left the former more vulnerable to the post-war depressions of the 1760s and 1770s. As the economy alternated between stagnation and expansion, working-class folks found jobs less secure.[16] The seasonal nature of work was another problem. Even during good years winter work was scarce for some people, while food and firewood rose in price. As the *New York Almanac* of 1747 noted, the month of January, distinguished by "piercing cold," proved little threat to rich people "with raiment, fire, and food," but it left poor people in "oppressive want and hunger's urgent pain." The poor rates, not surprisingly, rose steadily in the late colonial period: Gary Nash has noted that the average annual expenditure for the period 1751 to 1760 was £667 sterling; the following decade saw the rates rise to £1,667 sterling a year—a dramatic increase.[17]

Under these circumstances poor relief assumed even greater importance, although the basic features remained the same. Officials admitted more and more people to the almshouse, compelling the enlargement of the facility by 1766 and a separate bridewell (a house of correction) by 1775 next to the building. As the poor rates climbed upward between 1771 and 1775 to £2,778 sterling per annum, the almshouse itself became crowded with occupants: by 1771, 339 persons required shelter in the building; the next year the number rose to 425. And these numbers represented only a portion of the needy classes, for many people received assistance at home from the city welfare officers. In 1775 city officials dispensed over £6,000 in cash and goods, the latter being mainly dry goods or, presumably, clothing.[18] Voluntary subscriptions to aid poor New Yorkers were not unusual either; it was a normal practice in winter. In 1760 the *New York Gazeteer* reported "a considerable collection" raised to procure wood and all "the necessities of life for the poor." One account in the *New York Mercury* in 1752 even employed poetry to induce the more well-to-do to aid those less fortunate:

> Hail! Great good Man, hail! Patron of the Poor
> May Riches ever enter at thy door
> Be calm content, for ever in thy breast
> Because they did relieve the poor distressed
> With open hand, thou gav'st a large supply
> To help the needy who for help did cry.[19]

Attempts to employ poor people outside the almshouse attracted attention, too. In 1768 a committee appointed by "the inhabitants of the City of New York . . . to encourage frugality and employ the poor," urged citizens to reduce purchases of goods from abroad and to hire the "numerous poor" as well as tradesmen and other "distressed inhabitants." Plans to assist poor citizens by furnishing employment were complemented by the existence of several benevolent societies; the St. George Society and the St. Andrew Society, for instance, attempted to care for indigent English and Scots members. And, of course, the churches did their part.[20] Yet the continued influx of paupers into the municipal almshouse and the ever-rising poor rates reveal the modest level of success in combating poverty.

By the eve of the American Revolution the urban poor relief system was under siege, literally and figuratively. There remained the basic problem of caring for large numbers of paupers, who in the almshouse consisted of "the blind and the lame, numerous helpless orphans, tender distressed infants, foundlings, and decrepit old age in its last stage, the sick in body and distempered in mind." Then there was the political maelstrom of 1776 to consider. Under the control of the patriots, the city government tried to create order out of confusion by purchasing provisions and firewood for poor residents. Plans for employing "the industrious poor of the City in spinning and making manufactures" in January 1776 echoed the proposals of the 1760s. Such ideas, however, vanished once the prospect of a British invasion appeared probable by the summer of 1776. George Washington thought that the "shrieks and cries" of the destitute inhabitants would demoralize his inexperienced soldiers, who needed to concentrate their attention upon the enemy. The patriotic committee governing the city agreed with Washington's request to transport its poor citizens from Manhattan. They ordered that the "women, children, and infirm persons in the City of New York be immediately removed from the said City agreeable to General Washington's request," and by August the city's poor inhabitants had been placed in the surrounding countryside, where they would remain until the end of the war.[21]

Removing these poor citizens proved no easy matter. Transporting the occasional transient or vagrant to his or her last legal settlement was a relatively simple task compared to the job of removing some four hundred indigent folk from the almshouse as well as any other destitute folk wishing to leave. The fact that many of them were impaired, injured, or elderly made matters more difficult. Boats, carts, and wagons had to be found; food and shelter provided. In short, the entire operation involved a considerable amount of effort for the officials in charge and perhaps a degree of discomfort for the people being moved. Since no one rural community could easily handle such a large number, the poor evacuees were apparently divided into small groups and dispersed throughout the counties of Dutchess, Westchester, Ulster, and Queens. Local authorities in the towns then assumed the responsibility of maintaining the newcomers, with the state reimbursing them for their expense. Naturally, there were problems in an operation of this sort. One Colonel Lott, who oversaw the removal, informed the patriot authorities on October 3, 1776, that many of the people sent to New Windsor were "provided with provisions in a very expensive manner"; the Colonel, along with Major Parks, then became a committee to devise "a more economical mode of providing for them." As always, charity and economy went very much hand in hand in the minds of welfare officials. Sometimes the evacuees had difficulty in securing assistance from the villagers. Several weeks after Lott's report the patriot committee of New Windsor noted that six poor women with children from Manhattan could find no lodging in or near the town. What happened to them remains unknown.[22]

Local officials, in turn, ran into difficulties when it came to dealing with the influx. Rural villages were quite familiar with needy people, but they could hardly have been prepared for the sudden arrival of a large group of paupers, perhaps more than they had ever handled at one time before. The freeholders of Bedford in Westchester county had a unique opportunity to experience firsthand the difficulties so often faced by city officials when over two dozen paupers from Manhattan arrived in August. The patriotic committee governing the village hired a house for the destitute arrivals—perhaps because no one wished to board them. Even so, the separate lodging or poorhouse did not resolve the difficulty of tending these paupers, for as one of the local authorities reported in October:

> There is men and women in the poorhouse that is able to earn their living and not be chargeable to the public. They do little jobs about, which they are paid for, and they buy rum with and get drunk. They quarrel among themselves and make their complaint to me, which I can't do anything with them.

Whether this dilemma was ever resolved is uncertain, yet by December the villagers of Bedford were still complaining about needing instructions. Clearly, the welfare system, if still functioning, was in a state of disarray. Not until later in the war did some order emerge from the confusion.[23]

For the British, who occupied Manhattan during the Revolutionary War, poor relief was also a pressing matter. The war disrupted the normal order of things, played havoc with the economy, and created large numbers of loyalist refugees. Into the vacant almshouse swarmed three hundred such indigent persons, people who could not support themselves. Fires that broke out in the city left many people homeless and dependent upon aid. Trying to support the destitute by normal means, that is, by having the vestry collect a tax for their support, was well-nigh impossible, for many New Yorkers had fled the city at the approach of the enemy. New methods had to be adopted. A series of fines were levied against farmers charging above the maximum price of goods. Rents from buildings vacated by their owners were applied to relieve the needy. Individuals contributed funds, and Guy Carleton, a British officer, assisted children and orphans. According to one estimate £45,000 had been raised for the relief of the poor.[24]

With the end of the war and the subsequent evacuation of the British from Manhattan, city officials began the work of revamping the system of urban welfare. The disestablishment of the Anglican Church in 1784 did away with the offices of churchwarden and vestryman; instead, poor relief became the responsibility of the thirteen almshouse commissioners, although the aldermen of the Common Council continued to disperse small amounts of assistance. In other respects the system remained basically unchanged, for the state poor laws of 1784 and 1788, while offering some revisions, reaffirmed the colonial practice of local responsibility for poor relief and upheld residency requirements. The removal of non-resident poor persons was continued and even facilitated by the inauguration of a passport system, whereby migrating working folk presented the authorities with a certificate or passport that had their name and last legal settlement or residence. Penalties against poor people became harsher. As Raymond Mohl has noted, the poor law of 1788 required individuals to own more property than in colonial times in order to establish residency, while it increased the registration period for residency from forty days to one year. In Manhattan, the city fathers still relied upon the almshouse to assist and discipline the poor. New bylaws for 1784—the first since 1736—retained much of the philosophy of the earlier code, demanding proper behavior on the part of the inmates. In one section the new bylaws declared "none shall ever swear, abuse, or give ill-language to one another or be clamorous but all shall behave themselves soberly, decently, and courteously to each other and submissive to their superiors and Governors." Offenders could be placed in a dark room on a bread and water diet for disobeying the regulations of the house. So despite the political revolution that had occurred with the coming of independence, the urban welfare system remained in place much as before.[25]

The 1780s and 1790s also furnished little respite from the social and economic upheavals that had plagued welfare authorities before. The differences between rich and poor people were no less noticeable; nor did destitute immigrants cease entering the city. Manhattan officials complained in 1784 about the number of poor people being "greatly increased," and they specifically targeted the "idle and profligate Banditti," who roamed the city stealing and robbing. Vagrants and prostitutes also appeared to have increased, many of them left from when the British controlled the city. As always, these people, whether deserving or non-deserving, needed to be fed and sheltered. In 1785 a plot of ground behind the bridewell became a garden, presumably to supplement the inmates' diet, and William Sloo, the bridewell keeper, during the 1780s employed the vagrants in his care to catch fish for the institution, winning the praise of the Common Council for his endeavors. To make room the barracks behind the almshouse became a refuge for the sick poor in 1787.[26] Even so, poverty remained a compelling problem. Although the 1785 census for the almshouse reveals only 301 inhabitants—fewer than the 400 in 1776—the number of people on outdoor relief must have been considerably higher. Time and again, the city fathers needed to raise additional funds: the almshouse commissioners on February 5, 1785, informed the Common Council that it was no longer in their power to assist the multitude of poor people at home who were in "want of the common necessaries of life." Apparently, they lacked the financial resources. The Common Council responded by asking the city clergymen "to solicit contributions," which suggests that private charity had reached certain limits and needed an official request to raise more money. The city for its part furnished an additional £150. The following year another supplementary grant of assistance became necessary; if the Council did not provide extra funds many of the city's poor residents would be forced to enter the almshouse, which was "already much crowded." Again, the city raised more money.[27]

The almshouse commissioners also had their hands full in monitoring the people already in the institution. As we have seen, some of these people were quite willing to assert a degree of autonomy, protesting the need for more assistance or absconding from the institution. Much the same attitude existed in the 1780s and 1790s. In a city where working-class folk manifested a very real interest in everyday events, often displaying their outrage at unpopular political and economic policies through crowd actions and simple disobedience, it would be odd indeed if dependent poor people appeared passive or indifferent. Michael Katz in his study of welfare institutions has noted too that "individuals have used institutions and organizations for their own purposes, shaping them sometimes in ways quite at variance with the interests of their sponsors." The same was often true of poor Manhattanites. Although poor relief records usually suffer from a built-in class bias, they remain useful for illuminating the response of some poor citizens to poor relief. We know, for example, that sick persons in the almshouse in 1786 complained to officials about "a want of attention" from the institution's doctor. The city aldermen to their credit investigated the allegations on at least two occasions and in 1787 pronounced themselves satisfied with the treatment being administered. Other poor folk attempted to deceive officials, for during the 1790s the commissioners issued a directive to the almshouse keeper about people who bluffed their way into the building instead of seeking gainful employment. Elisabeth, a black woman described "as answering little," was actually an escaped slave, who probably entered the almshouse to avoid capture; after being discovered, she was returned to her master. John Armstrong sent his wife and three children into the structure, complaining of a "lame leg" that made it impossible for him to support them. However, the almshouse authorities noted that his injured leg did not prevent him from working as a ferryman. They charged him for the support of his family in the house.[28]

The 1790s also witnessed officials and inmates contesting with one another the issue of alcoholic beverages. Beer and perhaps rum had been dispensed to the poor during the colonial period; it remained available for much of the 1790s, but officials were intent on preventing the smuggling of any "strong liquor" as well as excessive drinking by the inmates. Such restrictions possessed merit, for an intoxicated or alcoholic inmate was a danger to her or himself and others. Yet alcohol, in whatever form, was also a staple for the great majority of city dwellers, rich or poor. Quite possibly, the inmates resented any limits being placed upon their consumption, deeming drink a necessity rather than a privilege subject to the control of their keepers.[29] And they were willing to go to unusual lengths to meet their needs. In 1793, for instance, the commissioners noted:

> Complaint being made that numbers of the objects of the almshouse who under pretext of fetching water from Chatham Street, were frequently seen in the tippling shops and begging in the streets; the water of our new well was again examined and concluded to be wholesome and sufficiently good to justify an abridgment of the privilege thus abused by the paupers of the house.[30]

What the inmates had done was to complain about the unsuitability of the water from the almshouse well, receive permission to leave the premises, and then procure liquor. The account also suggests a degree of organization among some of the poor—organization that was sufficient for a time to outwit the poor relief officials. Nor was this the end of the matter, for the almshouse occupants employed the same ruse to obtain alcohol in 1797.[31]

Monitoring the behavior of the needy and enforcing the rules of the institution was not the only task of the commissioners. It was also necessary for them to apprentice the children of indigent parents. The bonding of boys and girls to employers or masters was a common eighteenth-century operation; it enabled children to learn a trade and perhaps to improve their economic standing over time. The almshouse commissioners found bonding a convenient and humanitarian mechanism since it reduced the number of children in the house, while it provided a practical education for them. Usually, poorhouse children were placed on trial for a short time with a perspective employer in either the city or countryside. A formal agreement indenturing the child to the employer was later drawn up specifying the conditions of the contract and the number of years to be served. The same practice applied to children of destitute parents not residing in the almshouse, although the mayor and aldermen supervised this procedure.[32]

Of particular interest is the response of the poor to this aspect of public welfare. Working-class New Yorkers maintained an interest in the program and did not hesitate to alert authorities about possible improprieties in its operation. Indeed, the signing of the indenture failed to sever the emotional bonds between parents and child, and available evidence from the almshouse commissioners' records reveals a communication network in place among parents, siblings, and apprentices. In 1793, for instance, the sister of Jane Newman appeared before the commissioners to complain that Jane, an apprentice, "was ill-used being too frequently and cruelly beat and whipped and her schooling neglected." That same year the mother of Jane Green lodged a protest, testifying that the Widow Mary Sword, her daughter's mistress, corrected the child too much. Occasionally, parents even managed to maintain contact with their children after they had been sent to masters in the countryside. The mother of David Morrison implored the authorities for her son's release from his master in Ulster county, so he could learn a trade. Most likely, she had received information (from her son?) that his master was neglecting his education. Another mother went to greater lengths and visited her son's master in the same county, begging him to release the child from the contract.[33] Parents intervened to protect their children in other ways, too. The indenture of Isaac Van Dyck in 1792 had a written clause forbidding Walter McBride, his master, to leave Manhattan "without the consent of his [Van Dyck's] parents in the penalty of £50." Nor were these actions peculiar to the 1790s, for sporadic evidence from earlier eighteenth-century sources reveals similar instances of parental concern. In 1728 the Widow Mary Anderson testified before the local justices that Benjamin Blake, her daughter's master, "unreasonably corrected her." And parents might even ask the authorities to secure the release of children if better opportunities arose, as when the mother of Stephen Wood requested the city fathers in 1739 to release her son from his indenture, since the boy's uncle now agreed to train him.[34]

During the 1790s the commissioners of the almshouse acted as a general court of inquiry in these matters. They decided if a master had abused his or her charge, and they determined if the agreement between the two parties should be rendered void. Not surprisingly, they demanded proof that corrective measures were excessive. Eighteenth-century society found whippings and beatings a necessary means of punishment for unruly adults and children. Indeed, employers in Manhattan and the countryside often defended such actions by claiming their servants merited physical correction because of their various misdeeds. Thomas Thomas, for instance, acknowledged he had punished his female servant but only "when she deserved it," thus dismissing the charges of ill-usage brought against him to the satisfaction of the commissioners. The commissioners also agreed with the Widow Sword's reason for correcting Jane Green. The girl's "frequent running away" had made it necessary for Sword to discipline her. In a more extreme case of servant abuse the wife of Richard Amos admitted "her husband whipped the girl [his servant] with a horsewhip, but promised it should be done no more." The committee sent to investigate the charges against the couple then dismissed them.[35]

Nevertheless, welfare officials were not unsympathetic to the complaints of parents. The authorities at times voided indentures and took preventive action against any further possibility of abuse. In the colonial period officials overturned several indentures because masters had mistreated their charges, and in 1792 the commissioners noted that "some of the poor children placed at a distance in the country, have been very ill-used." They then agreed to prohibit masters from taking children into the country "without obtaining leave of the board."[36]

As urban officials retained the basic elements of their welfare system while struggling at times to administer relief and monitor its recipients, rural townsfolk north and east of Manhattan found themselves with a more serious dilemma. Poverty was no longer a casual concern; it had become a very noticeable phenomenon throughout much of the countryside by the middle of the century. Admittedly, the actual number and percentage of poor people in local towns appeared meager compared to Manhattan, yet destitute persons were still numerous enough to spark debate in town meetings. And with such debate came changes in the system of poor relief.

The economic and social developments, which had altered the response of urban society toward the destitute, eventually materalized in one form or another in several rural communities. For one thing, the rustic, often provincial environment so evident in the villages of the early 1700s declined in the wake of economic expansion, as towns and villages became drawn into Manhattan's commercial orbit. Communities in Suffolk, Queens, and Westchester soon found that distance from New York City provided fewer obstacles to the gradual process of economic interdependence. Villages increased their ties to the commercial world by building docks, starting ferry service across Long Island Sound, and improving roads. In eastern Long Island villages such as Sag Harbor in the town of East Hampton became important trading centers, engaged in whaling. Light industry also made an appearance as brick kilns, pottery works, and paper mills started to dot the countryside along with the ubiquitous grist mill. Farming, too, became more commercialized. Some yeomen, especially those who resided in Queens and Westchester, could supply Manhattan with garden crops, dairy products, and livestock more easily than they could before. The Anglican minister of Rye wrote in 1728, "Here are more hundreds of bushels of wheat sent to market in a year now, than single bushels twenty years past."[37] Driving cattle to market or transporting produce by wagons necessitated a better road system, and by 1724 an act passed the colonial Assembly requiring the connection of various roads on the Island. In Westchester, the Old Westchester Path Road served as a major artery for travelers and farmers alike. By 1758, moreover, the erection of a second bridge across the Harlem River indicated an increased volume of traffic between Westchester and the city. A further sign that contacts between the city and the countryside were on the rise came in 1772, when stagelines from Brooklyn to

Sag Harbor and New York City to Boston began regular service. The countryside was becoming firmly linked to the city.[38]

Uniting the rural village to the urban marketplace had certain social costs, however. If closer ties to Manhattan gave farmers a ready market for their surpluses, it also allowed them to feel the effects of economic depressions more readily; if ferry service and roads facilitated travel, it also gave transients better access to the rural hinterland. The commercial farming regions outside of the city, so typical of rural areas near urban centers, also witnessed the development of a more stratified social structure with fewer opportunities for advancement and, not surprisingly, the growth of a landless laboring class. Closer ties to the commercial world meant an end to rural isolation and left villagers on Long Island and Westchester with a set of problems similar to those of the city. Moreover, the close-knit social fabric of village life started to give way to a more individually oriented society caught in the process of economic development.[39] Nowhere was this more evident than in the evolution of public charity from a system that boarded poor persons among the villagers to one that increasingly favored such methods as poorhouses and pauper auctions. Old methods of assisting needy persons, with their emphasis on community participation, were frequently cast aside by local officials in a frenzied effort to find a more economical means of sheltering them. In the process, rural poor people came to be viewed less as objects of charity and more as costly burdens.[40]

The transformation of public welfare occurred first on eastern Long Island. Although removed from Manhattan's economic orbit, east end villagers in Southold, Southampton, and East Hampton had close commercial ties with Boston, shipping cattle, horses, sheep, and whale oil to the Puritan metropolis for the West Indies trade. Ships regularly sailed between eastern Long Island and New England. We do not know the degree of economic stratification within these communities, but we do know that in neighboring Brookhaven in 1749 the top 10 percent of the taxpayers controlled 46 percent of the assessed wealth; conceivably, east end towns had an equally stratified social structure given their degree of commercial activity. Then there was the problem of the soil. Eastern Suffolk, because of its thriving trade, was dependent upon the land to raise livestock and crops. Yet its ability to do so was hampered by overcultivation: generation after generation of farmers had planted crop upon crop in the fields, slowly wearing out the soil. As one nineteenth-century account noted for eighteenth-century East Hampton: "The lands had already begun to fail of their original productiveness; the crops were diminishing for want of attention to manure and the quantity of land under tillage decreased with the decreasing crop." To make matters worse a throat distemper struck East Hampton in the 1730s, carrying off large numbers of people and presumably raising the cost of public welfare. Distressed families needed medical attention, while those who lost a spouse or provider might become dependent upon the town for aid. Indeed, much of Suffolk appears to have suffered from periodic outbreaks of sickness during this period.[41]

Rural townsfolk in response began to revamp their system of public welfare. At first, these changes were almost cosmetic in nature—for example, when Southold appointed its first overseers of the poor during the 1720s. Poor persons, however, still appear to have been boarded out in the town. Yet by 1737 Southold residents appointed a committee "to make application to the General Assembly in order to inable them to build and keep a workhouse in this Town." Not only did they wish to lodge the town's poor residents in a separate structure, but the villagers believed that these people should be put to work. Three years later they did in fact make a motion to "hire a suitable house" as well as a keeper to superintend the inmates. In later years the freeholders oscillated between institutional relief and home relief, judging from the various accounts in the 1760s; nevertheless, they emphasized a degree of economy when it came to boarding out the poor. At one point in 1770, after going back to the boarding-out system, local officials gave poor individuals an opportunity to decide where to live. Indigent folks could then choose their particular keeper, subject to the overseer's approval. However, the town declared that the new keeper "must have no more for keeping them than the common price each one is kept at." The town of East Hampton followed Southold in regard to institutional relief. Up through the 1730s the villagers placed poor persons in private residences, but by 1747 the town voted to construct a house "for the ease of the town's poor."[42]

Developments of this sort proved even more common by the late colonial and Revolutionary era, as town after town considered alternative methods of poor relief. The process by which villages changed the system of relief was not always identical—some favored poorhouses and others preferred pauper auctions—yet it became clear that the traditional modes of assistance were less suitable. Old ways of tending poor people became suspect.

This transformation can be examined in depth by focusing upon the towns of Huntington, Hempstead, and Rye. All three communities shared a similar genesis, having been settled in the seventeenth century by God-fearing New Englanders, and all three had originally possessed similar social structures with only minor distinctions between rich and poor townspeople. In certain respects, they epitomized what Michael Zuckerman has termed "peaceable kingdoms," communities where the fine arts of conciliation and gentle persuasion existed in order to forge a workable consensus among the inhabitants to counteract occasional strains and tensions. In 1715, for instance, a dispute over the site of the Huntington meetinghouse, always a sensitive issue for devout Calvinists, ended when the town employed ministers from outside the community as arbitrators. Committees of private citizens also resolved boundary disputes between Rye and the colony of Connecticut. Not surprisingly, all three villages used the town meeting as a public forum to air issues of common interest, such as the admission of strangers, the granting of property, or the regulation of taverns. The desire to preserve order was so great, in fact, that even the establishment of the Anglican Church in both Hempstead and Rye, if far from welcome, received grudging acceptance over time by many of the inhabitants, perhaps because they still controlled the administration of the church through the election of the churchwardens and the vestrymen. The need to resolve differences amicably, to settle grievances fairly, and to agree upon political policy almost unanimously remained a salient feature of such communities into the eighteenth century.[43]

Internal tranquility, however, was sorely tested during the middle of the eighteenth century as the economic development engulfing the countryside disrupted the normal order of the villages. This period, labeled the "swarming time" by one account, witnessed the emigration of people from both the Island and southern Westchester, often to the frontier regions of the north. This exodus can be attributed in part to the continuing increase of the population during the 1700s and the limited supply of land available for cultivation. In a society where property remained crucial to wealth and social standing, a shortage of land could seem critical to farmers trying to preserve or expand their holdings. Queens had little or no common land after 1732, and in Rye only scattered parcels of available land existed after mid-century. By the 1760s, almost regardless of location, farmers had less property to bequeath their children.[44] What land did exist might engender heated debate, as happened in Hempstead during the 1740s, when the normally placid town meeting turned into an angry, factious assembly over the issue of the commons. Vocal groups of freeholders now publicly recorded their opposition for the records, a clear sign that a workable consensus was no longer attainable.[45] As might be expected, the social structure under these circumstances began to reveal a less egalitarian society than had existed in the seventeenth century. The top 10 percent of the taxpayers in Huntington controlled 37 percent of the assessed wealth by 1764. In New Rochelle, a town close to Rye, the most affluent tenth of the taxpayers owned a third of the total wealth. In other communities on Long Island the top 10 percent possessed as much as half of the wealth. Such proportions, in turn, indicate a more commercialized economy.[46]

These internal developments comprise only part of the larger social picture of rural society. The emergence of the commercial economy and the less egalitarian social structure may not have been immediately visible to everyone, but the presence of outsiders was known. As early as 1720 the town of Westchester had called attention to persons who entered the community to take shellfish from the town waters; by 1740, they passed an ordinance to seize the ships of people engaged in this shellfish plundering.[47] Similar concerns were manifested by other villages. In 1757, the same year that Huntington appointed its first overseers of the poor, the townsfolk decided to "join together to defend the town from strangers fishing and fowling anywhere in the Town." They extended the warning to prevent "foreigners" in 1765 from clamming in town waters. Rye took identical steps in 1753 to prevent individuals from destroying local clambeds: the village imposed forty-shilling fines on offenders, with one-half going to the informant and one-half going to the poor fund. The major reasons for these laws was not only to protect shellfisheries from misuse, sometimes from local inhabitants themselves, but more importantly to prevent commercial bandits from raiding town shores for clams and oysters, which could then be sold to city markets. These actions placed poachers in direct competition with the marginally poor of the town, a fact noted by the residents of Hempstead in 1769, when they declared poaching "a great deterrent to the inhabitants of the town, especially the poorer sort who receive great benefit from that part of the fishery."[48] Ironically, the proximity of the urban marketplace to the bays and inlets of Westchester and Long Island had made the countryside a competitive arena for both commercial smugglers and the poor—the former seeking to make a profit and the latter seeking simply to survive.

Warnings against strangers and foreigners were not always directed against people engaged in clam smuggling. Some of the individuals catching fish and fowl inside the towns fell outside the social network of the villages and formed the nucleus of a seasonal or casual labor force. We know, for example, that the freeholders of Queens by 1764 were so worried about these types of people that they petitioned the Assembly about how "several indigent persons in the said county, have erected small huts in the highways, or on small pieces of vacant land, in which vagrant persons are concealed contrary to, and longer for than the law allows."[49] The exact origin of this class remains unclear. Some may well have been the propertyless third- and fourth-generation descendants of the original settlers; others may have been from neighboring colonies, and still others could have come from Europe. A sample of three muster rolls from 1759—one from each of the three counties—furnishes some evidence for these assertions, since people born outside the counties where they enlisted comprised between 49 and 69 percent of all soldiers (see Table 3). Significantly, a sizable proportion of these outsiders worked at menial callings, either as laborers or as sailors, with Queens showing 46 percent, Westchester 57 percent, and Suffolk 43 percent of all non-county soldiers listing these occupations. A smaller percentage of outsiders worked as tailors, cordwainers, and weavers, ranging from 9 to 23 percent in the various forces.[50]

Equally informative is the high percentage of outsiders hailing from either Europe or New England. Immigrants from overseas had little or no trouble moving outward from the city toward the countryside, taking up positions in the local labor force. New Englanders also moved into these counties, although the majority seem to have found Suffolk far more congenial to their purposes than Queens or Westchester (see Table 4).[51] Even so, the ability of these counties to absorb such persons was decidedly limited in a land-scarce society. Nor were these the only outsiders coming

Table 3
Percentage and Occupation of Non-County Recruits, Queens, Suffolk, and Westchester, 1759

County	Born Outside County (%)	Non-County Laborers and Sailors (%)	Non-County Tailors, Cordwainers, and Weavers (%)	N
Queens	69	46	17	65
Suffolk	66	43	23	114
Westchester	49	57	9	93

Source: Second Annual Report of the State Historian of the State of New York (Albany and New York: Wynkoop Hallenbaeck Crawford Co., 1897), pp. 906-908, 941-944, 945-949.

to reside in the towns. During the French and Indian War some villagers played jailor to French prisoners of war, while others had to relieve French Acadians. The latter were political refugees, expelled from Nova Scotia (formerly Acadia) by suspicious British authorities and scattered across the colonies. One particular group of 150 Acadians arrived in New York in 1756. Such towns as Newtown and Hempstead supported these destitute folk, and they usually apprenticed their children. In turn, the appearance of such folk might have spurred both warnings against outsiders and more restrictive forms of poor relief.[52]

Table 4
Geographic Origins of Non-County Recruits, Queens, Suffolk, and Westchester, 1759

County	New York (%)	New England (%)	Europe (%)	Other Colonies (%)	N
Queens	7	24	60	9	42
Suffolk	5	59	29	7	75
Westchester	22	22	52	4	46

Source: Second Annual Report of the State Historian of the State of New York (Albany and New York: Wynkoop Hallenbaeck Crawford Co., 1897), pp. 906-908, 941-944, 945-949.

Other potential groups of dependent persons, moreover, caused concern among the villagers. Public welfare was not the sole preserve of white individuals, even if they comprised the largest numbers; it could also be given to blacks and Indians. The available, albeit limited, evidence indicates that both groups were now more liable than in the past to require some kind of relief. Although the great majority of black people were slaves and hence the responsibility of their masters, some could and did require public assistance. In 1770 the vestrymen of Rye supported Tondor Jack, the slave of a deceased member of the community, until he could be relocated with his master's son in Dutchess county; four years later he was still listed as a public dependent in the town of Rye. The town of Hempstead paid the Widow Thurston in 1761 for tending a black woman, and in the 1770s several destitute black and mulatto residents required aid.[53] In fact, the entire colony may have witnessed an increase in the number of poor blacks, for in 1773 the General Assembly passed a colonywide law to "Prevent Aged and Decrepit Slaves from becoming Burthensome," which indicted those masters who failed to provide for their slaves. The Assembly went on to note:

> Whereas there have been reputed instances in which owners of slaves have obliged them, after they are grown aged and decrepit; to go about begging for the common necessaries of life where they have not only been reduced to the utmost distress themselves, but have been burthensome on the humanity and charity of others.[54]

Such a situation, presumably, led to even higher public welfare costs.

Native Americans presented yet another concern for white officials. Tribal structure in the countryside had almost disappeared by the middle of the eighteenth century, with the exception of eastern Long Island, where several groups of Indians remained. Many Indians now lived with white families, presumably as servants, while others lived alone. Employment opportunities were rare. Indians became drawn into the white economy, selling sand (for cleaning floors) and bayberries to Manhattan housekeepers, or making baskets, brooms, scrubrushes, and fishing nets for whites to purchase. Others followed the sea as whale boat men under the command of white officers. Attempts to preserve autonomy under such conditions sometimes met with resistance, as happened in 1768, when the freeholders of Smithtown voted that "no squaw, mustee, or mulatto female" should have any "house or cellar or wigwam" standing in the town. As might be expected some Indians ended on public welfare. Thus, the town of Huntington in 1769 paid Masey Squaw to "nurse and keep Hannah Rumps squaw child"; several years earlier, in 1765, the town had assisted Free Peg, another Indian. Hempstead, too, had Indian paupers on the welfare rolls. Nevertheless, public assistance to Indians was not always a simple operation: Free Peg had to work off a seven-pound debt incurred when the town assisted her; and in nearby Brookhaven Isaac Brown, the Anglican minister, had to make a special plea in 1743 to the "Christian inhabitants" of the town to support Squaw Deborah "so she may not perish in our streets."[55]

Internal changes of a different sort were also noticeable in the countryside—changes that may have had some impact on the restructuring of poor relief. Communities divided more strongly along religious lines, especially between Anglicans and Presbyterians. Religious differences, of course, had always been present to some extent—except perhaps in staunchly Calvinist Suffolk—but the period from roughly 1750 to 1775 saw even greater disputes among members of different sects, which perhaps caused some to reconsider communal means of aiding the poor. Only Hempstead, with its diverse pluralistic society of Dutch Calvinists, Anglicans, Presbyterians, and Quakers, had learned by the 1760s to tolerate religious differences. Rye and Huntington were less fortunate.[56]

In Rye the division between Churchmen and Calvinists had never seriously interfered with the social cohesion of the community after the early 1700s. Despite the legal establishment of the church, Anglicans had to share power in the town; indeed, the non-church party, headed ironically by John Thomas, the son of an Anglican minister, commanded the loyalty of many villagers. According to a missionary from the Society for the Propagation of the Gospel in 1761, Thomas was

> so negligent and indifferent toward religion (in imitation of some of our great men) that it had been a steady method with him for many years not to attend public worship perhaps more than once or twice a year whose example has been mischievous. This man is not only one of our vestry . . . but has proceived that the majority of the vestry are men that will be governed by him. . . . The great majority

of whom I have all the reason in the world to fear are not hearty friends to the church.[57]

The uneasy truce between the two groups—apparently held together in the 1760s by alternately electing pro- or anti-churchmen as town supervisors—had crumbled completely by 1772. Feelings of animosity between the two camps, no doubt heightened by the approach of the Revolution, prevented the town from summoning a meeting of the freeholders until 1784. Not surprisingly, the failure of the community to agree among itself would soon have serious repercussions for poor residents.[58]

In Huntington, by contrast, disagreement among the populace was never great enough to halt the workings of the town meeting. The strong Presbyterian element prevented just such a situation. Nevertheless, this normally placid, staunchly Puritan village experienced an inner turmoil unknown in earlier days as members started defying the Presbyterian minister during the 1750s. Salary disputes between minister and flock forced the cancellation of the Lord's Supper. And by 1771 and 1772 town officials had appointed a committee to police the meetinghouse when the congregation became divided. In addition, the Presbyterians found their traditional foes, the Anglicans, gaining support in the village, as the efforts of the manor lord Lloyds north of the town led to the establishment of a church, a parsonage house, and a glebe by the 1760s. By 1769 the Anglican minister of the village could report:

> At Huntington I have a very decent congregation who almost constantly attend. Frequently a number of dissenters come to hear me, who behave with the utmost decency, and seem much pleased. Several times I have had the church so full that it could not conveniently hold more, and many were obliged to go away for want of room.[59]

No more could Huntington be considered a one-church, one-village society.

Further evidence hinting at a breakdown in the social cohesiveness of rural life was to be found in the Poor Law of 1773—the first significant revision since the statutes of the seventeenth century. This law was important mainly because it made family members legally responsible for supporting their relatives, permitting communities to use legal action against recalcitrant individuals who refused to support impoverished parents or grandparents, children or grandchildren. This measure served notice that informal methods of aiding poor persons needed the added authority of the law to be effective; community pressure alone was now apparently judged insufficient. In fact, the preamble to the Act stated as much, noting that "the laws of this colony relating to the settlement and support of the Poor are very deficient and ineffectual for that purpose," a sentiment with which the citizenry of the countryside undoubtedly agreed.[60]

Formal acts of the legislature told the settlers of Rye, Hempstead, and Huntington little they did not already know from experience. They only needed to observe the steady increase in the poor rates during the 1760s and 1770s. Villagers in the countryside now found themselves in a situation similar to that of the urban citizenry of New York, confronted by a growing class of paupers needing larger sums of money for their support. In Hempstead, the poor tax rose steadily during the middle decades of the century, eventually reaching an average of £350 per year in the 1770s (see Table 5). Equally significant were the reasons for this increase: available documents reveal a greater number of paupers who cost more to assist.

Table 5
Poor Tax and Public Dependents of Hempstead, 1751–1773

Year	£*	N	Year	£*	N
1751	115	5	1763	207	20
1752	180	2	1764	243	19
1753	100	7	1765	153	19
1754	130	9	1766	206	20
1755	130	13	1767	187	29
1756	70	13	1768	232	33
1757	180	13	1769	421	28
1758	180	7	1770	353	25
1759	130	11	1771	361	24
1760	120	16	1772	481	20
1761	226	8	1773	361	14
1762	201	17			

*The poor rate is in current money and rounded off to the nearest whole number. The number of listed public dependents does not appear to include every person who received support during a given year; in fact, some of the paupers had no stipend next to their names, making it impossible to determine their rate of support.

Source: Hempstead Town Records, MS vol. 5, 1709-1843, Town Clerk's Office, Hempstead, N.Y.

For example, fifteen paupers with listed rates of support averaged about five-and-one-half pounds per recipient in 1760; by the end of the decade in 1770, twenty-five paupers cost seven-and-one-half pounds to assist. Nor was Hempstead alone, for both Huntington and Rye experienced sharp increases in the poor rates during this time. Huntington saw welfare costs advance from a paltry £18 in 1755 to £112 in 1775—a sixfold increase in the rates. Public charity in Rye reached its highest level in the 1770s, averaging nearly £200 a year. In effect, the jump in expenditures created the preconditions for change in the overall system of poor relief. No longer was it possible for the villagers to perceive poor relief as a simple, informal operation; instead, it had become a costly responsibility.[61]

The high cost of aiding needy people, combined with the tensions manifested from within each of the three communities, compelled local authorities to reconsider their approach toward public charity. Increasingly, villagers adopted more formal methods of handling their destitute neighbors—methods that reflected a desire for less expensive kinds of relief. Like Southold and East Hampton before them, the residents of Hempstead, Huntington, and Rye found it time to act. And by placing an emphasis on frugality they signaled an end to the policies of the past, when they had once boarded poor persons among members of the community. This marked the emergence of a new relationship between destitute residents and the rest of rural society.

The first community to act was Hempstead. In 1771 the town elected a committee "to erect convenient buildings, in such places as they judge most suitable to accomodate such persons as now are or hereafter may become chargeable to the said town." The completion of the building shortly thereafter, along with "a place of confinement near the poorhouse" in 1773, illustrates the determination of rural officials to forego the customary method of farming out poor persons among the villagers. Although a few destitute persons still received relief at home, other paupers, presumably those requiring keepers to assist them, were summarily ordered into the building. Prior to the construction of the almshouse some unscrupulous keepers had either overcharged the town for tending the poor or refused to board them at all unless their price was met. This sort of economic blackmail was partly responsible for the building of the poorhouse. However, it was not the only reason. The town also considered the facility an appropriate place to commit sick Indians, blacks, and mulattoes. The vestry sent a "free negro wench . . . badly infected with disease" there in 1772, and they began preparations to admit "the Indians or mulatto children now sick nigh Westbury" in 1774. In addition, the town often required poor people to enter the poorhouse or else suffer the loss of any further support. Charity, therefore, remained available, but only to those who followed the dictates of the town officials.[62]

Paradoxically, the Hempstead poorhouse also symbolized the desire of civil officials to return to the customs of an earlier time when relieving needy people was less complicated and less expensive. Since certain individuals had corrupted the boarding out of poor people by demanding higher prices, what better way to restore the benevolent ethos of the past than by isolating the poor inside a separate building and treating them all equally? Under the supervision of a single official indigent people were protected from potentially exploitative keepers. There was the added advantage in that a single keeper was easier to police than a dozen or so freeholders sheltering the needy. Regrettably, we cannot determine the response of poor people in this instance to the change in public welfare. Whether every dependent person agreed to go into the house is impossible to say, but we do know that some could avoid incarceration. Possibly, this indicated a degree of resistance or independence on the part of a few to determine how they should be supported.[63]

While Hempstead busied itself with running the poorhouse, the citizens of Rye found other ways of tending its poor residents. The dissolution of town unity naturally made the traditional system of informally boarding out poor persons difficult, if not impossible, to maintain. By 1771, a year before the breakdown of town government, the vestrymen ordered the churchwardens in charge of the needy "to put out the poor of the parish of Rye at their discretion in as cheap and comfortable manner as they can"; several years later, in 1775, it was decided "that the poor of the town should be set to vendue to the lowest bidder," a scheme that reduced poor persons to the status of marketable commodities. Although people bidding for indigent persons in a pauper auction had an obligation to board and clothe them, they could put their charges to work, if possible, to supplement the town's stipend. Indeed, since destitute persons did go to the lowest bidder, it was perhaps only logical that they be employed in order to reimburse their new guardians.

Such a system, in theory, meant that the town paid lower prices and that the bidders gained a cheap supply of labor—a different scenario from the old ways of treating needy people. This plan for the disposing of poor people, however, proved short-lived. In 1776 the vestrymen noted that, "there not being a house and very few people appearing to take the poor," it was agreed to postpone temporarily the sale. Political dissension among the townsfolk had reached such an extreme that even a pauper auction could not be held. Only the offer of Captain Joshua Purdy, a noted Anglican with a charitable character, to shelter the needy persons inside his house saved the villagers from further embarrassment.[64]

In the town of Huntington the issue of poor relief did not reach a critical stage until after the Revolution. During the war the British garrisoned the town, requisitioned food and horses, and compelled the residents to engage in labor. Even with the disruption of local life the town continued to go about the relief of poor persons, depending upon the boarding-out system. The withdrawal of British forces from the town, although ending the military occupation of the village, removed any semblance of order for a time and left the freeholders unprotected from robbers and thieves. In fact, the post-war period was a time of confusion in Huntington, as the townsfolk attempted to restore order. One way to do so was by re-evaluating their previous policy toward poor people. In 1784 they voted "that if the trustees think proper to build an addition to the townhouse for the conveniency of the poor said addition to be built at the Town's expense." The town, it would appear, had decided to lodge poor persons in a separate dwelling. In 1785 the townsfolk agreed that "in case there should be an addition built to the poorhouse said overseers hath liberty to take away said poor when they think proper and pay those persons who had said poor for the time they have kept them," indicating again a poorhouse in readiness. The villagers also revamped the acts against outsiders during the 1780s. In 1785 the town passed an ordinance to prevent non-residents from "hunting, Hawking, Fishing, or Fowling" inside the town, citing as a reason the "necessity of the many poor inhabitants." Huntington, in fact, did more than institutionalize destitute persons and protect their food supply: by 1787 the overseers of the poor could "hire out" individuals whom the town had tended when ill in an effort to recoup the money spent upon them. Charity, insofar as the sick were now concerned, came at a price.[65]

The revolution of rural poor relief during this period was not confined to these three separate communities; other localities on the Island and Westchester adopted new mechanisms for assisting poor persons. Their reasons for doing so mirrored those already discussed. The emergence of a more commercial economy and a less egalitarian social structure was commonplace throughout much of New York. Periodic outbreaks of sickness such as smallpox may have been another reason for isolating poor people in separate buildings, similar to what Steven Ross has postulated for the origins of the Manhattan almshouse. Finally, there was the American Revolution, which must have exercised a tremendous impact upon rural villages. War not only meant casualties but occupation by enemy soldiers, who needed to be fed and sheltered, often unwillingly, by the villagers; it could also entail the destruction of property. Portions of Westchester became a sort of no man's land called the neutral ground, subject to raids and sorties by regular and irregular troops. War's end brought little respite as farmers now had to repair buildings and restore fields. Naturally, many would require some form of assistance during these troubled times.[66]

For some communities such as Brookhaven and Bedford the restructuring of public welfare followed a less than straightforward evolutionary path. Like nearby Southold, Brookhaven found relieving the poor a serious problem; so it compelled town officials to pass a resolution for a workhouse in 1769. After purchasing lumber to build the structure, however, the town reversed its decision. The boarding-out system stayed in place. After the Revolution, the villagers again reconsidered their policy toward its needy residents and decided by 1785 "to put out the Town's poor by way of public vendue at Coram," a local village in the township. What makes this decision even more curious is the low number of paupers on the welfare rolls: only four persons, two of them a mother and her child, needed to be auctioned. Quite possibly, the actual number of dependent persons in this instance proved less important to the villagers than the desire to save money. And the pauper auction provided one means of doing so.[67] The town of Bedford, as noted previously, had had the misfortune to shelter over two dozen urban paupers, who plagued officials with their behavior. This rude introduction to the city poor, although temporary, left its mark upon the citizens of Bedford. In fact, it seems to have prompted them to use similar tactics after the war upon the local poor. The town fathers turned a storehouse into a workhouse for needy persons by 1785, and they hired a keeper to oversee the operation. Like Brookhaven, however, the town's commitment to institutional relief was not permanent because by 1787 they had abandoned the workhouse and decreed that the indigent "would be sold to the lowest bidder."[68]

Other villages launched similar efforts. Increasingly, towns turned to either almshouses or pauper auctions as welfare options. While Smithtown, Oyster Bay, and Newtown employed separate buildings for poor people during the 1780s, the village of Riverhead by the 1790s instituted a pauper auction. The tiny community of Islip combined a traditional mode of relief with a curious twist, for they sent Johannah Hutton and her child, the only public dependents in the town, to every freeholder in the village, with the length of their stay determined by the wealth of each resident. Away from Manhattan's rural environs other villages resorted to the same devices. The village of Marlborough in Ulster county used a pauper auction in 1773 to provide for the town's lone pauper, but added, "If any person in the precinct of Newburgh will keep him for a smaller sum they are to have him." By 1796 the town poormasters hired a house for needy persons.[69] Outside New York other communities during the latter part of the eighteenth century altered their approach to public welfare. In the Pennsylvania town of Germantown, a commercially oriented community, the villagers first used a poorhouse, which was in place by 1775 and had twelve public dependents in it by 1790. Towns in Connecticut, moreover, witnessed increasing debate on public welfare after 1750, while a few communities comtemplated resorting to poorhouses. In neighboring Massachusetts the town of Ware was employing a pauper auction by the end of the Revolution; the town of Woburn in Middlesex county thought about a workhouse in 1794 and possibly even earlier. Northampton had acquired its poorhouse by 1768. And in Rhode Island such rural towns as West Greenwich and North Kingston had established institutions for the destitute by 1764 and 1769, respectively. The transformation of rural relief, then, was not confined to a few discreet localities, for it was a phenomenon evident throughout much of the northeast.[70]

Whatever the means employed, the normal policy of informally lodging poor people among rural villagers had seriously declined after 1750. The depersonalization of poor persons, to be sure, did not apply to everyone, for a few could always receive assistance at home from the community. Those with families to tend them or churches to render assistance seldom risked either poorhouse or pauper auction; those without close ties to the town were less fortunate in this regard. In any event, a crucial change in attitude had arisen concerning destitute people: many if not a majority of those poor persons unconnected to respectable townsfolk were now isolated from the other villagers in poorhouses or sold as commodities in pauper auctions. These developments also deserve mention, for they challenge some of the prevailing notions of rural poor relief for this period. David Rothman, as we have seen, believed the rural poorhouse to be almost non-existent before 1790.[71] This is incorrect. Not only did rural villages resort to poorhouses and workhouses, but some of them did so prior to the American Revolution. As for the pauper auction this also marked a major change, almost as radical as the poorhouse itself by virtue of the way it dispersed indigent persons to the townsfolk. What all this implies, then, is that the rural countryside did not lag far behind the city in its response to poverty; indeed, villagers revealed themselves to be quite adaptable and willing to change systems of welfare. In matters of poor relief the countryside had come to share the same philosophy as the city.

In Manhattan the evolution of urban welfare during the period reflects a refinement rather than a radical change in the system. Already committed to institutional relief, the city fathers had to maintain the facility and enforce order. This they did as best they could. Nevertheless, the growing number of indigent folk required additions to the structure as well as extra money. Then there was the matter of poor people and their reaction to poor relief. Some "objects of charity" manifested an independent spirit. Inmates might leave the house, beg for money, and buy liquor. Parents whose children were indentured out did not hesitate to notify the authorities of abuses. The operation of urban welfare saw both city fathers and the poor as active participants in the system.

CHAPTER IV
The Almshouse Triumphant?: The Response of City and Countryside to the Poor, 1790-1830

*I*n 1794 the Common Council of the city of New York called attention to the ruinous state of the municipal almshouse. The two-story grey stone structure that had served as the cornerstone of the public welfare system since 1736 was now deteriorating at a rapid pace, so rapid, in fact, "as not to justify the expending of any monies thereon in repair," according to city officials.[1] Several generations of paupers had finally taken their toll upon the building. Repeated maintenance would no longer work. Concern over the physical structure of the building was matched by apprehension over the crowded conditions inside it. Even when city officials sent some of the needy persons to the bridewell or other nearby structures, the almshouse remained far too small to handle the several hundred paupers still residing there. Indeed, by 1795 the commissioners of the almshouse warned the mayor and aldermen that the building was "incapable [of] accommodating with conveniency but little more than half the number of our care; not to say anything of the extremely decayed state of most of the old buildings in which the poor are placed."[2] These damning judgments by civil officials responsible for the destitute illustrate the difficulties confronting the public welfare system.

Away from the city in the rural counties of Queens, Suffolk, and Westchester the issue of poor relief required less drastic solutions by the 1790s. The spirit of urgency that had initially compelled farmers and freeholders to alter traditional mechanisms of charity began to diminish, as the social, economic, and political uncertainty of the Revolutionary period ebbed and faded. There was, to be sure, a continuing interest in destitute people: the newly created village of New Castle in Westchester appointed a committee in 1796 to meet with the representatives from North Castle and Bedford to decide upon "the erection of a house for the reception of the poor," and that same year the villagers of North Hempstead in Queens considered abolishing home relief of indigent persons, much as South Hempstead (henceforth Hempstead) had done at an earlier time.[3] Nevertheless, the question of how to assist poor people lacked the political importance it had once inspired. As rural freeholders readjusted themselves to a world of changing circumstances—a world where older notions of community behavior began to revive—interest in the needy lapsed, especially when rural methods of poor relief appeared to be functioning smoothly. A thriving economy fueled by high grain prices also promised more prosperous conditions for the rural citizenry, rich and poor.[4] Although rural residents and urban dwellers believed in curbing poverty, they did not adopt similar techniques of public welfare. Instead, a patchwork mechanism of old and new methods was employed outside the city with some communities emulating Manhattan's use of the almshouse, others turning to pauper auctions, and still others clinging tenaciously to home relief. Poverty and public charity, insofar as they affected the rural environs of the city, still remained a local matter to be handled as each town thought best during the 1790s.[5]

Efforts by urban and rural officials to address the problems of needy persons received added emphasis during the early 1800s. This was an age when political leaders and social reformers worked to understand the causes of poverty, to prevent its spread, and to deal with its existence. Unlike earlier years, when the urban-rural reaction to poverty had been characterized by unsystematic attempts to deal with the indigent, this age strove to establish a tighter structure of control over poor people, to police their behavior, and to regulate their movements inside such public institutions as almshouses, workhouses, and bridewells. In certain respects, the decades from 1790 to 1830 represented a transitional period between the colonial era, with its first crude attempts at institutions, and the antebellum years, with their unabashed championship of almshouses. The time between these two periods, then, was one of trial and experiment as old methods of handling poor people at home or inside institutions were almost totally abandoned. These changes in public charity also reflected alterations within the society itself as the last vestiges of the moral economy crumbled before the unfettered competition of the marketplace.[6] Increasingly, the values of the marketplace—the emphasis on thrift, frugality, and savings—infiltrated the basic structure of public charity, while it often relegated poor people to items in a ledger. City and countryfolk alike incorporated these values into their respective systems of public welfare.

New York City and its rural environs during the late eighteenth and early nineteenth centuries were two relatively distinct societies that shared a similar problem, namely, how to assist the poor. The mechanisms they developed often took into account the social and economic structure of their particular localities. Plans for dealing with poor people were often developed with a very real sense of the possible, an awareness that certain policies could never be accomplished given the contours of the society from which they sprung. No urban officials or reformers proposed abandoning the almshouse in favor of universal home relief, nor was there any suggestion in the Common Council about auctioning off destitute persons to keepers, as had been done in the countryside. Criticism of the almshouse existed, but officials and reformers directed it primarily at the operation from within and not at the actual institution. In village society, on the other hand, no single plan for tending poor persons predominated; almost any method, apparently, was agreeable to village officials so long as the actual cost remained at a reasonable level. Ironically, the yeomanry of the villages, so often perceived as provincial and narrow-minded, were far more willing and indeed able to experiment with different ways of helping poor people than their city counterparts. Until the widespread adoption of institutional relief in the late 1820s, towns sometimes employed several different policies of poor relief, alternating among pauper auctions, poorhouses, the contract system, or home relief.[7] While city officials modified the internal workings of the municipal almshouse and resolved policy disputes, rural officials prepared themselves to adopt more sweeping changes, transforming both the external form and the internal mechanism of public charity in their search for an effective system of relief.

For urban officials of the 1790s the issue of public charity was dramatized by the construction of the new almshouse. Faced with a rapidly deteriorating building impossible to repair, the members of the Common Council had little choice but to erect another, larger, structure if they wished to assist dependent poor people, while monitoring their behavior. The city government passed a resolution to establish an £11,000 public lottery to raise the necessary funds for construction—a sum that exceeded the annual cost of poor relief.[8] The public lottery had the advantage of dispersing the costs among the would-be gamblers of Manhattan rather than burdening the taxpayers with additional levies. Even so, enacting the measure proved easier than attracting people to participate in the actual program: the summer of 1795 saw the lottery drawing postponed due "to the slow sale of tickets," and the outbreak of yellow fever during succeeding months temporarily turned attention away from the lottery.[9] Indeed, it was not until 1797, three years after the initial resolution condemning the old building, that the new municipal almshouse was completed near the site of its predecessor.[10]

The need for a larger facility also reflected the existing social conditions within the urban metropolis of the 1790s. Like so many seaport cities of the period, New York experienced a rapid rate of growth; its population almost doubled between 1790 and 1800 from 33,000 to 60,000, as Manhattan became the premiere seaport in the nation.[11] Even if the percentage of paupers in the overall population had remained steady, an increase in the number of the indigent would have occurred. In addition, the social structure of Manhattan exhibited a greater division of wealth between rich and poor. In the words of one historian, the years from 1789 to 1796 saw "by far the highest concentration of wealth recorded in New York during the eighteenth century"; in fact, the "bottom fifty percent of the population suffered a further major decline in their relative position."[12] The wealthy importing merchant residing in a three-story mansion attended by servants or slaves had a very different style of life from that of the carters, laborers, and sailors who inhabited rented quarters near the docks or in the less than respectable neighborhoods of the interior. Although rich and poor citizens might rub shoulders in the streets on their way home or to the market, they still remained separated by an economic chasm often symbolized by their ability or inability to own a freehold estate. Divisions in wealth proved particularly noticeable within certain wards of the city as economic segregation became more pronounced. The lower wards of southern Manhattan bordering on the East River remained a haven for the more affluent classes, for as much as 40 or 50 percent of the adult male population there owned a freehold estate valued at £100 or more (see Table 6).[13] Further north a different setting existed: the majority of individuals here were mechanics and laborers, often too poor to own any real property. In the sixth ward of the city, near present-day city hall, almost 85 percent of the adult population lived in tenements, which cost only a few pennies a week to rent. Perhaps not surprisingly, this ward had a reputation as one of the most dangerous and poverty-stricken neighborhoods of Manhattan, a place where immigrants, blacks, and destitute native whites mingled together.[14]

Such an extensive lower class obviously created difficulties for the city welfare system. These were the people who needed firewood in the winter, who required food in times of dearth, and who merited medical treatment when sickness spread through their neighborhoods. Disease was of particular concern to poor people and officials alike. In 1795 and 1798 two attacks of yellow fever

Table 6
A General Account of Electors in New York City, 1796

Ward	Freehold Estates, £100 or More (%)	Freehold Estates, £20–£100 (%)	Tenements, 40 Shillings (%)
First	34	0	66
Second	49	1	50
Third	40	0	60
Fourth	32	0	68
Fifth	28	1	71
Sixth	15	0	85
Seventh	26	0	74

Source: Journal of the Assembly of the State of New York, 19th Session, 6 January 1796 (New York: J. Childs, 1797), Microfiche Collection, SUNY-Stony Brook, p. 31.

brought business to a standstill. While the more well-to-do citizens fled the city with their families to the relative safety of the country, working-class folk generally remained.[15] The "filthy cellars, boarding houses, and tippling houses," where many artisans and laborers resided, provided ideal conditions for the spread of disease, especially when these structures had been built on low, swampy ground. Indeed, a report to the Common Council in 1799, after one such epidemic, noted that those dwellings were "the last resorts of sailors and the lower classes of emigrants and other disorderly persons; where drunkeness and debaucheries of many kind were committed, which often produced diseases of the most serious nature."[16] Although this report confused moral behavior with the spread of sickness, there was no denying the serious effects of these epidemics in working-class communities plagued with poor sewage and inadequate sanitation. And it is not surprising that the charitable resources of the city were stretched in assisting the sick poor.

Living conditions were only partially responsible for the large numbers of people seeking assistance. Another reason for the apparent surge in the number of poor applicants for relief over the decade was due to the steady stream of immigrants arriving in Manhattan: from 1789 to 1794 approximately three thousand immigrants a year landed in the city.[17] While many found employment as artisans, shopkeepers, or laborers, a certain proportion of immigrants always appeared ill suited to life in the urban metropolis. Some had come to the city in poor health, exhausted from their long sea voyage; others had arrived penniless. Many such folks ended in the almshouse, much to the dismay of poor relief officials, who saw them as a potentially expensive group to support. A report presented to the mayor and aldermen by the commissioners of the almshouse in 1796 illustrated the severity of the situation: "We cannot help being alarmed at the enormous and still growing expense of this department, arising not so much from the increase of our own poor, as from the prodigious influx of indigent foreigners in the city." These newcomers, among whom "the Irish were the most numerous," had landed in Manhattan "destitute and emaciated," and they often found shelter in "cellars or sheds about the shipyards." Unable to support themselves or their families, they turned to the almshouse, swelling the numbers of that already crowded institution.[18]

These various factors easily explain the need for another almshouse during the 1790s. Confronted with a noticeable lower class consisting of both citizens and immigrants, who were unusually prone to catching fever in their squalid quarters, city officials of necessity embarked upon the only feasible alternative—the construction of a larger almshouse. Yet the new building, while alleviating briefly the problem of overcrowding, failed to attack the actual causes of poverty.

While city officials pushed for and constructed a new almshouse, they were not unmindful of providing a certain standard of care. Of course, their definition of care might sometimes run counter to that of some of the inmates, yet both officials and paupers did share some common assumptions about the quality of assistance. In matters of medical care the city did try to ensure proper conditions, conducting investigations during the 1780s and 1790s in regard to the treatment of sick inmates. At one point in 1793 the complaint of a pauper against John Henry, a medical student, for "personal abuse" led to Henry's being barred from the premises. The Common Council established committees, launched investigations, and ferreted out corruption in other ways, too. They found and corrected a situation in which the almshouse commissioners had provided poor-quality goods to the inmates. Another commissioner was caught trying to enrich himself by furnishing the paupers with inferior shoes. Equally troublesome to the city fathers was the inefficient government structure of the institution. As Raymond Mohl has noted, the thirteen commissioners of the almshouse were unable to coordinate policy properly, especially since they shifted responsibilities to different members with no apparent order or design. The fact that these men were volunteers rather than paid professionals made a bad situation worse, for these men spent more time with their businesses than with the almshouse.[19]

The late 1790s and early 1800s witnessed a substantial administrative restructuring, as urban officials experimented with different governing structures. In 1798 the city revamped the system by replacing the thirteen-man board with a five-man committee to run the almshouse. The following year the Council appointed several aldermen "to report to the Board a more perfect system of government and management of the Almshouse and Bridewell, particularly as it respects to the mode and manner of keeping the accounts."[20] Meanwhile, hints of internal corruption received further proof that year, when the authorities dismissed Peter Coles, the bridewell keeper, on charges of corruption and negligence; several years later, in 1802, they removed Samuel Dodge, who had been the almshouse keeper since 1784.[21] Changes of another sort were also being accomplished: in 1800 a three-man board consisting of two paid professionals and one volunteer replaced the five-man board. The first commissioner, who bore the title of superintendent, dealt with the daily activities concerning the running of the building; the second commissioner handled the financial aspects. Along with the third commissioner they acted as a tribunal, screening all applicants applying for assistance and putting to work all healthy individuals admitted into the house. Inmates who distinguished themselves by their labor could be rewarded with small gratuities—no doubt to encourage further disciplined work habits among them. Concomitantly, individuals who proved unwilling to work or disobedient of authority were punished, with the penalties ranging from public admonition to removal to the bridewell. Those sent to the bridewell could then reconsider their behavior in the company of vagrants, prostitutes, and criminals. And to encourage the supervision of the poor inmates, all "decent and well-behaved persons" among the urban citizenry were now "invited to pay a vigilant attention to the almshouse and its management, to note every abuse that may take place, and to suggest such improvements as may occur to them in confidence."[22]

The decision to invite the public to scrutinize the operation of the almshouse reveals the changing social milieu surrounding public charity. No longer was almsgiving placed in the hands of inept administrators; no longer were amateurs permitted to supervise the institution. Instead, a more professional attitude was encouraged on the part of citizens and officials to promote efficiency. The commissioners could also look with favor upon the passage of a statewide law in 1798, which allowed for additional funding to assist poor immigrants. The next year the city enacted an ordinance to compel ship captains to post bond for each foreign immigrant they landed.[23] In theory, the weapons were at hand for dealing with urban poor people.

Further attempts to restructure Manhattan's welfare system sometimes encountered resistance from working-class individuals. New York City artisans were an independent group bound together by the shared experience of the workplace and a keen sense of their own autonomy. In addition, they were actively involved in the urban political process, casting their votes for candidates who favored their positions. Officeholders almost irrespective of party knew better than to dismiss the workers' demands, for this might mean disaster at the polls. Robert Livingston, the Republican mayor, had conceived a plan in 1803 for developing public workshops to train immigrants, sick and handicapped persons, orphans, and ex-convicts in the various craft industries. Learning a trade would enable these otherwise unproductive individuals—who comprised a large percentage of the poor—to subsist without charity and thereby lessen costly public expenditures.[24] This bold plan failed to win the support of the working-class community; many artisans saw it as a thinly veiled threat to their own positions, for an added influx of skilled tradesmen would only depress wages. The General Society of Mechanics and Tradesmen rejected the Mayor's proposal, termed it "inexpedient," and vowed to fight its implementation. Not surprisingly, the idea was eventually shelved.[25]

Other problems relating to the operation of public welfare resurfaced despite the efforts of urban officials. Poor non-residents of Manhattan continued to enter the almshouse, prompting a report in 1805 to the Common Council. What made the report a bit unusual was its source—the almshouse superintendent, Philip Arcularius. Unlike past officials, who recorded abuses but rarely advanced solutions, Arcularius called for the transportation of all non-residents lodged within the structure, citing the summer "as the most favorable season for their removal." Upon disposing of one small group of paupers that year he took pains to remind the Common Council about "this important and necessary duty."[26] Not content to focus upon just the non-resident poor inmates of the building, Arcularius drew attention to people receiving assistance outside the almshouse who had no need of it. Such people were "imposters" to the zealous Superintendent. Equally troublesome to Arcularius were those poor parents who refused to apprentice their children. As we have seen, parents attempted to exert what influence they could upon the binding out of their offspring, and some parents, apparently, preferred to keep them at home with them. Such actions failed to please the Superintendent, for he considered it an additional expense to the city, having to support both parents and children. His solution was draconian and simple: parents who failed to bind out their children should lose any chance of public support.[27]

Reformist officials such as Arcularius had a limited impact upon the structure of urban welfare. While they could thunder against irregularities and advocate solutions, such people still had to contend with the unyielding organization of the system itself—an organization that had become increasingly drawn into the vortex of partisan politics. During the first decade of the nineteenth century political loyalties played an integral role in the appointment of the almshouse superintendent: Richard Furman, a loyal Federalist, lost his post when the Republicans came into power, appointing Arcularius in his place. This situation, in turn, enabled partisan newspaper editors to launch campaigns against incumbent welfare officers. William Coleman, the Federalist editor of the *New York Evening Post*, wrote incessantly about Arcularius's poor performance in office. His replacement, William Mooney, another Republican, received similar treatment from Coleman. Indeed, Mooney's actions as superintendent even disturbed the Republicans, who conducted an investigation into his alleged drunkenness in 1808. To make matters more confusing, the administrative structure of public welfare was altered again in 1808; this time a separate superintendent operated the system in conjunction with five "unsalaried, non-professional commissioners," in effect returning to the way things were in the 1790s. Such developments along with the fierce partisan infighting, in the words of Raymond Mohl, "negated social welfare reform."[28]

Agitation over the operation of urban public charity during these years contrasted sharply with the tenor of rural poor relief. While city officials implemented reforms, established rules, and launched investigations, their country counterparts started to undo in some instances the work they had begun, switching from poorhouses to pauper auctions and other kinds of public charity. Unlike the Revolutionary era, when rising poor rates prompted profound alterations in the mechanism of welfare, these developments aroused little excitement among the townsfolk. With but few exceptions relative calm prevailed during the 1790s and early 1800s. For the majority of towns, poor relief remained a peripheral social issue that merited but brief consideration.

The rural villages of Queens, Suffolk, and Westchester presented a society caught between the echoes of the past and the sirens of the future, an environment where modern codes of social behavior founded on individual autonomy and a desire for self-improvement and learning competed with traditional notions based on resistance to change and innovation. If certain elements of rural society heralded the future, such as the rapidly expanding market economy, other elements such as the use of stocks for punishing criminals symbolized the past.[29] Visitors and residents of the countryside observed this dichotomy firsthand: while John Jay of Bedford in 1812 noted the active trade in farm produce to the city by the farmers, among whom "the state of the market here is always well known," others remained awed by the scenes of rural decay and rustic provincialism. William Strickland described Westchester in 1795 as a place where "there is appearance of want of substance in the owners which disables them improving their homes and cultivating their land, they seem in general to possess but little beyond mere necessities." A visiting Scotsman, who traveled to the Westchester community of South Salem in 1821, regarded its freeholders as a "people not much disposed to local changes or distant affinity," further adding that their farms "yield half [the] produce they should."[30] In 1804 Timothy Dwight, the acerbic Federalist from Connecticut, found that, while the farmers of Suffolk eagerly exported cordwood to Manhattan and imported potash for fertilizer, they still clung to old-fashioned notions of neighborliness, making it impossible for lawyers "to get a living in Suffolk county." In fact, the flourishing export trade between the city and the Island could not shake off the provincial trappings of the citizenry, whose concerns were "largely confined to the house or neighborhood," the latter of which seldom extended "beyond the confines of a small hamlet."[31]

Knowledge of market conditions did not always threaten a villager's allegiance to traditional social norms. It was possible to participate fully in commercial networks and to retain old customs and practices. What appeared as contradictory impulses to men such as Dwight were actually evidence of social flexibility, with villagers accepting the advantages of the marketplace while remaining loyal to traditional relationships. No dichotomy existed in their minds; old values could persist, endure, and survive despite alterations in the economy. And the persistence of such values in part explains the rural response to poor relief.[32]

During the Revolutionary period many rural communities had

substantially revamped their system of public charity in order to meet internal and external conditions. Now, however, a sense of ambivalence or perhaps uncertainty crept into their actions. In Huntington, the course of public welfare circled forward and backward as the villagers vacillated between pauper auctions and poorhouses. In 1784 the overseers of the poor had received permission from town officials to place destitute persons in a poorhouse if necessary; by 1785 the town considered proposals to expand the structure. Yet this particular institution seems to have been short-lived, for by the 1790s the town assisted a few paupers inside private dwellings, while no mention of an operating almshouse appears after 1790. A proposal to spend $750 in 1800 "for the purchasing of a suitable lot of land and house or of building a house convenient for the lodging and accomodation of the poor of the town" indicates that the previous structure was in disrepair, if not actually abandoned. This proposition, which mentioned "setting such poor persons to work" inside the building, met a quick demise, however. Five years later the pauper auction had become the cornerstone of poor relief in Huntington.[33]

This approach to public charity was characteristic of other rural villages. The residents of the towns appeared less committed to restructuring public welfare and continuing the poorhouse than their city counterparts. Indeed, in several instances they turned away from institutional relief: Smithtown purchased a three-acre lot for a poorhouse in 1786, yet the town sold the poorhouse by 1803 and the property by 1810. In Southold, which had been among the first rural communities to propose a poorhouse in 1737, the villagers by 1795 had decided "to vendue the town poor." Oyster Bay also lost interest in institutional relief. The villagers had replaced their 1780s poorhouse with either a pauper auction of some other plan of relief by the early 1800s, and in 1806 a vote reaffirmed their current policy and rejected a motion for "the poor [to] be put out on a new plan."[34] Even repeated efforts by local authorities to place destitute people in an institution could come to naught, as happened in the Westchester community of New Castle. Resolutions to provide a house for poor people first appeared in 1794 but failed to win acceptance. The town voted in 1800 "that the poormasters and justices of the peace provide a place for the building of a house for the use of the poor"; this motion reappeared almost word for word in 1802 and 1803. On all three occasions the motion failed. Finally, in 1813 the town simply decided to relocate destitute persons to any "workhouse in this state."[35]

Other towns followed the time-honored tradition of sheltering indigent members of the community in the homes of the local citizenry, emulating the practices of the colonial period. East Chester, apparently, retained this method of public welfare, for none of the town meeting records mention a pauper auction, yet documents exist showing keepers tending paupers in their homes. Quite possibly, private bargaining between keeper and officials determined where those persons needing assistance would be sent. In the Westchester community of Scarsdale a similar policy of home relief may have been followed. A nineteenth-century account of post-revolutionary Scarsdale, although not specific about the mechanism of assistance, noted that poor people caused "little anxiety" and that the poor rates were low, in contrast to some other communities. Such conditions may have allowed villagers there to retain the boarding-out system. In addition, the town of Islip seems to have stayed true to its 1784 policy of boarding out its poor citizens among the residents. The fact that these three communities had under one thousand inhabitants, ranking them among the smaller towns in the countryside, may also explain their adherence to older methods of relief. There were only so many paupers in their community, and these were best handled in a more traditional fashion.[36]

While it is easy to understand why smaller communities might continue such means of public welfare, what can explain the desire of other, larger, towns to do away with institutional relief? A number of communities had found poorhouses necessary during the Revolutionary period and even earlier; some towns even contemplated setting poor people to work in them. And yet by 1800 poorhouses disappeared in town after town, or they encountered resistance among the villagers, who thwarted efforts to erect them.

One reason for this change in policy might have to do with the local economy. The 1790s and early 1800s, in general, proved to be a profitable time for farmers, who found a ready demand for their products. New York City produced a dramatic effect upon the rural economy in this regard: the expanding seaport, which had doubled in population between 1790 and 1800, provided a profitable market for farmers. In fact, the pull of the urban economy was so strong that even residents of Suffolk abandoned their traditional trading connections with Boston in favor of New York City. Small sailing

ALMSHOUSE TRIUMPHANT

vessels put into the bays and inlets of the Island and carried away farm produce. In Brookhaven, for example, the Strong family maintained a steady intercourse with city buyers, sending cattle on foot to market and paying close attention to prices. Whale oil was yet another valuable commodity. From east end Long Island communities such as Sag Harbor whaling ships set sail; some of the whale oil from these voyages ended in either Long Island or Manhattan homes, furnishing a source of illumination. New York City residents, moreover, required substantial quantities of cordwood, and much Long Island wood found its way to this destination. Villagers in Westchester benefited in much the same fashion. Their proximity to Manhattan enabled farmers to ship livestock and crops. Prices for crops, according to one account, were "almost fabulous," especially since demand from Europe rose in response to the Napoleonic Wars at this time as well. To handle the increased volume of trade more roads appeared, and by 1800 a turnpike had been constructed from East Chester to the Bryam River. Queens, of course, was similarly affected by these developments. In fact, not only was farming in good shape but light industry seemed to prosper, for a paper manufacturer in 1797 recorded that "making paper . . . at this time is more lucrative." Prosperity was the order of the day.[37]

A surging economy benefited rural communities in regard to poor relief. With farmers assured a decent price for crops, livestock, and lumber, it was perhaps easier for transient laborers, the "strolling poor" of an earlier age, to find employment. This meant less chance of ending up on the welfare rolls. Moreover, people who could not work for one reason or another may now have been more easily assisted through private means; marginally poor neighbors, friends, and relatives could perhaps do more for their destitute fellows when they themselves had steady employment.

The strong economy alone cannot explain the decline of the almshouse. Equally important was the existence of other poor relief options, most notably the pauper auction. As we have seen, several villages, after employing poorhouses for a time, decided to rely upon the public vendue of the destitute; Bedford, Huntington, Southold, and other communities did so. Despite the economic advantage of placing all poor people under one roof with a keeper, the pauper auction may well have appeared even more cost-effective to the villagers. Consider how the public sale of the poor worked. A number of townsfolk, primarily farmers, gathered together, looked over the assembled paupers, and bid for them. The low bid won custody of a pauper. The competitive aspects of the auction would help to keep the cost down, while the bidders could expect to put at least some of their charges to work. Although we have no direct proof of this in regard to Long Island and Westchester, Benjamin Klebaner in his study of the New England pauper auction notes several instances where some of needy persons were eagerly coveted as laborers. The same was probably true for New York villages.[38] The public vendue of indigent persons also permitted a larger number of people to participate in the operation of poor relief than would have been the case with a poorhouse. This proved an important consideration. By making the citizenry rather than officials mainly responsible for the destitute via the auction system, villagers reaffirmed their belief in basic republican principles, which upheld the primacy of the people. In a sense, the auction became the extension of the town meeting—inviting the public to bid for paupers much as the town meeting invited the public to elect officials. The auction provided a degree of continuity with the colonial boarding-out system, only this time the ethos of the marketplace had replaced notions of benevolence.[39]

Nor should we ignore other possible explanations for the popularity of the auction over the poorhouse. An institution for the poor, even if it was only a crude dwelling, had to be constructed or purchased. This meant additional local taxes needed to be levied. While the poorhouse may have been cost-effective in the long run, it could appear to tax-conscious residents to be costly in the short run, which might explain why some towns failed to follow through on proposals for these buildings. Placing indigent persons in a separate structure also deprived some of the villagers of an extra source of income as well as a supply of labor—something less well-to-do farmers may have resented. Economic factors aside there is another reason to consider: several rural poorhouses owed their genesis to the social dislocation and economic disarray of the Revolutionary period, when transients and refugees swarmed through the countryside. The sudden appearance of these people, many of them non-residents too impaired to be transported, might have prompted residents to isolate them in separate structures; few residents probably wished to take in outsiders even at a price. When conditions righted themselves and when dependent poor persons were drawn more from the community, villagers perhaps found it easier to resort to the pauper auction.[40]

Such factors explain why rural officials seldom maintained poorhouses between the 1790s and early 1800s, and why the issue of public welfare aroused only moderate attention. Pauper auctions and the boarding-out system provided villages with two alternatives, each of which was easily implemented. While a few communities such as Hempstead maintained their allegiance to institutions, other towns opted for different systems of charity. Thus, rural communities witnessed a weakened commitment to poorhouses as the normal pace of life reasserted itself and the pauper auction handled the needy.[41]

Distinctions between urban and rural mechanisms of public welfare faded over the next two decades. Such events as the Embargo Act of 1807, the War of 1812, and the Panic of 1819 adversely affected city and countryside, causing public officials to devise more efficient methods of relief as economic conditions deteriorated. Unemployed sailors, carters, and laborers demanded public assistance from the city, joining the ranks of the elderly, disabled, and orphaned applicants. Indeed, the spiraling poor rates brought on by the increasing number of individuals needing assistance compelled urban officials to build yet another poorhouse by 1811, less than fifteen years after the completion of the previous structure. The new facility at Bellevue in 1816 was as much a factory as an almshouse, a place where paupers, vagrants, and petty criminals were expected to learn the value of disciplined labor. Emphasis on reforming poor people through work emerged as a dominant theme in urban poor relief. Outside Manhattan an equally dramatic restructuring of public charity occurred: villages once hesitant about the usefulness of a poorhouse now viewed them more favorably; groups of concerned citizens called special meetings and adopted resolutions in favor of institutions. Although the path to institutional relief remained studded with obstacles, the almshouse, ultimately, became a common sight in the countryside. And by 1830 most communities had access to one.

Harbingers of this change manifested themselves at an early date in the seaport metropolis. During the first decade of the 1800s persistent complaints about street beggars and vagrants aroused the attention of officials. One anonymous author writing to the *New York Evening Post* in 1801 expressed alarm about "the hordes of beggars, some of them very young and many of them sturdy that infest our streets and houses," adding "that presently it will be unsafe as it is now annoying to walk the streets."[42] Although the editor of the paper considered the account fictitious, city officials evidently agreed with the writer's assessment and enacted special measures in 1805 and 1807 to remove "all vagrants, negroes, common prostitutes and other persons likely to become chargeable," following, it seems, the advice of Philip Arcularius. In 1809 the Common Council acknowledged "that our streets swarm with beggars."[43] Private citizens seconded these observations and complained increasingly about disorderly elements inhabiting the streets and neighborhoods of the city. William Dunlop, a theater owner, placed ads in the newspaper about his establishment being frequented by "crowds of idle boys and disorderly persons"; others petitioned the Common Council to enforce measures against public drunkenness, for example, in East George Street—a haunt of lower-class individuals—and to prevent "Houses of Ill Fame" from spreading there. Concern over like developments prompted the distraught citizens of Bedlow Street in 1808 to form a private society for "public peace and the suppression of immorality and vice" in their neighborhood.[44] For many, these complaints illustrated the inability of the city to police itself adequately. While beggars, prostitutes, and drunkards had always been present in the seaport metropolis, the fact that officials and citizens alike now called repeated attention to these unruly lower-class elements suggests a heightened sense or perception of social problems and a desire to eliminate them. It also reveals an underlying fear that the traditional props of society, that is, the family, the church, and the community, were powerless to hold in check such social deviants unless assisted by the government.[45]

Of equal concern to the majority of the citizenry was the state of the urban economy. New York's position as a center of commerce was all but assured in 1800, when it surpassed both Boston and Philadelphia as the leading seaport for shipping. Manhattan's prosperity, in turn, provided employment for hundreds of unskilled and semi-skilled individuals such as sailors, porters, stevedores, laborers, and carters, while it permitted skilled artisans such as carpenters, caulkers, coopers, and ropemakers to thrive. One visitor to

ALMSHOUSE TRIUMPHANT 117

New York in 1807 observed "streets jammed with carts, drays and wheel barrows; horses and men huddled promiscuously together having little or no room for passengers to pass."[46] Yet in a year's time this image would vanish with the passage of the Embargo Act.

The Embargo Act of 1807 had its origins in the Napoleonic Wars, which pitted England and France against each other. America, by virtue of its position as the leading neutral shipper, was caught in the middle between the two warring powers, each of which might seize American ships for trading with their enemy. Unwilling to use military force, the national government employed a policy of economic coercion, banning American exports in hopes of bringing European powers to heel. For New Yorkers, however, the politics that inspired the act proved less important than the economic consequences they reaped. Closing the port of Manhattan caused suffering among the urban populace, as everyone connected with maritime trade—merchants and brokers, carters and sailors—reeled under its impact. A visitor to Manhattan, John Lambert, noted:

> The port indeed was full of shipping, but they were dismantled and laid up. Their decks were cleared, their hatches fastened down and scarcely a sailor was to be seen on board. Not a box, bale, cask, barrel, or package, was to be seen upon the wharfs. Many of the counting houses were shut up and advised to be let; and the few solitary merchants, clerks, porters, and laborers, that were to be seen, were walking with their hands in their pockets.[47]

In response, private groups of citizens formed charitable organizations, such as the Assistance Society, which aided several hundred families. The city, too, stepped up efforts to assist its impoverished citizens as charitable expenditures leaped from $46,000 in 1807 to $78,000 in 1809. Not surprisingly, the almshouse population rose in the wake of economic dislocation from 976 to 1,217 in the years between 1807 and 1811. Overcrowding became a serious problem. The superintendent of the almshouse warned the Common Council in 1810 about the lack of space in the structure, adding "it would be necessary to accomodate some of the paupers at Bellevue . . . or to procure room next to the Almshouse."[48]

Such circumstances again dictated another almshouse. This time the search for a new almshouse site was coupled with an ambitious scheme to tighten the requirements for charitable assistance, to reduce, if possible, the dispensing of outdoor relief, and to institute far-reaching reforms within the operation of the new municipal almshouse. Growing concern over the character of the urban poor population had led some officials to question the effectiveness of distributing alms to needy persons outside the almshouse. Paupers on the outside were not subject to the same controls as those inside the institution. When in 1809 the Common Council declared that the streets swarmed with beggars, they qualified the statement by adding it was not from lack of charity, since poor people were "regularly supplied at the almshouse" and by private "humane institutions," but because these persons sought to increase their already sufficient stock of provisions by street begging. Another indictment against outdoor relief came from a public official employed "to report upon the situation of the outdoor poor." He remarked: "It is universally admitted that the giving of money is the worst method of relieving the poor."[49] The Reverend Ezra Stiles Ely, the almshouse chaplain, also agreed in 1811 "that to give street beggars of this city is not well directed charity." Although Ely and others made allowances for so-called "proper objects" of charity such as the laboring poor, their chorus against the disreputable segments of the lower classes drowned out much mention of deserving poor people.[50] Perhaps the harshest judgment against outdoor assistance occurred in 1812 from a committee report to the Common Council, which stated:

> In their opinion there is no cause in which the public are more liable to imposition of fraud than in the distribution of alms. It is often difficult to discover the real necessities of the applicant and the clamourous importunities of the profligate mendicant, are often more successful than the meek and retiring wants of the virtuous poor.[51]

These remarks signaled the inability of civil officials to sort deserving poor persons from the undeserving; it also testified to a growing belief among urban authorities that many destitute persons were untrustworthy, more intent on making the rounds of charitable institutions, municipal and private, than in procuring work. So, too, criticism leveled in 1809 against dispensing money to poor people suggests a fear that they would spend it on alcohol instead of more wholesome nourishment. In a city where in 1810 the Humane Society estimated that one out of seven families supported themselves by "selling poison," and where in 1811 over 1,300

ALMSHOUSE TRIUMPHANT 119

groceries and 160 taverns were licensed to sell "strong drink," not to mention the unlicensed grog shops, it is little wonder that civil authorities and private citizens voiced concern over outdoor relief. Nor was their fear unjustified; many poor persons, as we have observed, went to great lengths within the almshouse to obtain liquor. Those outside the institution had much easier access. The solution, then, was to curb home relief, forcing at least some poor people to enter the institution. Once incarcerated, these people would be removed from tavern society, and their moral reformation could be begun.[52]

The new almshouse facility started at Bellevue in 1811 was designed to meet these concerns. Well north of the city line, the institution's location on the shores of the East River away from the centers of population symbolically separated poor New Yorkers from the urban community, a fact made even more apparent by the stone walls that surrounded the complex. Plans for dealing with the incarcerated poor received added impetus in 1814, when Thomas Mercein, the city comptroller, advocated a further innovation. Calling attention to the steep rise in the poor rates—a rise that exceeded the growth of the urban population—Mercein suggested transforming the Bellevue almshouse into a combination factory-poorhouse for the destitute classes of the city. He believed "much useful industry" could be extracted from those "in want." According to Mercein, the "great improvement in labor saving machinery," its "simplicity of operation," would provide ample opportunity for many poor people, including the children, "to be profitably exercised in the lighter branches of manufactories." Not only would youngsters be set upon the right path, but sturdy vagrants, who usually proved so troublesome in Manhattan's streets, would be transformed into useful members of society. As Mercein noted, "No habits however confirmed or laziness however riveted but by wholesome regiment of discipline may be corrected." The same methods could also be applied to the non-resident poor persons who continued to bedevil city authorities. One month after accepting Mercein's proposals, the Common Council decided that disciplined labor more than confinement or corporal punishment was appropriate for this class of paupers.[53]

Transforming the almshouse into a place of industry reflected the high hopes many Americans held for early manufacturing enterprises, and the beliefs of social reformers that supervised labor might reform the poor population. The language used by Mercein echoes that of Alexander Hamilton and Tench Cox, each of whom saw the development of industry as a way of further securing the nation from unfair foreign competition.[54] Even Jefferson agreed with this philosophy up to a point. Although opposed to subsidies and tariffs and committed to free trade and unregulated development of the economy, Jefferson and his followers approved of manufacturing under certain conditions; they believed it could be used as a "pallative for idleness and vice."[55] Putting poor people to work inside the almshouse had another advantage as well. Unlike Livingston's public workshop scheme, which had posed a threat to the artisan community, this plan involved machine trades rather than craft industries for the most part, minimizing its effects on carpenters, blacksmiths, coopers, and glaziers.[56] Traditional artisans would then be unaffected.

The opening of the new almshouse in 1816 came at an appropriate time. During the War of 1812 the authorities had managed as best they could, confronted with a crowded almshouse and ever-increasing numbers of poor persons demanding relief. The presence of a British blockade squadron in 1813 only made matters worse; it disrupted commerce and that in turn led to greater unemployment. The arrival of peace in 1815, although welcomed, witnessed economic dislocation and the large-scale resumption of foreign immigration. Equally devastating was the Panic of 1819. Bankruptcy became the order of the day for many businessmen, and unemployment rose. The New York Society for the Prevention of Pauperism estimated that there were 8,000 paupers in 1819 drawn from a population of 120,000; by the next year the number of poor residents in their estimate stood at between 12,000 and 13,000.[57]

The new almshouse saw plenty of use. While social reformers looked with dismay upon the growing number of paupers and often condemned their intemperate behavior, they could at least be pleased with the three-story almshouse at Bellevue. Here in relative isolation from the harmful atmosphere of the outside world, individual paupers would commence the necessary retraining. The operation of the facility, in fact, drew praise from city officials. An unannounced visit in the summer of 1819 by aldermen and assistants brought the remark that the almshouse included "apartments in as good order and generally free from filth and offensive smells as could be reasonably expected." In addition, the visitors noted that the "manufactories are also in good order and apparently well conducted." A later visit in November by another group of aldermen observed that three hundred out of about one thousand adult paupers were "kept constantly at work, some at the stone quarry in breaking out and dressing stone, . . . others at caulking, spinning, weaving, shoe manufacturing etc. by which means nearly the whole of the clothing used by the paupers is manufactured by themselves."[58] Indeed, the successful operation of the woolen factory convinced the almshouse officials in 1821 to appoint John Closback, a pauper, to direct the enterprise at a salary of $200 a year. Nor were these the only manufacturing enterprises. That same year the city granted the petition of Thomas Hayes to establish a "pin manufactury" inside the institution capable of employing a hundred individuals.[59] Work and relief were now joined hand in hand for some of the incarcerated poor.

Segregating destitute people in a workshop environment accorded with the expressed desires of city officials and social reformers. The entire Bellevue establishment represented by the almshouse, the public hospital, and the penitentiary was a centralized operation designed to meet the needs of indigent, disadvantaged, and criminal persons. In theory, the almshouse complex alone offered every appearance of a model community, providing living and working quarters as well as a school room for the children and a chapel for the religious. On the grounds could be seen a bakery, icehouse, greenhouse, stable, and soap factory—all signs of an established community.[60] John Stanford, the almshouse chaplain, was also inspired in 1826 to employ a similar metaphor to the institution, describing it as a "sort of world in miniature," inhabited by a cast of characters as varied as those in any city or town.[61] Like a rural community in microcosm it seemly promised a more perfect, orderly life than that already existing in the lower-class neighborhoods of Manhattan.

As the authorities placed poor people to work the state legislators began to revise the poor laws. For some time it had been obvious that the forced removal of destitute persons worked inefficiently: some individuals proved too weak or ill to be transported; others seemly had no well-defined legal residence. And when people could be removed, towns might refuse to accept them. The result might be a court case to decide the matter. Manhattan had more trouble in this regard than rural villages. Not only was the city a haven for poor transients, but it became a refuge for poor immigrants; these persons could be returned to New York City (their port of entry) from other towns if they had not obtained residency status and then required assistance. Thus, Manhattan had a steady number of paupers to assist. State legislators complicated matters with their redrafting of the poor laws, for by 1824 they ended the policy of transportation across county lines. Determining a person's residency became less important, too. Manhattan officials, surprisingly, were furious. Although they stood to benefit from not having to worry about poor immigrants being returned from other localities, they still believed that transportation of the domestic poor was an effective tool of public welfare. Their complaints were to no avail. Transportation was no longer an important tool of public welfare.[62]

By 1830 city officials still debated the best means of assisting its poor people. The almshouse, of course, was considered an essential part of public welfare, yet city officials continued to disperse outdoor relief in the form of fuel, potatoes, and money. Disagreements centered upon how best to reform poor persons inside the almshouse, while striving to keep costs under control. No one denied the advantages of labor. But a committee appointed by the city government to investigate the operation of the almshouse stressed the advantages of agricultural labor, in emulation of rural poor farms. The commissioners of the almshouse remained unconvinced. Even so, despite the disagreement, city officials and welfare officers alike could take a certain pride by their standards in the operation of public support: the cost of assisting one inmate per week in Manhattan came to only sixty cents in 1830; by contrast, Baltimore spent seventy-five cents per week and Boston seventy-eight cents. By their own frugal standards the almshouse was a success.[63]

Manhattan's desire to control costs and develop efficient methods of assistance was hardly unique. Philadelphia is a case in point. As Priscilla F. Clement has shown, the Quaker city during the first half of the nineteenth century found itself home to many needy immigrants, who comprised a substantial proportion of the welfare rolls. Like Manhattan, Philadelphia experimented with different policies to reduce the spiraling costs of relief, often adopting draconian measures. After 1815 the city fathers not only put the institutionalized poor to work, but they attempted to limit outdoor relief to the most serious cases. Able-bodied poor persons, in fact, were seldom allowed assistance either within the almshouse or inside their homes. A more callous attitude toward the poor population had emerged.[64]

As urban authorities in large municipalities attempted to incarcerate and reform poor people, ever mindful of public welfare costs, rural towns in Long Island and Westchester also acted to restructure the workings of public welfare. Almost imperceptibly a few scattered voices in the communities called for change—voices that grew and multiplied with the aftereffects of depression and war. Increasingly, towns started to abolish home relief and pauper auctions in favor of institutions.

The Embargo Act provided the first incentive for altering normal modes of assistance. Long Island and Westchester farmers, who depended heavily on city markets for their exports, found that prices had plummeted. As John Lambert observed, "The farmers refrained from cultivating their land, for if they brought their produce to market, they either could nor not sell at all or were obliged to dispose of it for only a fourth of its value." In eastern Long Island the Embargo crippled the port of Sag Harbor, while farmers complained about the lack of a market for their crops and cattle.[65] Under such circumstances some of the poor residents must have been hard-pressed; those who at one time could depend upon casual employment from farmers were probably dismissed. And some dependent poor persons, who previously relied upon support from private sources, that is, marginally poor friends and relatives, may now have been driven onto public relief rolls. Although we cannot fully document this process, we do know that in several instances the poor rates in the towns rose. The town of Huntington saw the rates jump from $1,100 in 1806 to $1,500 in 1807; the following year it reached $2,000. Bedford witnessed similar occurrences as expenditures advanced from $200 in 1807 to $500 in 1808—a 150 percent increase. And in Smithtown the poor tax went from $400 to $600 in the same two years.[66] Even so, several communities weathered the recession quite nicely, for Rye and Hempstead posted modest declines in their poor rates during the period. Islip showed no change at all (see table 7). Yet the Embargo may have reinforced a commitment to institutional relief among some towns. On eastern Long

Table 7
Poor Rates for Selected Towns, 1806-1809

Community	1806 ($)	1807 ($)	1808 ($)	1809 ($)
Brookhaven	1,000	1,000	800	—
East Chester	200	—	150	—
New Castle	250	—	225	200
North Hempstead	1,100	1,100	900	600
Oyster Bay	1,000	600	600	600
Rye	500	350	250	350
Smithtown	400	400	600	—
New Rochelle	450	500	800	—
Islip	100	—	100	100

Source: *Records of Brookhaven, 1798-1856* (Port Jefferson, N.Y.: Steam Job Print, 1888), pp. 109, 116, 124; *Records of the Town of East Chester, New York* (6 vols.; New York: East Chester Historical Society, 1964), 4: 168, 175, 178; Town of Islip, Town Board Minutes Resolutions, 1720-1850, Microfilm Collection, SUNY-Stony Brook, reel 33, 1806-1809; *Historical Records, North Castle/New Castle: Colonial History and Minutes of the Town Meeting* (2 vols.; Armonk and Chappaqua, N.Y.: Towns of North Castle and New Castle, 1975-1977), 2: 104-110, passim; Town Book of North Hempstead, Records of the Poor, 1785-1833 Microfilm Collection, New York State Archives, Albany, 1806-1809; John Cox, ed., *Oyster Bay Town Records* (8 vols.; New York: Tobias Wright, 1931), 8:27, 30, 33, 35; Jeanne A. Forbes, ed., *Records of the Town of New Rochelle, 1699-1828* (New York: Paragraph Press, 1916), pp. 397, 399, 400; Transcript Minutes of the Town Board of Rye, 5 vols., Microfilm Collection, New York State Archives, Albany, 2: 155, 156, 158, 160; William S. Pelletreau, ed., *Records of the Town of Smithtown* (Smithtown, N.Y.: Town of Smithtown, 1898), pp. 138-140.

Island Southold once again returned to the poorhouse, after having employed a pauper auction for assisting needy persons in the 1790s. By 1806 the town decided to "hire or rent a suitable tenement to be improved as poorhouse" for a one-year term. In 1808, although some residents favored an alternative method of welfare, the almshouse remained in operation. The transformation of public welfare had begun in the countryside.[67]

Over the next few years more towns emulated Southold's approach, either abandoning pauper auctions and home relief in favor of institutions or else devising yet other methods of charitable assistance. Like Manhattan, rural communities suffered from economic dislocation, such as the Panic of 1819. Although the Panic struck financial centers hardest, farmers, too, probably found their prices for crops reduced, especially since European markets had dried up with the end of the Napoleonic Wars. A ripple effect from merchant to farmer to laborer must have arisen. Nor should we ignore climatic conditions and their impact upon the agrarian economy. In 1816, the year "without a summer," farmers throughout the eastern seaboard states experienced freakish weather; prolonged frosts late in the year and an unusually dry summer were some of the features. Crop damage was inevitable. Prices, of course, rose, ensuring profits for some, but many more farmers may have faced economic ruin.[68] Poor relief rates began a steady increase in most communities, and townsfolk called special meetings to discuss the topic of public welfare—clear evidence of serious concern. Poor relief in Oyster Bay increased in cost from $700 in 1810 to $2,000 in 1820; local officials responded early by summoning a special meeting in March 1812 "for the purpose of making such alteration respecting the putting out of the poor as may lessen the growing expenditures of the town." After an initial period of uncertainty regarding the best approach to poor relief, the townsfolk resorted to an almshouse by 1825.[69] The neighboring community of North Hempstead also found public welfare a pressing issue: in 1815 it ordered the overseers of the poor to "hire out" as many paupers as possible (perhaps as farm laborers and servants?), and to apply their "earnings" toward the support of other, presumably disabled, paupers. Yet even this bold scheme of work relief fell by the wayside in 1816, for the town overseers had been instructed by the local officials to cooperate with nearby Flushing to procure "both house and land for the needy of the two villages."[70]

The desire to devise a workable and inexpensive means of relief proved a common goal among other towns. After the War of 1812 several communities in Westchester considered the idea of institutional relief more favorably—so much so that the county government may have felt confident enough in 1815 to request that the towns meet together to purchase land for a county almshouse at Mount Pleasant. Although the plan failed to win widespread support, perhaps due to strong localist sentiment against expanding the power of the county government, institutional relief was not unattractive to some towns. They preferred, however, to tend needy residents by themselves. For instance, the residents of Rye seem to have developed their own poorhouse in unison with the village of Harrison in 1815, rather than accept the county's scheme. Time and again, the independent citizens of Rye rebuffed calls for a county facility in 1820 and 1822, preferring to work together with their sister town or "with any other adjacent town or towns in providing a suitable place for the accomodation of the poor."[71] A county facility had no place in their immediate plans. Quite possibly, the same spirit of localism motivated New Rochelle to do the same. A vote in 1820 declared that the "town will not join [the] association for the building of a poorhouse," and in 1822 the townsfolk defeated an identical county proposal by a vote of fifty-two to seven.[72] Other towns, meanwhile, gave serious thought to building their own poorhouses or at least considered proposals to do so. Bedford heard several resolutions in support of an almshouse between 1819 and 1820, some of which had been championed by the leading citizens of the community in alliance with local officials. And in the town of New Castle the overseers of the poor had received virtual carte blanche to place destitute persons in an institution or "to dispose of the poor in any way they think proper" by 1825.[73] While both Bedford and New Castle wavered about reaching a definite decision over the almshouse plan, support for institutional relief mounted during the 1820s. Both Mount Pleasant and South Salem used institutions during the early years of the decade, and by 1827 the county, too, could claim a victory because it constructed a facility, also at Mount Pleasant, to serve all the towns.[74]

In Suffolk an even stronger spirit of localism prevented the establishment of a county facility until the latter half of the nineteenth century. This most New England-like of all New York counties, viewed by Timothy Dwight as a replica of Connecticut, placed the bulk of government power in the towns rather than the county.[75] The towns, in turn, preferred to shoulder the burden of poor relief alone. And after 1815 they had sufficient opportunity to do so, for the rates continued to edge upward. Smithtown went from $300 in 1815 to $800 in 1819, while Huntington went from $1,000 to $1,400. Islip saw an even higher percentage increase, going from $100 to $500 during the four-year-period.[76] In Brookhaven the increase in the number of paupers along with mounting expenses led the overseers of the poor in 1817 to buy a house and ten acres of land for their public dependents. Ever frugal, town officials permitted some needy residents to be relieved outside the building, provided "they could be supported elsewhere as cheap as in the poorhouse." Cost, it seems, was the primary concern. Not surprisingly, the town officials largely copied Manhattan's approach for dealing with the institutionalized poor; they expected the inmates to cultivate the land, pick oakum, and labor at "domestic manufacturers." The facility, apparently, met these criteria. The town supervisor remarked in 1821, "I am confident that the poor are better supported in our town, and at least one-third cheaper, than they were before we procured a house for them."[77]

Throughout Suffolk the result was usually the same, even if the path to institutional relief sometimes followed an indirect course. The post-war period was characterized by several experiments in poor relief reforms, similar to those in Westchester and Queens, where different policies had been adopted and then abandoned. While convinced of the need for reform and innovation, the freeholders sometimes possessed less conviction and perhaps less certainty over how to alter the system of public welfare. The confusion was natural. For towns caught between the fading traditions of the past and the fast-approaching ways of the future, the path forward occasionally remained uncharted in regard to poor relief. Should, for instance, the poorhouse supersede the pauper auction, bringing rural communities in line with the urban metropolis? Or should the pauper auction itself be modified by allowing persons, commonly known as contractors, to bid competitively for poor people as a single group? Some towns opted for the latter practice. The idea of putting out poor people "in bulk" or "in gross," as village officials so quaintly phrased it, won acceptance in principle from both Smithtown and Huntington. Although Huntington failed to adopt the plan, perhaps because no one contractor ever bid low enough to satisfy the town fathers, Smithtown employed contractors in 1821 and 1822 before farming out its destitute residents in 1823 on an individual basis. In time, both communities turned to the almshouse.[78]

Despite the emphasis on cost-effectiveness, which figured so prominently in town resolutions, still other reasons help to explain the rural response to poor relief. Of particular interest here is the reason that people suddenly decided to opt for institutions. Was the economic climate of the post-war era, climaxed by erratic weather conditions and the Panic of 1819, causing farmers and artisans to dismiss servants and field hands, journeymen and apprentices? Did such unemployed folk then require relief? Were dependent poor persons now less able to rely on private charity, hence the increase in the rates? While most townsfolk agreed that the number of paupers had risen, sometimes exceeding the percentage rate of population growth, and while there is evidence to indicate a noticeable class of propertyless laborers during the 1820s, other factors must be examined in order to understand the local dynamics of institutional relief.[79]

Economic alterations provided the preconditions of change, for they set the stage for a group of rural citizens to agitate for reform. What sparked the campaign to revamp the structure of relief, then, was several forward-looking persons, who rejected what they saw as the traditionalism of village life. These persons, many of them local officials or prominent citizens, some of them affluent and active in church affairs, attacked the boarding out of poor people at home and the pauper auction; they condemned such policies as corrupt, costly, inefficient, and immoral. Opposed to them stood a number of residents, probably farmers, who viewed the matter of poor relief quite differently. This group favored non-institutional forms of relief. In certain respects, the campaign to remodel rural welfare pitted the forces of reform, that is, the local elite of the village, against the forces of tradition, who comprised the commonality. And this campaign dramatized the divisions that had arisen among the townsfolk as rural villagers found it increasingly difficult to achieve consensus on the issue, an issue that involved comparatively large sums of money and that eclipsed, for a time, any other local questions. The "peaceable kingdoms" of the eighteenth century, which had survived in battered form the aftermath of the Revolution by reliance upon old customs, now became drawn into the vortex of factionalism so characteristic of the Jacksonian Age. The movement for institutional relief helps to illustrate this change.[80]

Evidence of elite participation in the campaign for the rural poorhouse is best revealed in the communities of Bedford and Huntington. Each village witnessed a major effort to employ an almshouse for its needy residents, and each village has sufficiently detailed records to give us some sense of the actors involved in the enterprise. Both villages, moreover, typified rural communities in Queens, Suffolk, and Westchester during the early nineteenth century; they were dependent upon agriculture, yet each had a commercial or manufacturing base of modest proportions. Bedford possessed grist mills, fulling mills, and seven distilleries by 1821. Huntington not only had grist mills and fulling mills, but it was home to a woolen factory by that date. Thus, a degree of diversification existed within the rural economy.[81]

The town of Bedford had wavered between institutional relief and the public sale of poor people since the Revolutionary era. By the early decades of the nineteenth century the town boarded out indigent residents among the villagers, most likely by means of a pauper auction. A glance at the extant records for 1806 shows that Ned Bundage was "keeping" Pat Mason and his children for $86.96, and Lucretia Clark was tending Samuel Carrywood for $25.00; other names of keepers and paupers appear, too. This system of relief continued uninterrupted until 1815, when the town meeting "voted that the overseers of the poor be authorized to rent a house and land for the use and accomodation of the poor for one year." Welfare costs may have been a factor in this decision. The villagers raised $650 for poor relief in 1815, while in 1814 they had needed $550 and the year before that $450. Nevertheless, the villagers resorted to placing poor persons among private residents in 1817, even though the estimated cost for tending them was $825.[82]

Some people remained convinced that a poorhouse should be employed. During the annual spring meeting in 1819 the townsfolk organized a committee "to examine and report . . . the most eligible situation for a poorhouse, the sum of which will be necessary to raise for the purchase of the same—the quantity of land which will be proper to buy, and the advantage which in their opinion will result from the purchase." To head the committee, the town selected three individuals, all of whom were local officials, two overseers of the poor and the town supervisor, David Miller. The wording of the resolution, while perhaps not guaranteeing an almshouse, would seem to indicate that a large number of citizens were at least willing to entertain proposals for an institution.[83] That was as far as it went, however. No almshouse appeared that year. The freeholders, apparently, did not consider the proposal worthwhile. Yet by February 22, 1820, several citizens, refusing to concede defeat, submitted a petition for a special meeting, claiming that it was "highly important to the interest of the said town that a house should be speedily provided in which the poor of the said town may be maintained." The persons who signed the petition represented the social elite of the community, ranging from William Jay, noted Episcopalian and the son of John Jay, Revolutionary figure and the wealthiest freeholder, to the aforementioned David Miller, former militia captain and town supervisor from 1808 to 1830. Among the eleven other signers of the petition were several more prominent folk, four of whom had real estate and personal property that put them in the wealthiest 10 percent of the population, according to the 1815 assessment list for the town. Some of those not in the upper strata were the sons of affluent parents. In addition, almost all of the signers had been local officials or would be, while William Jay would go on to become a well-known county judge and an active social reformer.[84]

The proponents of the almshouse apparently managed to make their point since the town clerk set a special meeting for March 15, 1820. Once again, the issue of institutional relief came before the villagers, as the town drafted a set of resolutions similar to those mentioned the year before. This effort also failed. By 1822 the town was still trying to "place all of the poor . . . in one place." Poor relief records still show that destitute persons were boarded out; the names of paupers along with the cost of their support appeared throughout the 1820s. People interested in institutional relief had to wait until the county facility opened in 1827.[85]

Efforts to employ a poorhouse in Huntington proved more successful. Like Bedford, this Suffolk community had experimented with both institutions and pauper auctions after the Revolutionary War. By 1805 they settled upon the pauper auction and for almost twenty years it remained in operation. Year after year in spring the freeholders had the chance to bid for the poor. And as the years went on the price of supporting the destitute citizenry rose, as did their total numbers: the eighteen public dependents in 1806 became forty-nine by 1820, while welfare expenditures surged from $774.70 to $1,532.05.[86] A few people at least were now beginning to pay more attention to poverty and public welfare. In the local newspaper, the *American Eagle,* the editor reminded the villagers during the winter of 1823 about how wealthy persons should "display the magnanimity of generous funds, . . . then will the poor subjects of destitution, bless their benefactors with a grateful remembrance, whose name will live in posterity." Another issue on November 11, 1824, ran an item on the Salem, Massachusetts, "Almshouse Farm," calling it "one of the most successful experiments in agriculture that we have ever known." The timing of this article is probably significant, for in the spring of that year town officials had set the stage for an almshouse. Although the pauper auction continued, town officials gave the overseers the power to commit indigent persons to a poorhouse "at their discretion." Such commitment began later that year.[87]

Locally prominent figures stood in the forefront of the almshouse movement. One of these men was Nathaniel Potter. Bearer of a well-known Huntington name, Potter had been trained as a silversmith and then had emerged as a local businessman by the first decade of the 1800s, running a general store; later he achieved a measure of fame by serving as a state assemblyman and county judge. A devout Presbyterian, he left a sum of money on his death to the First Presbyterian Church, the oldest church in the town. Assisting him in the campaign was Devine Hewlett. An Episcopalian, Hewlett was engaged in commercial and manufacturing enterprises, and his family ranked among the wealthiest in the town. Hewlett had also participated in the pauper auction on occasion. Yet by 1825, if not earlier, he had become a believer in institutional relief. Potter and Hewlett received moral support from Samuel Fleet, who was the local publisher and principal of the town's academy. In 1825, Nathaniel Potter, now president of the town's trustees and an overseer of the poor, along with Devine Hewlett, also a trustee and overseer of the poor, completed the transformation of the poor relief system. Together they ended the pauper auction. Assistance now centered upon the twenty-four-acre poor farm, and those who refused "to conform" to this arrangement would have no support except in "extrodinary cases at the discretion of the overseers of the poor."[88] From the perspective of these people the almshouse more than paid for itself. In 1826 Samuel Fleet in the *Portico,* another local paper, demonstrated the savings by comparing the costs of the pauper auction in 1823 and 1824 that totaled $3,360.04 to the $2,954.38 it took to run the poorhouse in 1825 and 1826. He also praised Potter and Hewlett for their achievement:

> The above comparison speaks for itself—it is a handsome experiment and the gentlemen involved who effected so great a revolution in our pauper system and made so great a savings to the town, deserve the thanks of all. They are entitled to much credit for their enlightened views and for their perserverance in accomplishing the object of their undertaking—for abolishing the custom of exposing the poor at public sale—a custom whose every feature was savage and which was productive of increasing and sore evils.[89]

Even in Huntington, however, the campaign for institutional relief had geographic limits. While supportive of the local poorhouse, residents refused to join with other towns to establish a county facility. An article in the November 23, 1826, issue of the *Portico* did mention support for a county almshouse among "many of the inhabitants," but it was insufficient. Poor relief remained a local issue.[90]

What made the triumph of the Huntington reformers so impressive and the defeat of the Bedford forces so unsurprising was the nature of the opposition arrayed against them—that is, the participants of the pauper auction. The "increasing and sore evils" referred to by Fleet may well have been an oblique reference to what many rural reformers considered the internal corruption of the pauper auction. In theory, the auction presented the appearance of competition, with bidders vying against each other at successively lower prices; in reality much the opposite occurred, with many bidders deliberately encouraging impoverished friends and relatives—whom they might have assisted at no cost to the town—to enter the auction. Both parties could then rely upon the stipend. After all, why should bidders assist friends and relatives out of their own pocket when money could be obtained via the auction? Farmers, too, had reasons to maintain the auction; it allowed them in some instances to procure workers—people whose labor would only benefit the town with the adoption of institutional relief. Then there were the marginally poor persons themselves, who might have found the auction system a way to keep off the welfare rolls. The stipend they received from the town might just have been enough to make ends meet.[91] Town officials were aware of these facts. In Mount Pleasant, for example, many poor residents did not enter the poorhouse because they had "friends," according to one official, who would support them. The town even agreed to provide a stipend if it proved to be less than the cost of institutionalization. In North Hempstead, the placing of poor people in private residences, perhaps by means of the pauper auction, was abolished since many needy persons ended up with "connections," as a town official phrased it.[92] Huntington and Bedford officials were also no doubt aware of these things, hence their campaign to install poorhouses.

Another reason why the almshouse may have encountered resistance had to do with the local attitudes of the residents—attitudes based perhaps less on economic and social factors than on a simple unwillngness to embrace new ideas. The belief in tradition may have been especially strong in portions of Westchester, where the presence of the market economy did not necessarily entail a restructuring of daily life. Consider the observations of Horatio Spafford. The editor of the 1824 *New York Gazetteer,* a compedium of information, he had access to state census reports and letters from people scattered across the state. Spafford noted that the residents of the eastern half of Westchester "are wanting in enterprise, if not in ingenuity, compared with their neighbors in Connecticut." In fact, the men "followed the plough, content, if the surplus of their farms enabled them to become their puchasers." Extending his coverage, Spafford mentioned that the eastern side of the state—which included Westchester—was burdened with the support of its poor citizens, yet the residents failed to create a "House of Industry connected with a farm," which he believed would eradicate pauperism.[93] Some residents, quite simply, had no desire to change their way of doing things, even when pressed by rising poor rates.

Reformers, of course, viewed matters differently than did many local residents. Although the pauper auction or boarding-out system may not have always been corrupt, and although a certain amount of rigged bidding was perhaps tolerated by the residents, the economic expense involved in supporting poor people had become too great for them by the 1820s. Some of these reformers, as we have seen, were also among the wealthiest taxpayers—the group that would shoulder the heaviest share of the poor tax. This was another reason for them to favor new forms of relief. So, too, when reformers noted that some of the bidders or purchasers of destitute persons treated them "like brutes," while spending the stipend on alcohol, they felt compelled to act. Reform, then, became a double-edged sword; it enabled the Hewletts and the Jays to try to save money, while it appealed to their religious and moral sensibilities—each of which was an important consideration. And the almshouse seemed to provide the right tool.[94]

The democratic character of the pauper auction lost its appeal under such circumstances. For some, it was better to rely on institutions and emulate the city than to depend on the supposed good intentions of the populace. The battle over poor relief, then, became a conflict between the forces of change and the forces of tradition. On the one side stood the farmers along with friends and relatives of the poor, persons who preferred to have their poor neighbors with them; on the other side stood men such as William Jay, Devine Hewlett, Nathaniel Potter, and others. The latter group, although landowners, had an interest in politics and business that divorced them from the soil-tilling yeomanry; they were willing to question old practices and do away with them.

And then there were the poor people themselves. What did they feel? Perhaps the clearest response came from Thankful Soper. This Huntington resident, long a public dependent, was both destitute and ailing, yet she was no fool. In 1825 she refused an order to enter the almshouse, as did two other paupers once served by the pauper auction. These people would rather take their chance on the outside. Some could expect relief from the village; others could not. Poor relief officials for their part could be pleased: in town after town in the 1830s poor rates declined. The deterrent effects of the almshouse had become evident.[95]

In retrospect, the establishment of the almshouse in both city and countryside illustrated the concern of citizens and officials to reduce poor relief expenditures. It further revealed a belief that needy people were better treated inside an institution safe from temptation and exploitation. Both urban and rural officials sought to make destitute persons as self-reliant as possible by means of work, and both succeeded in a small way. Yet their path to this goal was different: the city establishment at Bellevue represented a logical step forward over previous kinds of institutions; it stressed disciplined labor for both sick and healthy inmates in what was basically a separate community closed off from the world. This was the culmination point of the institutionalization process. In the countryside, on the other hand, the path forward was less well charted, as communities often abandoned their poorhouses only to return to them again at a later period. Residents of the countryside debated about what method to use, and the debate featured two distinct groups of people, either for or against almshouses.

If the city remained truer to the concept of institutional relief over the years, the countryside, too, knew how to employ such devices. Indeed, villages surpassed the city in their efforts to eliminate outdoor relief. Manhattan's attempt to reduce outdoor relief could never be fully realized in a populous urban environment, where the inclemency of the winter, the uncertainity of the economy, and the baneful effects of epidemics forced many to require temporary assistance. It was impossible to house them all. In fact, an 1833 report on public assistance in the city revealed 5,179 persons incarcerated in the almshouse and 3,830 families or 19,150 individuals supported outside the institution. Rural towns, however, usually had only several persons at any one time receiving relief at home. They could impose a structure to poor relief that the city fathers could never match. Despite all that has been written about the provincial character of country life, there seems little doubt that in matters of public charity rural folk would become among the most faithful disciples of institutions.[96]

CHAPTER V

Paupers and Wanderers: The Identity of the Rural Poor, 1800–1830

On December 8, 1819, Henry Thaler appeared before the justice of the peace in the town of Huntington prepared to submit testimony "touching upon his last legal settlement." Thaler described to Justice Moses Rolph his birth in Germany and later arrival in America as a soldier in the British army during the Revolution. Deserting at the close of the war, he had found work on Long Island in the town of Oyster Bay before moving to Huntington and laboring for John Jones; one year later he had gone to sea for an unspecified period of time, returned to Huntington, married a woman from Oyster Bay, and soon started traveling "from place to place" in search of work. During these years he had never purchased a freehold estate or rented a house for more than twenty-five dollars a year. Now residing in Huntington and "unable to labor and destitute of the means of support," Thaler was requesting charity of the local authorities. He received one dollar per week.[1]

On January 26, 1821, another petitioner stood in front of the local justice of the town. This applicant was a free black man named Prince who had been manumitted by his Huntington master, Abraham Van Wyck, almost twenty years earlier in 1802. Unlike Henry Thaler, who went to sea and traveled to different locations, Prince had worked the "principal part of his time for Isaac Hewlett" and leased "sundry tenements" from his employer, either in the town or

136

in neighboring Oyster Bay. He never paid more than fifteen dollars a year in rent. Like many laborers during the winter, Prince proved unable to find employment and hence was "destitute of fuel." No record exists of his receiving aid.[2]

These two examples reveal some of the difficulties that beset so many destitute persons, black and white, in the rural countryside during the early national period. Individuals no longer able to support themselves by necessity sought charity from local officials. Aged and crippled persons, those who were sick or unemployed, men and women, adults and children, formed the nucleus of this unfortunate class of rural poor persons. While a few owned small freeholds, others were propertyless artisans, laborers, and servants, persons who traveled from town to town in search of employment. The road was often their home. Over several years they could move among nearby villages or go across counties and even states, working for a time and then moving on yet again. Some might settle in one location and attain a moderate subsistence, yet illness, injury, or old age could cause them to request assistance. For many, life represented little more than a marginal existence, a constant struggle to eke out a living. Some of these facts are well known. Fernand Braudel's description of the European pauper as a "man who barely scraped a living from his work" could equally apply to the American pauper; poverty, after all, had certain universal features.[3] Less certain, however, is the identity of rural poor Americans and their relationship to the society—in particular, how they functioned in a republic that championed the virtues of social mobility in the age of the common man. Nor do we really know much about the course of their travels despite the work of Stephen Thernstrom, Peter Knights, and others. Rural working folk moved often, but their pattern of travel needs to be more clearly detailed in regard to the distance and frequency of each journey. This chapter, then, seeks to illuminate the identity and movement of rural poor New Yorkers during the early nineteenth century.[4]

Descriptions of rural poor people varied. Everyone recognized the need to assist the less fortunate, especially "the poor widow and the fatherless," who qualified as "deserving objects" of charity through no fault of their own. Towns and churches freely rendered assistance to them, providing food, clothing, shelter, and medicine. Individuals, too, might be disposed to give alms under certain circumstances; in 1800, for example, Samuel Thompson, a Brookhaven farmer, aided one William Thompson, "who came here with some credentials as a seaman [and] asked charity. I gave him a dollar and a nickel of it."[5] Less deserving, however, were the "idle and dissapated," who customarily sought relief "in the inclement seasons of the year," according to one account from Long Island in 1823. Samuel Chipman, a temperance advocate, concluded in 1833 that the state poorhouses were overflowing with the victims of alcoholism; he observed that a majority of the 205 inmates in the Westchester almshouse were intemperate, with another 70 considered "doubtful" in regard to sober behavior.[6] Equating poverty with alcoholism proved a common theme for social reformers—so much so that they never missed an opportunity to link the two. In 1827 a Westchester newspaper contributor described a "company of ill-favored, strolling wretches from 15 to 20 in number . . . covered with remnants of blankets, quilts, carpets, and cast-off clothes," who set their children to beg in the streets in order to obtain a "gallon of whisky." Similarly, a young woman from New Castle confided to her diary in 1800 about a needy family in neighboring Bedford, once "counted one of the foremost," but now, due to the husband's "inattentiveness . . . to business and incessantly drinking strong liquors," reduced to a state of penury.[7]

Less descriptive but equally informative accounts of rural poor people appeared during the 1820s. Concern over rising poor rates prompted frightened officials to determine the exact number of dependent paupers in each township. By 1824, the Yates Report, named after New York's secretary of state, provided the first detailed glimpse of rural poverty in New York City's environs. Despite the jeremiads of local officials decrying inadequate poor laws and costly poor relief expenditures, the number of paupers was low; in fact, most townships dispensed assistance to fewer than 2 percent of their citizens.[8] The majority of these dependents in the counties of Queens, Suffolk, and Westchester appear to have been women and children rather than adult men. While adult men occasionally outnumbered adult women—as was true in Hempstead, Mount Pleasant, and Brookhaven—they almost never exceeded the combined total of women and children (see Table 8). Widows, single mothers, and orphans received the bulk of public assistance.[9]

The high proportion of female paupers reflected their limited

Table 8
Public Dependents in Queens, Suffolk, and Westchester, 1822-1823

Community	Men	Women	Children
Queens			
Hempstead	26	16	24
Jamaica	6	12	3
North Hempstead	28	28	33
Oyster Bay	6	16	6
Suffolk			
Brookhaven	17	16	6
East Hampton	4	5	0
Huntington	22	29	10
Riverhead	1	9	2
Smithtown	2	8	3
Southampton	15	24	12
Southold	6	14	2
Westchester			
Mount Pleasant	26	20	21
New Castle	5	9	3
New Rochelle	3	1	1
Rye	4	2	2
South Salem	9	14	7
Westchester	19	22	15

Source: "Report of the Secretary of State in 1824 on the Relief and Settlement of the Poor," in David J. Rothman, ed., *Poverty, U.S.A.* (New York: Arno Press, 1971).

economic skills and restricted geographic mobility. Women remained confined to the household, and their moral role relegated them to restricted economic tasks for the most part. Of course, some women might teach in the village school, instructing the sons and daughters of the villagers for brief periods of the year; others could operate small businesses. Yet the great majority stayed tied to household occupations, which promised considerable drudgery and unvaried routine.[10] This was especially true of house domestics—often the lowest-paid rural wage workers. Unattached women who lacked a benevolent employer or family could find their positions compromised when sickness or injury occurred. A widow with a large family often fared similarly. Both women might then turn to the town for support. Some women possessed yet another disadvantage, for few white women above the "laboring classes" could go on the roads unescorted; it was expected that they have a male companion or protector. And yet many such women, suddenly reduced in circumstance, might have no friends or relatives elsewhere, forcing them to stay in the immediate locality. Men faced no such difficulties, moving where they pleased in search of work. The ability of most women to rise above a modest standard remained limited.[11]

Regrettably, this analysis of male and female paupers cannot be carried further. Later tallies of dependent poor persons generally avoided identifying them by sex, concentrating instead on the total number of paupers in the respective townships. Although the state census of 1835 reveals a majority of male inmates in the Westchester almshouse, this may be the result of the institutionalization process rather than any dramatic shift in the sex ratio of needy persons. Men normally outnumbered women in poorhouses during the antebellum period, as women continued to remain more on home relief.[12] Even so, later records still prove useful in determining if the number of paupers had risen. The state censuses for 1825 and 1835 supply information on the number of public dependents.

The census of 1825 furnished a statistical portrait of New York's inhabitants. Various categories listed the number of males and females, aliens and paupers, untaxed blacks and taxed blacks, while other tables concentrated on the handicapped. For our purposes, the most remarkable feature was the decreased number of paupers since the appearance of the Yates Report. Several towns even witnessed a dramatic decline: North Hempstead's pauper class went from fifty-six to twenty-five, Jamaica's from eighteen to five, Huntington's from fifty-one to seventeen, and Mount Pleasant's from forty-six to nine.[13] The few exceptions to this pattern recorded only slight increases. For instance, Smithtown's pauper population rose from ten to thirteen, and East Hampton edged upward from nine to thirteen; the one lone exception, New Castle, had a 50 percent increase, from fourteen to twenty-one (see Table 9).

Stricter mechanisms for dispensing public charity explain much of the decline. As we have seen, rural reformers attacked what they perceived to be the corrupt features of poor relief, whereby friends and relatives of destitute persons received monetary support for lodging them. Reformers considered this assistance unnecessary, a convenient profit-making scheme for persons who normally might have assisted family members or companions free of

Table 9
Public Dependents of Queens, Suffolk, and Westchester, 1825

Community	N
Queens	
Jamaica	5
Hempstead	14
North Hempstead	25
Oyster Bay	14
Suffolk	
Brookhaven	23
Huntington	17
East Hampton	13
Riverhead	7
Smithtown	13
Southampton	27
Southold	15
Westchester	
Mount Pleasant	9
New Castle	21
New Rochelle	3
Rye	3
Westchester	27

Source: *The Journal of the Senate of the State of New York, 49th Session, 3 January 1826* (Albany: Craswell, 1826), SUNY-Stony Brook.

charge. Moral responsibility was forgotten in favor of procuring a town stipend—or so reasoned many rural reformers.[14] One way of reducing the strain on the town budget was to develop alternative mechanisms of relief. In Huntington, the new almshouse completed in 1825 effectively dissuaded many from going there to receive relief. The nine persons lodged inside the house and the seven "supported out by their labor" compared favorably with the fifty or so individuals assisted by the town during the last years of the pauper auction's operation. The adoption of institutions in other rural communities undoubtedly contributed to similar results.[15] In addition, several towns experimented with a contract system that pemitted needy persons to be supported in bulk by a single contractor. These contractors were often notorious for exploiting their charges, putting them to work at various tasks and occasionally mistreating them. Rumors of such treatment compelled some people to care for less fortunate relatives themselves, diminishing the welfare rolls further.[16]

Pauper rolls were trimmed again in the 1830s. Although Westchester had a centralized county facility for destitute persons, Suffolk and Queens preferred to administer poor relief on the town level, with local officials deciding policy. Conceivably, local control lent itself to lower poor rates since villagers were better able to regulate requests for charity. Then there was the spectre of the poor farm, which continued to deter people from requesting relief. In any event, such towns as North Hempstead and Brookhaven registered one-third fewer public dependents in 1835 compared to 1825. Other towns, although assisting more public dependents, had also experienced a substantial population growth during the ten-year period. Local populations often increased by 15 percent and sometimes by as much as 25 percent (see Table 10). And this may explain in part the increase in the number of poor persons.

A strong economy also eased the demand for rural poor relief. With the revival of commerce and the rapid growth of manufacturing enterprises during the early 1820s, employment opportunities blossomed. Indeed, both the 1820s and 1830s have been considered a crucial period for the American economy in general, for it witnessed the beginnings of a manufacturing economy as well as a burgeoning commercial sector. While individual historians differ as to the exact date of this economic revolution, there appears little doubt that the period between the Panics of 1819 and 1837 proved prosperous for many Americans. The stronger economy, although of little direct benefit to handicapped and maimed citizens, did furnish employment for able-bodied poor persons, which allowed them to support themselves and their families.[17]

The identity of the rural poor population and their relationship to the greater society is illuminated by consulting the extant poor relief records from Huntington, Brookhaven, and East Chester. These accounts vary in the quality and quantity of information they provide, ranging from little more than a few sentences regarding a particular poor person to lengthy legal depositions submitted by the poor people themselves to the authorities; taken together, they permit a uniquely personal insight into a class of citizens often depicted as lifeless statistics. Legal depositions, in particular, increase our knowledge not merely about dependent poor Americans—those

Table 10
Growth of Population and Number of Public Dependents, Queens and Suffolk, 1825-1835

Community	Population Growth			Public Dependents		
	Census of 1825	Census of 1835	% Growth	Census of 1825	Census of 1835	% Growth
Queens						
Hempstead	5,295	6,654	25.6	14	30	114.2
Jamaica	2,401	2,885	20.1	5	4	-20.0
North Hempstead	2,827	3,360	18.8	25	16	-36.0
Oyster Bay	5,005	5,083	1.5	14	9	-35.7
Suffolk						
Brookhaven	5,393	6,866	27.3	23	16	-30.4
East Hampton	1,556	1,819	16.1	13	12	- 7.6
Huntington	4,590	5,498	21.1	17	16	- 5.8
Riverhead	1,816	2,138	17.7	7	16	128.5
Smithtown	1,677	1,580	-5.7	13	4	-69.2
Southampton	4,561	5,275	15.6	27	15	-44.4
Southold	2,456	3,236	31.7	15	21	40.0

Source: *Journal of the Senate, 49th Session: The State Census of 1835* (Albany: Croswell, Van Benthwysen, and Bush, 1836), Microfilm Collection, SUNY-Stony Brook.

who required assistance—but marginally poor ones, that is, people who managed without public support. Individuals entering the community with uncertain economic prospects could be called before the justices and compelled to recite an account of their travels. Such information, in turn, allowed the justices to transport paupers to their last legal settlement, if they should become public dependents. This practice lasted until 1827. Afterward, towns in Suffolk continued taking testimony from such persons, for they could still charge other towns in the county for their support.[18]

The rural poor persons who appeared in the official records of the early nineteenth century resided in a slowly changing society. Old customs, as we have seen, could linger long in some villages despite evident economic alterations. Yet change did occur. The consensual political communities of the eighteenth century, which stressed unity and agreement, were less recognizable by the 1820s and 1830s, as the forces of pluralism spread and sometimes flourished in the countryside of southern New York. Religion was one example. What had once been mainly a Calvinist domain with some Anglicans and Quakers now blossomed into a more diverse religious society, as Methodists, Baptists, and Universalists attracted adherents among the countryfolk. The agrarian economy, while still dominant, geared itself more for export as farmers sought out profitable markets in Manhattan. Westchester had "hours of the day when the roads it is said were fairly blocked by the heavy traffic upon them, and eyewitnesses declared that at night even the floor of the bars and sitting rooms of the taverns were spread over with the sleepers tarrying to rest themselves and their teams for a few hours on the way." In East Chester grain mills and saw mills dotted the landscape, while residents engaged in trade with Manhattan from the town's landing. On Long Island much the same situation existed, with farmers selling wood, crops, and cattle. And in Huntington the woolen factory promised "constant employment" for weavers, preferably "men with families," who could find homes provided by their employers.[19]

These three communities, however, remained quite unchanged in one respect—their suspicion of people from outside the town. Statutes enacted in the eighteenth century served warning to prevent strangers and foreigners from fishing, hunting, and clamming during much of the 1800s. Local residents alone could reap these resources. Similarly, officials manifested much the same attitude toward people asking alms, for they forced outsiders to give an account of their origins. East Chester even had employers report upon anyone they had hired in an effort to identify potential public dependents. Local authorities, it seems, left little to chance.[20]

Perhaps the most common outsider to appear in these communities was the rural laborer. Unlike many farmers, shopkeepers, or artisans, the country worker remained an individual of decidedly modest means, owning little or no property and few personal possessions. Day laborers proved a distinctive feature of the rural landscape, clad in "yellow buckskins or leather breeches, a checkered shirt, and a red flannel jacket, . . . heavy shoes with huge brass buckles and a leather apron."[21] At work on the farmstead, they plowed the fields, planted the seeds, and harvested the crops in accordance with the demands of the season, when not busy mending fences or cutting wood. Few tasks appeared beyond their skill. Indeed, William Cobbett, the English political essayist who resided on Long Island, considered them jacks-of-all-trades: "Every man can use an axe, a saw, a hammer. Scarcely one who cannot do any job of rough carpentering and mend ploughs or a wagon. Very few of them who cannot kill and dress pigs and sheep and many of them oxens and calves. . . . In short, a good laborer here can do anything that is to be done upon a farm."

Although rural laborers worked the whole day, their movements were slow and deliberate rather than fast and hurried, with periods of rest during the hottest part of the day and occasional holidays. Both farmer and hired hand depended on a steady rhythm of work, unbound by the constraints of the clock. Cobbett wrote: "An American laborer is not regulated as to time, by clocks or watches. The sun, who seldom hides his face, tells him when to begin in the morning and when to end off at night. Here there is no dispute about hours. 'Hours were made for slaves' is an old saying; and really they seem here to act upon it."[22]

Nor were such laborers interested in changing how they did things. James Harriot, an Englishman who purchased a farm in Queens in the 1790s, could observe firsthand the behavior of his employees in this regard—behavior he evidently disapproved of. After procuring help with some difficulty, Harriot was amazed to discover the unwillingness of his men to work as he directed in some instances. They refused to do half the tasks assigned. This was hardly due to any inherent difficulty, according to Harriot, but because "they have not been accustomed to do it in such a way." Resistance to new methods complemented a remarkable degree of anti-black feeling. White laborers would work alongside blacks, yet disliked eating with them at the same table. In fact, two of Harriot's white laborers left several days after one such incident.[23]

Living arrangements varied among poor people in general and laborers in particular. Hired hands enjoyed the option of boarding with their employers or renting separate dwellings, depending on their circumstances. A fortunate few owned a house and property. Whatever course they chose invariably depended on such factors as family size, wages, and rents: single persons with little capital probably favored living with their employers, sacrificing some autonomy and higher wages in return for bed and board. In East Chester John Tubs hired a fourteen-year-old boy who had arrived at his house in 1813 "looking for work," while Gilbert Shute took forty-year-old Eanack Mills into his family to work with him in 1810. Workers disenchanted with this living arrangement could always leave—something hired hands often did without warning.[24] Married men with children generally rented separate dwellings from their employers or another local landlord. The need for privacy and sometimes the unwillingness of employers to board entire families contributed to this result. For between ten and thirty dollars a year laborers could rent a dwelling, which one observer likened to a "shell of boards," and perhaps enough land for a small garden. Those with a house and a freehold estate of several acres fared best of all, for they could avoid paying rent and perhaps escape taxes due to their modest status. Their small plots might enable them to plant crops, reducing puchases from farmers. Such a situation, presumably, would permit landed laborers to save more money than renters or boarders. Nevertheless, even this elite class of workers had to be cautious; their small tracts might be located on poor soil, which would produce low yields. And constant cultivation might ruin the land further. So, too, freakish weather conditions or a sudden swarm of pests might devastate their crops more than those of a substantial farmer. Their margin of security was limited.[25]

Some poor people might not even hire themselves out to employers, preferring to live as squatters along the seashore or within the pine barrens that extended across Long Island from the Hempstead Plains to Peaconic Bay. Such people remained almost independent of the cash economy; they worked rarely, if indeed at all, for any employer. Waterfront citizens harvested the sea's bounty of fish, clams, oysters, and mussels, while they occasionally pillaged shipwrecked vessels beached upon the shore for whatever objects they might use or sell. This was especially true of southern Long Island. The land here was too poor in many places to support farming; hence people relied upon the shellfisheries to survive.[26] Although individuals of this description probably appeared seldom before the authorities for relief, we do have an account of one such person living in Hempstead in 1842:

> We tramped several miles along the beach . . . and on our return stopped at the Hammocks, where a large hut had been erected and was maintained; peradventure it might prove a shelter to some poor bayman, or maybe to some wrecked sailors. The hut was occupied by Ize Johnson with general consent its accepted keeper. Now poor Ize was a vagrant throughout. We do not mean a vicious loafer, but a dreamy idler who takes life indifferently having found the art of arts that of being without—a cultivated savage—this is no contradiction, it is near the perfection of manhood. We looked in the hut, but did not enter, the atmosphere was far from agreeable. After giving Ize all the tobacco in our party, we left for camp.[27]

Another class of people who seldom rose above the position of laborers and often remained distant from the cash economy were the Indians. Few of them were left in Westchester, but upon Long Island could still be found scattered settlements of native Americans, coexisting after a fashion with the white inhabitants. Indians who resided near the villages resorted to the manufacture of baskets and brooms; the profits from these enterprises could then be used to buy blankets and powder, as well as "such indulgences as it exceeds their art to manufacture." Many of them still hunted. Long Island had a variety of wildlife, and Indians continued to take advantage of this bounty. In regard to housing, many Indians still lived in shelters of largely traditional design. James Fenimore Cooper, who visited Long Island during the 1820s, described one such structure as a "wigwam of a most primitive construction"; it "consisted of a few made chairs, baskets, and a bed that was neither savage, nor yet such as marks the civilized man."[28] Cooper's cultural bigotry aside, Indians did live simply and frugally for the most part. One Brookhaven Indian woman, Silva, who became a public dependent in 1809, had a household inventory of £2-18-0, which was a low amount indeed compared to some of the white poor. Among her modest belongings could be found plates, pails, pots, cups, and utensils, along with such items as a smoothing iron valued at two shillings and an iron candlestick holder assessed at one shilling. Silva slept in a straw bed with an "old sheet" and "old blanket" for warmth. Such was her material world.[29]

Such accounts, however, are rare. No other Indian pauper appears in the town records of Brookhaven or Huntington. Despite their evident poverty, most Indians, it seems, preferred to remain apart from the white world, using what they could in the way of goods and staying mostly to themselves.[30]

Black applicants proved to be a more common sight among welfare officials. In the towns of East Chester and Huntington they could occasionally comprise as much as 20 percent of the public dependents during a given year, although generally the percentage was lower. Nor should this be surprising: black persons were an integral part of the rural countryside as well as a destitute class of people. The 1825 State Census showed 265 blacks in Huntington out of a total population of 4,540, while in East Chester there were 148 black inhabitants residing in a community of 931 persons. Neither town had many black taxpayers, that is, persons who owned a freehold estate valued at $250 or more. The 1825 census showed two such persons in East Chester and none in Huntington. As might be expected, most blacks worked as laborers, fishermen, and domestics. And such persons were sometimes candidates for poor relief.[31]

Not surprisingly, blacks were frequently required to submit testimony to the justices regarding their last legal settlement, even those able to support themselves. White officials remained deeply suspicious of free blacks—as they did of itinerant whites—and hauled them before the justices whenever the opportunity arose. Many such black people, freed under the provision of the Emancipation Act of 1799, furnished information on their early lives as slaves, detailing their sale to different masters and their eventual manumission. For some, life as a bondsperson during the waning years of the institution meant serving several masters in different towns, as white owners attempted to profit from the gradual freedom clauses of the Act of Emancipation. Peter Fleet remained with his first master until the age of ten, when he was sold to Gilbert Fleet, who in turn sold him to Augustine Fleet. All three owners resided in Huntington. Peter Fleet later served two masters in Oyster Bay, one in Brookhaven, and one in North Hempstead before acquiring his freedom. He then returned to Huntington, where his wife remained in bondage. Other blacks moved among branches of the same family: Ceasar, a bondsman of Annias Carll, later worked for Jesse Carll, and Elijah Cooks served both Isaiah Whitman and Jarvis Whitman.[32] While many rural masters promptly manumitted their bondspersons, some appeared decidedly lax in fulfilling the necessary legal steps. Elijah Ferris told the Huntington justices that he had never been manumitted "according to law." Elijah Cooks, after working for the Whitmans, went to other masters in Long Island and New Jersey until forcibly taken from New Jersey by the "people called Quakers and manumitted by them." Peter Prince achieved freedom without the assistance of any benefactors, for he deserted his Westchester master after seven years' service. Later, he returned to his former master to obtain the legal documents certifying his status as a freeman. Prince also obtained a promise of support from him if he should ever become a public dependent.[33]

The depositions of these recently emancipated persons illustrate the obstacles peculiar to many black workers, obstacles that seldom confronted poor whites. The right of freedom was sometimes hard to acquire. Unscrupulous masters might stand in the way. Yet what did such freedom bring once it was obtained by blacks in the rural countryside outside of Manhattan? How did they function in the local economy? What was their relationship, if any, to the white majority during the first decades of freedom? Could they depend upon support when ill or injured from former owners or did they rely upon public welfare? And did they develop a cohesive community with a sense of solidarity, or were they merely a group of individuals with little actual autonomy engulfed by white authority?

The structure of the free black community during the early national period has been covered in some detail over the past few decades. Historians readily acknowledge the secondary position of Afro-Americans in white society, agree about their meager economic status, and accept that few had the right to vote. Both Arthur Zilversmit and Leon Litwack have added tremendously to our knowledge in this regard, while more recent works by Leonard Curry and

Gary Nash show us where the field is headed.[34] Most of these works deal with the urban black population, however; the position and status of rural blacks have been less well studied.

Those rural free blacks who continued to live with white families as domestics or hired hands after their emancipation probably had only a limited degree of physical freedom and perhaps autonomy. Like most live-in domestics and laborers—white or black—their time was seldom their own during the day; they worked long hours, often in close proximity with their employers or other white laborers. Those who lived apart from their bosses may have been in a better situation. They could at least retire by day's end to the security of their dwelling, however modest, and be among themselves. Black farmers and fishermen were even better off. Not only did they live among themselves, but they could dictate their own hours and pace of work, free of possible white interference. Most likely, such folk had a different kind of social existence from their fellows who resided in white households.[35]

The black community of Huntington provides some insight into this issue. Although former slaves and their children lived on the borderline between subsistence and privation, eking out a living in manual occupations, social divisions of a sort did exist among them based upon their relationship to the white majority. During 1790 most Huntington blacks were slaves, who resided with their masters; the 320 bondspersons identified in the federal census of that year lived inside their masters' households or in adjacent buildings of the estate. Such blacks had daily exposure to white members of the household, for few Huntington masters owned more than three or four slaves. Free blacks, too, often ended up as lodgers in white households, with the census listing forty-three blacks living among whites and thirty-one living on their own. Almost all of the latter had white neighbors. Census entries reveal that the few black households were located near to white residences in almost every instance. Indeed, only Charles Potter and Leuis Tilleson may have resided next to each other; their names appear in sequence on the census roll, suggesting some proximity. No free black community existed in 1790 save in the most rudimentary sense.[36]

Emancipation effected profound alterations, however. Freedom offered the opportunity for increasing numbers of blacks to forge an almost separate residential existence by renting tenements or by purchasing plots of land. Benjamin Hammond, a former slave of the manor lord Lloyds, bought a freehold estate for $125 in the town and "actually paid the money," according to his deposition. His neighbor, a free black man named Jonah Mott, may have also owned property. Steven Ogden leased a ten-dollar-a-year tenement, purchased an acre and a quarter for fifteen dollars in 1810, and paid twenty-five dollars for a house that he moved to his property in 1819.[37] The trend to greater black autonomy increased over the century. The 1820 manuscript census for Huntington lists several black households, including at least two interrelated families, residing close to each other. Indeed, the four male-headed households totaling twenty-two individuals presumably comprised a black community in microcosm; they numbered six families or thirty-six individuals by 1830. Nor were these people alone: the 1830 census reveals that 53 percent of the black population lived on leasehold or freehold estates (N = 362). The 1836 coastal survey map of the Island further illustrates the geographic dimension of black settlement, detailing at least one small group of households clustered together—perhaps the aforementioned group in the censuses—in southern Huntington; it also shows several blacks who lived apart in the woods of central Huntington.[38] Clearly, some kind of community had developed.

Greater residential and social autonomy was not always possible. Living alone, of course, implied a certain measure of independence, a certain social distance from possibly meddling whites; but spatial or geographic appearances often failed to guarantee economic freedom. Testimony supplied by blacks reveals many who rented lodgings from white landlords or employers. Residential distance from a white employer belied the economic chain of command that continued to link the two races together. In fact, single blacks seldom had the opportunity to live alone in a separate dwelling, rented or otherwise, and none was recorded as doing so by the Huntington census marshals in 1830. James Benson, for instance, rented a room in 1825 from Nathaniel Potter at four dollars a quarter, working as a common field hand for his landlord. And Lydia, a single woman, lived with her Oyster Bay employer until she was discovered to be pregnant with a villager's child in 1824. Whole black families occasionally resided with whites, as did Elias Hearden, his wife, and his stepson, who took a farm on "shares" from the Widow Harrison. Others simply rented tenements from whites.[39]

Black property owners sometimes lost their holdings, becoming renters or boarders. And for some destitution was the result. The case of Charles Potter from the 1790 census helps to illustrate this sequence of events. Sometime before 1790 Potter purchased two acres of land for twenty dollars in Huntington, where he constructed a house and raised his family. He eventually sold the property for $62.50. What prompted this decision is uncertain, but we do know that Potter "went to work by the year for Townsend Hewlett" in Oyster Bay, presumably as some kind of laborer. He later leased a dwelling in Huntington. In 1818 this aging free black man, now apparently alone, his wife and children gone, turned to Devine Hewlett, the son of his former master, for assistance. Hewlett permitted Potter to build a "small house" on his land, lent him a team of horses to cart stones for the structure, provided timber, and furnished him with provisions for the next two years. Yet limits, apparently, existed to Hewlett's charity. In 1821 Potter requested assistance from the Huntington overseers of the poor.[40]

The independence of the black community was thus circumscribed in some instances. Many who lived away from their employers still leased dwellings from them or other whites and lived beside white neighbors on borderng tracts of land. Although cherishing their physical independence, rural black people possessed only a modicum of economic independence from landlords and farmers. Nevertheless, a few managed to acquire property; a house and several acres of land meant much to a people recently freed from servitude and well aware of their tenuous position in society. Those fortunate enough to live among fellow blacks even possessed the semblance of a separate community. And yet, if some black persons created a life for themselves divorced from white landlords or employers, some failed to achieve this goal. Freedom was eventually bequeathed to all; its fruits, however, proved unevenly distributed.

Huntington was hardly peculiar in these respects. Census rolls and other sources reveal that black communities flourished in many other Long Island townships. The town of Islip had six households headed by blacks in close proximity to one another as early as 1790; by 1820, another settlement of similar size was discernible. In Hempstead, a town once described as a place of "dissapation," where neither master nor slave displayed a fondness for work, nine free black families, almost fifty individuals in all, appeared in sequence in the 1830 census, most of them bearing the same surname.[41] Other black people lived with white employers, either

PAUPERS AND WANDERERS 153

unable or unwilling to sacrifice immediate job opportunities. Some communities, however, with large numbers of blacks—leaseholders, freeholders, or squatters—alarmed white authorities. Jamaica officials forbade "persons of color" in 1814 from assembling one hour after sundown "in any streets or highways, lanes, alleys, or any stoop . . . to drink, play, sing, dance, and wrestle," subject to a five-dollar fine. The authorities also penalized tavernkeepers twenty dollars for selling liquor to free blacks one hour after sundown because it "produced disorder and licentiousness among them." Nearby Flushing adopted a harsh attitude toward black residents, too. Blacks there participated in "outdoor dances, equivocal serenades, and barbecues at night," which led the white citizenry to complain about the lost sleep that resulted from these "drunken brawls" during the 1820s. White retaliation proved swift. Bands of young men, known as the Rotten Egg Club, hurled eggs at the evening revelers and compelled the "dusky orgies . . . to retreat from the public square to the shanties of Crown Hill and Liberty Street." Here, perhaps, black people could live as they wished. Even so, blacks who ignored white perceptions of proper social behavior risked reprisals.[42]

Did such attitudes by white officials and villagers affect the treatment of black persons on public welfare? The answer to this would appear to be no. As we have noted, eighteenth-century black individuals could and did receive welfare from local officials; much the same arrangement continued into the nineteenth century. Consider the town of East Chester. Until the completion of the county almshouse in 1827, East Chester depended upon household relief of the indigent. Town officials, for example, boarded two black men named Toney and Nero in the 1790s at the home of the Widow Fowler, much as they lodged white paupers in other households. Johannah Jackson and her daughter Mary lived with two different keepers in private homes from 1803 until the mother's death in 1809. Sums of money paid their guardians often exceeded £30 a year, a stipend equal to or greater than that given white dependents. Indeed, officials allowed mother and child to remain together, although it was often policy to bond out pauper children from their parents at an early age. Another black woman received assistance at home from 1821 to 1825—assistance that was increased from $15.50 in 1823 to $33.00 in 1824, when she delivered a child.[43] Nor was East Chester unusual in this regard. In Huntington the public vendue of the poor applied equally to whites and blacks; both huddled together waiting to be sold. Treatment, too, was probably similar, judging from the sums of money spent on different paupers, for the condition of the person—age, injury, or illness—rather than race was the prime concern of potential keepers. By such means black paupers went to live in different households: Ruth Kit resided with four keepers from 1805 to 1817, as did Samuel Starr from 1820 to 1823. Others remained with a single keeper. Sometimes blacks could rely for assistance on their fellows, who perhaps allowed their charges a greater degree of autonomy than they might have had in a white household. Enos Sampson, Benjamin Lloyd, Israel Veil, and Dig Wicks assisted fellow blacks at different times. Some blacks such as Benjamin Hammond did not even have to go through the pauper auction, receiving assistance at home.[44]

Blacks could also rely upon private forms of assistance. They sometimes preferred to remain independent of white municipal relief, whatever the form. The free black community of Oyster Bay banded together in 1788 for just such a purpose, after it had received permission from the town "to associate themselves for the purpose of raising a sum of money to support the aged and indigent." Quaker-sponsored charitable societies in North Hempstead and Oyster Bay complemented black efforts at self-support, while a few masters might assist former slaves. In Hempstead, members of one family aided several blacks "during the winter months," when employment opportunities became scarce. Some masters, however, needed to be reminded of such obligations by former bondspersons. In Newtown a soon to be freed elderly bondsman drove home the point that his master had a responsibility to him, declaring, "Well, Old Massa, you have had de flour, I guess you must had de bran too." He got his support.[45]

Not all black people were so charitably treated. An unidentified black man, presumably a non-resident pauper, was "carried" to New York City from East Chester in 1824, and that same year a court case between New Rochelle and East Chester took place over the legal settlement of Jerry Santon, a destitute black man. Similarly, Brookhaven authorities removed black persons to such towns as Smithtown, Albany, and Brooklyn during the early decades of the century. Towns, however, employed identical measures against white non-resident paupers. Race was not a factor in regard to transportation.[46]

Rural working-class whites had their own share of difficulties. Greater legal and political rights did not always ensure greater economic benefits or status—far from it; such whites might have few material advantages over free blacks. Impoverished whites may have been despised more as shiftless, lazy vagrants. Like rural blacks, such whites often relied upon manual labor to support themselves and their families, while living in rented quarters or with their employers. Elkhanah Rogers leased a house from Nathaniel Potter in 1827 for twelve dollars a year and worked at splitting fences, butchering livestock, and harvesting corn—much as James Benson had once done. Although neither man became a public dependent, each performed tasks common to most rural working poor men, laboring at farm chores.[47] Not everyone was engaged in tilling the soil. Benjamin Johnson, who did appear before the justices in Huntington in 1839, had worked in the town woolen factory two years before and probably resided in one of his employer's cottages. Jeremiah Terry was a sailor, which made it difficult for the Brookhaven justices to determine his legal settlement in 1821. Changing jobs was not unusual either. Henry Nicols worked in different towns across Long Island, apparently as a laborer, and signed on a whaling ship out of Greenport in the 1830s. James Martin worked as a cook on land before going to sea and eventually ended up in the Brookhaven poorhouse by 1825. Of course, individuals might acquire property. John Van Nort contracted for a piece of land in Huntington worth two hundred dollars—perhaps as much as ten or twenty acres—while Nathaniel Ketcham bought two acres in the same town for fifty dollars. Alexander Raynor at one time paid two hundred dollars for a parcel of land in Riverhead before moving on to Brookhaven. Other potential dependents could at least claim connection to more well-to-do relatives. Guy William Augustine Hait informed Huntington officials in 1819 that he was a teacher, who had once resided on his parents' freehold valued at one thousand dollars. Charles Cuthing may have been the proverbial poor relation, for he informed the same officials in 1820 that his brother had assisted him over the years with three thousand dollars' worth of support, some in cash and some in goods. Private charity, it seems, kept Cuthing and his family solvent.[48]

Property ownership provided no guarantee from privation. A small freehold was insufficient security in the event of sudden misfortune, as several people testified before the Huntington justices.

Stephen Nicolls owned a house and property valued at one hundred dollars, but he continued in indigent circumstances due "to an infirmity of the eyes." Similarly, Samuel Conkling's freehold became almost valueless once "ill health made him unfit to labor"; and Stephen Stratten's land was hardly an asset when sickness and old age encumbered him too much to work.[49] Under different circumstances such people might have been considered responsible lower-class members of the community—landed laborers who modestly supported themselves raising a few crops, harvesting shellfish, and working for local farmers. In fact, Conkling and Ketcham could both claim distant kinship with some of the town's early families. Yet ancestry proved of little value in these conditions. Their inability to labor altered dramatically their position in the local social structure, transforming these once self-sustaining citizens into public dependents. Not surprisingly, both men upon their deaths received a pauper burial courtesy of the town.[50]

Poverty was also an inherited social position to some. A landless laborer could bequeath few skills and less money to his children as they grew older; indeed, many children of poor families undoubtedly struggled along the same path as their parents, starting out as bonded servants and becoming laborers and domestics. Those who suffered from physical handicaps were further cursed. John Stiverson, according to his testimony, had been bonded out as a servant at the age of seven in 1816. For the next fourteen years he served Isaac Hewlett, member of a prominent Oyster Bay–Huntington family. During this period Stiverson accompanied his master when he relocated, moving from Huntington to Flushing and then again to Huntington. Stiverson ended his term of servitude in 1830 at the age of twenty-one. Now on his own, Stiverson worked for a year in both Huntington and Oyster Bay, probably as a farm laborer. Then on January 1, 1831, a Queens county judge, William Jones, ordered him into the county poorhouse. Stiverson remained there until April, when the overseers of the institution told him "he must go away from [the] Poorhouse and get his own living"; it would appear that Stiverson, like other laborers in winter, had no means of support until the spring planting. In 1832 Stiverson experienced much the same difficulty, for he came before the Huntington justices in January in need of relief and ended in the poorhouse until April. He had an additional handicap in being "subject to fits." Even so, he managed to find employment in Oyster Bay over the next two years, until his current employer in 1834 sent him to the Huntington poorhouse when he became "badly burnt." Disabled by epilepsy and the product of a broken marriage—his father and mother lived in separate towns—Stiverson was a classic example of a rural pauper.[51]

Women as well as men required relief. Their limited economic opportunities combined with social restraints made working-class women possible candidates for public welfare. Recently, such historians as Thomas Dublin, Alice Kessler-Harris, and others have depicted the experience of women at work in the home or in factories.[52] Legal depositions furnished by rural women before local justices provide an additional insight into the world of working-class women—an insight that complements further the study of women in early national America. As might be expected, women who appeared before local officials were often in desperate straits. The disappearance of Sabrina Worth's husband in 1835 left her with four children to raise and no means of support except her "household function." On the other hand, Fanny Frost had to leave her husband in 1830 because he stole her "earnings to buy rum" and "beats and bangs her so." Huntington officials assisted both of them—Worth in her home and Frost in the poorhouse.[53] In Brookhaven the authorities in 1811 helped the Widow Margaret Ludlow, although she was actually an inhabitant of Oyster Bay, since her poor health prevented her removal. Another poor woman, Jane Butler, apparently moved from town to town, never acquiring much in the way of employment. Born in Brookhaven, she later lived for a time in Orange county until returning to the Island and eventually ending in the Oyster Bay poorhouse in 1818 or 1819. Southampton officials in 1820 sought to remove her to Brookhaven because she was "likely soon to become chargeable."[54]

Sexual exploitation was another compelling reason for assistance. Working women, often servants, could be victimized by men promising marriage in return for sexual favors or by lecherous employers with few moral qualms about seducing their domestics. Other men took advantage of women, abandoned them, and disappeared from their lives—leaving the villages to deal with the situation. Nancy Hallek furnishes one such example in this regard. Orphaned shortly after birth, she had been bonded out by Manhattan welfare officials at the age of eight to a Huntington master, whom she served for eight years. She then "worked in different places." In 1820 William McKinn, an itinerant mason from New York City, seduced her in Huntington. Hallek petitioned the justices for assistance on January 12, 1821, and she admitted in a subsequent deposition the same day that McKinn was the father of her expected child. Three months later she gave birth to a stillborn baby girl. Sometimes, however, local officials could locate the father of illegitimate children. In 1806, for example, Phebe Davis of Brookhaven delivered a boy and named Timothy Mills of Smithtown as the father. Brookhaven officials then ordered Mills to pay ten dollars for Davis's lying-in costs plus an additional fifty cents a week for the support of his son.[55] Occasionally, women were compelled to take a different course of action when confronted with the prospect of a bastard child. Catherine L'Homedine, a bonded servant, lived with her master Platt Brush in Huntington, until

> about last of January or first of February [1823] . . . she the deponent was delivered of a male bastard child and on the next day of birth she the deponent was married to John Noon and is informed that said Noon had another living wife at the time she married and she believes first wife still living and the aforesaid Platt Brush is the father of the bastard child and that she is now in indigent circumstances and asks relief.[56]

Catherine L'Homedine was only fifteen years old at the time.

These accounts illustrate the existence of an almost distinct lower-class culture among elements of the rural poor. This was not in itself especially new. Cases of fornication and immorality abounded among servants in eighteenth-century rural communities; it was also not unusual among respectable folk to conceive children several months before their marriage. Yet this activity on the part of women and itinerant artisans such as Hallek and McKinn in the nineteenth century—an age of stricter moral codes of conduct—may suggest a willingness to disregard emerging social codes. Many such affairs stem from sexual exploitation, but when individuals with no economic connection "frequently cohabited together," as one desposition revealed, this was something different.[57] It may well be that some working-class folk simply resisted the imposition of what they perceived to be middle-class norms.

Interestingly, there are far fewer records of illegitimate births among blacks, a group of people whom whites usually regarded as promiscuous. In Huntington from 1800 to 1830 only one out of nineteen women testifying in cases of bastardy was black. Whether Huntington blacks hid their sexual indiscretions from prying white authorities or policed themselves remains uncertain. Nevertheless, the one instance where a black woman did appear to testify is suggestive: when Lydia's employer dismissed her upon the discovery of her pregnancy in 1821, she "removed at Huntington at the house of Peleg coloured man where she was delivered . . . of a male child." Her first reaction, then, was to avoid white officials, even though they had every reason to assist her in finding the father, who was liable for child support. Perhaps other black women also shunned town authorities, preferring internal systems of relief and emotional support. In any event when black women did petition for assistance it was not for reasons of illegitimate chldren.[58]

The testimony of impoverished blacks and whites reveals much in common. Whites with their larger freeholds did describe rosier economic conditions, but a number of them lived no differently from free blacks, working as day laborers and renting rooms from their employers. Personal distress sent individuals of both races to the overseers of the poor and the local justices. For some whites, a request for assistance revealed their downward descent from still respectable village families, which had grown so large and diffuse that poorer cousins could not claim familial assistance from them. They had to turn to the town for support. Blacks, however, could sometimes rely on former masters for support; the relationship between masters and former bondspersons was not always severed by the process of emancipation. In addition, black women required far less public charity as a result of illegitimate births than did their white counterparts.

Individuals requiring public welfare, men and women, black and white, were not always "destitute of the means of support." Everyone examined by the justices of the peace, with the exception of young children, had supported themselves at least part of their lives. Even John Stiverson secured occasional employment despite his condition. Men could find work as laborers, loggers, and sailors, while women generally stayed in household endeavors. Yet if the kind of work seldom varied, the employer and the work site often did. The individuals who appeared before the local officials displayed a remarkable degree of geographic mobility, similar to that of later nineteenth-century working-class folk. The availability of work and the type of job determined if and when they would move. While some were classic examples of "betterment migration," that is, people who traveled to improve their economic position, others followed a general pattern of "subsistence migration" that entailed searching for work wherever it could be found. When these people testified as to the location of their last legal settlement they sketched a profile of their various movements—something that most historians have been unable to plot. Thus, the legal depositions of poor people provide a rough gauge of working-class movements during the early national period.[59]

All such rural transients had to deal with the available transportation system. Itinerant laborers presumably gauged distances in relation to how far a man might walk in a day, an important concern, since neighboring townships on Long Island required a "moderate day's journey," according to one traveler of the time. Westchester townships varied in size but some such as Rye, Harrison, and Scarsdale were small and close together.[60] During the early 1800s Long Island and Westchester afforded easy access by sea via coastal vessels and ferries. Land travel was another matter. Despite regular stage service along major roads, not everyone could afford commercial transport; such folks walked alone across fields, woods, and countryside. Roads were sometimes troublesome, especially when frozen in winter and muddy in spring. Then there was the constant exposure to the weather. Anyone trekking across the Hempstead Plains would doubtless agree with the eighteenth-century cleric who declared it "very troublesome in the heat of summer and cold of winter" to traverse an area "sixteen miles long without shade or shelter."[61] So, too, travelers might become lost on unmarked paths and lanes that crisscrossed the main routes. As one person noted at this time:

> The roads of Long Island are exceedingly numerous and difficult for strangers. There are three principal avenues running nearly the whole length of the island which are distinguished as the North, Middle, and South Roads. They are not only intersected by others leading from one town and neighborhood to another, but in the most uninhabited parts there are numerous woodpaths well worn by constant carting which vary little from the course of the main road and not infrequently appear the most direct and most used that the

PAUPERS AND WANDERERS   161

stranger is constantly liable to go astray, and that too where he might remain a whole day without meeting a person to set him straight.[62]

Additional trouble might arise in securing lodgings for the night. One of the depositions mention the matter directly, but other sources suggest that this was a concern for itinerants new to the area. When Sojournor Truth, the noted black abolitionist, traveled to Long Island in 1843 to begin her work as an evangelical preacher, she encountered considerable difficulty. With her bundle and packet in hand she perhaps looked no different from other wanderers who carried their meager possessions. She found white animosity widespread, especially in the homes of the well-to-do. Shelter was often denied her. At other times lodgings came with peculiar conditions attached to them. The owner of a tavern, which doubled as the village jail, would admit her only if she agreed to be locked in at night. A white couple who offered her a place to stay also asked that she accompany them to a party. Accepting her benefactors' invitation, Truth was astonished to find the festivities held in a "dirty hovel," crowded with "an assemblage of people collected from the very dregs of society, too ignorant or degraded to understand much less entertain a higher or brighter idea." This room of whiskey-drinking people shocked her moral scruples; "it is a dangerous thing," she remarked, "to compel anyone to receive that hospitality from the visicious and abandoned."[63]

Other wayfarers of less sensitive character might have welcomed such offers of hospitality. Certainly, a transient such as John Thuilby, who slept along the seashore one night, would have appreciated a more comfortable shelter. And Joseph Still, the eleven-year-old son of an abusive woodcutter, would have been no worse in a tavern setting than at the home he had left. What Truth considered a hovel, despite her welcome by the white revelers, was perhaps a congenial enough surrounding for some working-class folk, a place for unsupervised recreation.[64]

Laborers native to the region probably had little trouble in traveling the roads and finding shelter, using their knowledge of local farmers and landlords to good advantage. Many of these individuals, in fact, easily found positions in the countryside and limited their movements to discrete localities. George Tigney, although a native of Smithtown, labored "most of his time in Huntington," the adjoining community to the west. Jeremiah Haff's family worked in Islip, Huntington, and Smithtown before returning to Huntington—either renting tenements or living on farms. Equally typical were Richard and Platt Jones. These two married brothers found work in Oyster Bay or Huntington. Black laborers might follow similar patterns. Ceasar divided his time between Smithtown and Huntington, while David Helms alternated between Brookhaven and Huntington.[65] Less detailed but still useful records of transported paupers furnish an added insight into the movements of poor New Yorkers. In Brookhaven between 1800 and 1820 the authorities transported or received seventeen public dependents and their families. Although one case involved a removal to Oneida county in upstate New York, the other sixteen involved communities on the Island. Such towns as Southold, Smithtown, Riverhead, Hempstead, and Brooklyn had two or more public dependents associated with them; other communities with only one transient included Huntington, North Hempstead, Oyster Bay, and Southampton.[66] Such transients, it would appear, possessed little incentive to leave the immediate region, perhaps restrained as much by familial ties as by economic opportunities. Certain paupers clearly had relatives in the general vicinity; their surnames were common in some villages. These family connections, if difficult to measure precisely, could well have exercised a restraining influence and prevented any long-distanced travel on the part of some.[67]

Other migratory working folk had broader horizons, moving among towns in Long Island, New Jersey, Connecticut, and other parts of New York State. Such persons may well have been more ambitious than purely local migrants, willing to leave their homes for more faraway regions. And they formed a recognizable segment of the labor force in Long Island. Eneas Cook and Elijah Smith left their homes in New Jersey and Connecticut and slowly reached Huntington, laboring at various jobs along the way. Occasionally, people native to Long Island might travel further afield: both Conkling Wicks and Samuel Conkling had spent some time in Manhattan before returning home to Huntington. These men, however, were not itinerant wayfarers drifting aimlessly from town to town, but individuals with a set destination—New York City. Similarly, Catherine Nicolls, a "woman of colour," had been born in Flushing, served in Brookhaven when bonded out as a servant, and

PAUPERS AND WANDERERS 163

then relocated on her own to New York City. By 1824 Manhattan welfare officials had returned the now impoverished woman to Brookhaven. Clearly, the city exerted a powerful influence among some migrants regardless of race.[68]

Long-range travelers were not uncommon either. Immigrants, for example, evinced a tendency to travel several hundred miles or more in quest of employment. Nor should this be surprising. Such folk were unbound by family ties, having already made a decision to sever connections with relatives and friends. Like their local counterparts they might work varying amounts of time with an employer ranging from a week to a year. And then they would push on yet again. John Thuilby was perhaps typical in this respect. An English immigrant, he first arrived in Canada in 1821 and passed through Quebec to Montreal before entering northern New York by way of Ogdenbury—a popular entry point. His odyssey led him from Ogdenbury to St. Lawrence county, "where he labored for twelve months," and then he pushed south to Utica for a month of work before finding employment on "the canal near Schnectady for a month and a half." Future localities of work included Saratoga and St. Lawrence counties. He also found employment among the Quakers in an unspecified location. Leaving the Quakers to work in Jefferson county during the winter of 1824-1825, he again headed south with eighty dollars in his pockets, a substantial sum for a laborer. Nevertheless, constant travel and exposure to the elements had taken their toll upon Thuilby, leaving him too ill to work. Huntington officials found him in June 1825 on the shore with only a few clothes and three dollars. He died in the town poorhouse a few weeks later.[69]

James Martin followed a similar path south from Canada. He, too, was an Englishman who went from Quebec to Montreal, arriving in the United States by way of Vermont. He worked there through the summer and winter of 1820 before removing to nearby Plattsburgh in New York. After a year and a half there, Martin procured employment as a cook for two months in Troy. He worked another month in Catskill and then arrived in New York City. His testimony before the Brookhaven justices indicates that he had some skill as an artisan, for Martin mentioned having "wrought in various kinds of work" over several months until suffering a fall that hospitalized him. Upon recovering, he performed "different little jobs," presumably in Manhattan, and then went with Captain

Bartlet Sanford in the sloop *Experement* to the village of Moriches in Brookhaven in December 1824. Once off the ship he appeared before the local authorities. Like Thuilby, his destination was the almshouse.[70]

Both of these men illuminate the opportunities and setbacks that long-distance travelers might experience. Migrants from Canada and northern New England could earn high wages in New York's booming lumber industry during the period. Others could always work on farms or in service positions, switching locations and occupations as the need arose. Quite possibly, the more sparsely settled sections of the state caused these itinerants to move greater distances; unlike local migrants, such folk often traveled from county to county instead of town to town in a single county. Geography, then, may have been a factor in influencing such treks as much as the state of the local economy. Together these two factors help to explain in part why some people traveled as they did. Then, too, a simple desire to see new lands could be a reason for such jaunts; single, unattached men divorced from kin and countrymen could wander until they found a place that suited them. Like the hoboes of a later period, these persons were able to wander as they pleased.[71]

Such travelers did not always journey from sparsely settled regions to more populous locales. Southern New York and its neighbors to the east and west drew in their share of long-range transients. Richard Haply, for one, roamed across New York, Pennsylvania, Connecticut, and New Jersey after his arrival from Ireland in 1811. Eventually, he reached Long Island and worked in both Smithtown and Huntington by 1832. Jarvis Smith adopted an almost identical course of movement, leaving his native town of Fishkill at the age of fifteen to work in Connecticut, Pennsylvania, and Connecticut again. He then left Connecticut by sailing across Long Island Sound and arrived in Lloyd's Neck just north of Huntington by 1834. Another such person was a Smithtown native, Stephen Nicolls. His movements, however, suggest a pattern of betterment migration, for he seems to have attempted to improve his economic status on each journey. Nicolls started without property, bought a freehold in Huntington, sold it, and moved to Manhattan and leased a tenement. From the city Nicolls next traveled west to Allegheny county, where he advanced steadily upward as a carpenter, landing a three-hundred-dollar contract and eventually buying 150

PAUPERS AND WANDERERS 165

acres of land—far more than he could have purchased on Long Island. He now possessed solid middle-class credentials by virtue of his calling and property. And yet Nicolls decided to abandon this life, selling his land and returning to Long Island by around 1811. His new home in Islip sat on a tract of land that measured only nine square rods. By 1823 he had to request public assistance.[72]

Despite whatever prompted them to move, the success of such people in being accepted into the local labor force was clearly evident. Consider the experience of Jarvis Smith. Arriving on Long Island in 1834, Smith worked on Lloyd's Neck for eighteen months and then labored in Huntington for a year; he was later employed during the spring and summer of 1837 "in various places part in Huntington and part in Lloyd's Neck."[73] Increased familiarity with local employers perhaps explains this more frequent shifting of jobs. The Englishman James Riggs provides a detailed account of his employers on the Island. Arriving in New York by way of South Carolina, Riggs

> came to Long Island, Islip South, and worked for Dr. Udle about two years and worked for Harvey Vail and some for George Cornish and thinks he worked for John Carll in the winter of 32/33 in Huntington and thence to Crab Meadow to work for Joseph Scudder about two months he thinks and from thence to Great Cow Harbor to work for Robert Perot between one and two months and upon March, 1834 he went to Smithtown to work for Silas Strong and worked about three months and thence back to Huntington for John Carll four or five months and a few days for Nathan Tottin and a few days for Joseph Lewis and then worked for Robert Perot again and was in his employ when he broke his collarbone.[74]

This deposition reinforces the notion that laborers often had little trouble in hiring themselves out. The brief periods of employment mentioned by Riggs testify to the highly commercial character of the rural economy during the 1830s, which permitted a laborer to choose among several employers in a relatively small area. Farm families once dependent almost totally on offspring now turned more often to hired hands; merchants and professionals such as Nathaniel Potter and Dr. Udle also found them useful for cultivating the parcels of land.[75] Indeed, the diversification of the economy made itinerant laborers increasingly necessary as more people abandoned farming to work in other callings. Laborers, too, took advantage of this demand for hired hands, selecting carefully where they might work.[76]

Movement, however, was sometimes restricted by social considerations rather than economic opportunities. Few transients permitted the marketplace totally to chart their movements; they may have known that some regions were unfriendly to particular types of newcomers. Blacks, it seems, followed a prescribed pattern of migration that contrasted sharply with that of more geographically mobile whites. Testimony of black deponents reveals that most remained on Long Island, with only a few coming from nearby New Jersey and Connecticut. None of the black deponents could match the movements of a Thuilby, Martin, or Nicolls. Free black folks remained almost stationary by comparison, with Long Island serving as their area of travel.[77] What can explain this pattern? Quite possibly, blacks evinced acute pessimism about establishing themselves in more distant locations. The lure of the frontier with the chance of improved prospects and cheaper land also meant facing in some instances unsympathetic white settlers determined to prevent their arrival. So, too, relationships between former slaves and masters might have been a limiting factor; it was sometimes possible for black men and women to depend on assistance from their former owners, as we have seen. Scattered evidence also suggests a degree of social cohesion among the Island's black residents, who could live alone in isolation or in small settlements. Not only did blacks have access to one another, but they also had their own churches by the 1830s and 1840s. Given such factors it is perhaps not so surprising that blacks curtailed their movements more than whites: Long Island was no better or worse than other places and for some black people it was home.[78]

Poverty was a universal social condition for both blacks and whites; its agents—sickness, injury, old age—produced grave effects on working-class individuals, compelling them at times to seek public charity. Yet the shared experience of poverty among members of both races was distinguishable in certain respects. Blacks seem to have avoided the kinds of sexual entanglements that led whites to seek public assistance in Huntington. Unlike several whites who could claim distinguished ancestry yet still require public support, some black inhabitants could look to former masters and effectively bypass public welfare. Even so, the success of the black community needs to be weighed against its failures, in particular, its inability to achieve autonomy save in rare instances. Blacks often lived under the indirect supervision of whites, dependent upon them as employers and landlords. They were also less mobile. The latter fact is important. Whether by choice or lack of alternative, remaining where they were or moving only short distances trapped rural blacks in the web of the local employment network. The guarantee of work in prosperous years might be rescinded in depression years, and unlike mobile whites, who could move substantial distances, the free blacks rarely traveled far. In effect, many remained ensnared within the local environment, unable to realize material success save in occasional instances. Poor whites and their offspring probably had a better chance to move upward. Even poverty at times could reveal a set of different standards for different people.

CHAPTER VI
This Confusion of Dialects: The Dependent Poor of Manhattan, 1800-1830

On March 24, 1811, the Reverend Ezra Stiles Ely, preacher to the almshouse and the public hospital of the city of New York, recorded in his journal the unusual variety of paupers present during a prayer meeting: "When we attempt to praise God in the almshouse the dialect of almost every nation is heard for the English, Scotch, Irish, Dutch, German, Spanish, and Italian as well as the American poor, have met together. I have now become so accustomed to this confusion of dialects that it does not disturb my devotions."[1] The babble of voices that greeted Ely and other visitors to the building testified to the large number of destitute immigrants who had made the institution their home—some for the remainder of their lives. It was also a domicile for the native-born poor of the city unable to survive without assistance, and for "needy adventurers from almost all parts of the nation."[2] If early nineteenth-century Manhattan was renowned for its varied ethnic society comprised of many different foreign nationalities, so too was the municipal almshouse.

Ethnicity also proved a crucial factor in determining which groups were more prominently represented inside the almshouse between 1800 and 1830. While poverty was an economic fact for many Manhattan residents, domestic and foreign, the response of indigent persons to charity could take different forms, with some choosing to be relieved at home and others preferring the shelter of the almshouse. Although historians have discussed the evolution and function of public institutions, they have sometimes paid scant attention to their occupants, considering them a minor feature.[3] Yet the question of who received aid inside the almshouse is as important as the origins of the institution. Those who preferred charity outside the almshouse—either from the city or from private benevolent societies—evinced a desire to remain independent of administrative authority, avoiding the regimented environment of such structures. Foreign and domestic paupers who ended in the almshouse revealed their own lack of alternatives.

The purpose of this chapter, then, is to provide a social portrait of dependent urban poor people—those individuals who needed assistance—while attempting to chart their response to different kinds of charity. Various censuses, removal records, and municipal accounts provide an ideal starting point for deciphering the identity of the destitute. Unlike eighteenth-century officials, who seldom bothered to furnish detailed accounts of the poor, later generations of officials in the 1800s took this task seriously and compiled extensive reports. The superintendent of the almshouse submitted yearly and sometimes quarterly censuses on the inmates to the Common Council, dividing the destitute on the basic of age and sex into such categories as adults or children, males or females. Some censuses even separated whites from blacks and foreigners from domestic paupers. Increasingly, the second and third decades of the century saw accounts that labeled indigent persons by age, sex, and nationality; the last classification employed various subdivisions that divided the domestic paupers of Manhattan, New York State, and the United States, while distinguishing among French, German, Irish, and English paupers. City officials, moreover, compiled records on people who received support outside the almshouse. Such information when used in conjunction with data from private charitable sources allows an insight into the identity of non-institutionalized poor people. Together, these records of private and public charity prove useful in constructing an image of destitute city dwellers and their reactions to public welfare.[4]

Visitors to the almshouse often described the inmates in different tones, careful to distinguish among the various types of destitute individuals. Although one visitor to the almshouse at Bellevue in

1824 called it an "asylum from the bitter shafts which cold penury hurls at her unhappy victims," depicting the indigent inmates as people trapped by circumstance, others voiced more critical opinions. The Reverend Mr. Ely divided the almshouse population into "decent people," those who were "morally upright," and the "vile," whose "filthy conversations" transformed the institution into a "second Sodom." The Reverend John Stanford, another almshouse chaplain, agreed with this assessment in 1826, noting that some of the needy "represented a stately castle fallen in ruins; while others collected from the dregs of society, lay as a cumbrous load upon the public bounty."[5] The division between respectable and non-respectable poor persons, the moral and the immoral, was characteristic of the way evangelical Protestants judged destitute people. Where they actually came from seems to have mattered less to them than how they behaved.

A more dispassionate account of dependent poor persons emerges from the census records of almshouse officials. These lists of paupers substantiate Ely's description of the house in 1811 as a home for wayward foreigners; indeed, the censuses reveal that even his account did less than justice to the unusually varied assortment of people drawn from different parts of the western world. According to the 1805 census the almshouse had English and Welsh, Scots and Irish, Germans and Swiss, Dutch and French, as well as Africans—all of whom shared quarters with New Yorkers, New Englanders, and Southerners. Other nationalities appeared in later years. By 1813 the first West Indians entered the structure, to be joined two years later by Spaniards and Italians. And in 1830 Swedes and Prussians sought shelter there.[6]

The existence of so many different nationalities under a single roof was hardly surprising given Manhattan's position as America's busiest seaport. The deep-water harbor handled shipping from almost every corner of the globe; packet ships from Europe unloaded cargo and passengers on a regular basis, providing a steady flow of business. Then there were vessels from the West Indies and South America, which shared dock space with coastal brigs and schooners that plied the domestic trade. The harbor, in effect, was a forest of masts and sails during the early national period. New Yorkers themselves proudly proclaimed their city a "great commercial capital," where "adventurers from all parts of the world would resort."[7] On the streets of the city native New Yorkers jostled the crowds of newly arrived immigrants from Europe and migrants from bordering states. Visitors to Manhattan could not help but notice the mixture of people and the many languages they spoke. One account from 1827 commented that the "number of foreigners from all countries is great. One hears the French and Spanish language almost in every street." Another described New York in 1817 as "thronged with British and French emigrants." An unknown Scotsman, who visited the seaport for the first time in 1821, marveled at the diversity of foreigners: "The aspect of society here is amazing from the vast conflux of foreigners. The nimble Frenchman dancing rather than walking along the streets is a contrast to the stiff Scotsman lately come over or the no less heavy Dutchman from the interior. The Irishman is always the same wherever we find him . . . lounging out at the sides of the streets . . . or in an old cart."[8] Here, then, existed a rich ethnic mix, perhaps unsurpassed by any other city of the United States.

A more discerning visitor might have noted where these immigrants lived. Although foreign-born persons resided throughout the city in the various municipal wards, some sections of the urban metropolis clearly attracted a larger number of aliens than others; it was evident that economic status played a role here. The relatively affluent wards of lower Manhattan possessed an immigrant population of under 1 percent in the second ward and 3 percent in the third ward in 1821. Further north aliens could compose over 9 percent of a ward's inhabitants, as was true in the fourth, seventh, and ninth wards (see Table 11).[9] While many immigrants lived in respectable middle-class neighborhoods among merchants, shopkeepers, and artisans, those dwelling in parts of the fourth, sixth, and seventh wards often found themselves in less pleasant surroundings. The sixth ward, in particular, was one of the poorest sections of Manhattan, already renowned for its working-class denizens, black and white, who frequented the numerous brothels and taverns that lined the streets and alleyways.[10] Impoverished immigrants drawn by cheap rents gathered in these neighborhoods, and it was from such locales that many indigent aliens entered the almshouse.

The foreign-born formed a significant and quite stable proportion of the total almshouse population, ranging from 30 to 40 percent during any given year (see Table 12). From 1800 to 1830 these people retained a considerable edge over paupers from other

Table 11
Percentage and Number of Foreign Nationals, 1821

Ward	%	N	Total Population
First	3.3	406	12,085
Second	0.8	66	8,214
Third	2.9	271	9,201
Fourth	10.2	1,096	10,736
Fifth	1.2	156	12,421
Sixth	3.9	611	15,309
Seventh	11.3	1,478	13,006
Eighth	0.6	88	13,766
Ninth	9.3	1,048	11,162
Tenth	0.9	170	17,806

Source: Census of 1821, located in Horatio G. Spafford, *A Gazetteer of the State of New York* (Albany, N.Y.: B. D. Packard, 1824), p. 352. These figures understate the true percentage of the foreign-born. Naturalization laws allowed many immigrants full citizenship.

states as well as New York State, and in 1826 they actually exceeded the number of Manhattan-born poor persons—an event that had never happened previously in the century. In fact, foreign-born poor people may well have enjoyed numerical superiority over the Manhattan-born poor during other years if their offspring, born after they had arrived in Manhattan, were counted as foreigners instead of Americans. A sample entry taken from the admission and discharge records of the institution in December 1826 illustrates this fact: when the Mackie family entered the almshouse, officials labeled James Mackie and his wife, Sarah, as Irish, while their children were designated as New Yorkers. The same held true for other immigrants with offspring.[11] In effect, the actual percentage of foreign poor persons was higher than the figures would indicate. This fact was known to city officials, too. In 1819 a committee of aldermen visiting the Bellevue establishment concluded that many of the needy persons inside "the almshouse [were] aliens and their children."[12] For civil officials, then, public charity had become associated to a large degree with sheltering the foreign poor.

One reason for the preponderance of poor immigrants was the lack of any legal ordinance for expelling them. By 1797 the city

Table 12
The Foreign and Domestic Poor of Manhattan's Almshouse, 1800–1830

Year	% Foreign	% Domestic	Total N
1800	32	68	874
1801	32	68	903
1802	33	67	895
1803	32	68	931
1804	34	66	904
1805	33	67	941
1806	32	68	955
1807	33	67	976
1808	32	68	1,017
1809	32	68	1,051
1810	33	67	1,066
1811	33	67	1,271
1812	32	68	1,409
1813	34	66	1,265
1814	29	71	1,506
1815	31	69	1,322
1816	33	67	1,525
1818	29	71	1,506
1824	39	61	1,476
1826	40	60	1,468
1828	41	59	1,627
1830	41	59	1,627

Source: Figures for 1800–1816 taken from Raymond A. Mohl, *Poverty in New York, 1783–1825* (New York: Oxford University Press, 1971), p. 86. The other census material can be found in the almshouse folder of the City Clerk's Files for the years mentioned at the Municipal Archives of the City of New York.

could no longer expel foreign-born poor persons to their homeland, leaving Manhattan defenseless against the increasing number of destitute foreigners. As William Cobbett so aptly wrote: "It is notorious that whatever may be the number of persons relieved by poor rates, the greater part of them are Europeans, who have come hither, at different periods and under circumstances of distress."[13] Although overseas removals had been few in the 1700s, the appearance now of thousands instead of hundreds of needy arrivals might have prompted the city fathers to begin a massive reshipping program, provided they possessed the legal authority. Yet even this possibility, however remote, was denied them. All that could be done was to require ship captains to post bond for their passengers and to enact special tax levies for their upkeep. The immigrant poor would continue to come.

Among the large percentage of foreign paupers entering Manhattan, several types of immigrants admitted into the almshouse were clearly noticeable. The melody of accents that greeted Ely in his visits to the house was undoubtedly drowned out on more than one occasion by the sounds of an Irish brogue. The tones of the Irish were certainly heard more often than those of the Scots or the English. The Irish had the dubious distinction of outnumbering all the other foreign poor, if those from England and Scotland were excluded, and they remained the largest ethnic group during the early decades of the century.[14] Starting in 1805, when they formed almost 20 percent of the inmate population, the Irish never totaled less than 13 percent and sometimes amounted to 27 percent of the institution's inmates (see Table 13). The Irish often held a two-to-one majority over the English and Scottish poor, who represented the second most dominant group of aliens; later on they registered a three-to-one majority.[15] Not surprisingly, their sheer number and their Catholic religion caused them to stand out from the usually Protestant paupers in the building. Ely referred to Irish individuals

Table 13
Irish Inmates in Manhattan's Almshouse, 1805–1830

Year	Irish N	Irish %	Total Inmates
1805	107	18	586
1813	246	19	1,265
1814	163	14	1,201
1815	169	13	1,293
1818	256	17	1,506
1824	339	23	1,476
1826	370	25	1,468
1828	433	27	1,627
1830	479	26	1,876

Source: See the Almshouse Folders, City Clerk's File, NYMA.

specifically in his notebook, without once mentioning the British, French, or German poor. Unable to convert them, he contented himself with various observations as to why they required assistance, perhaps betraying his sympathy for these unfortunate people. He noted how one Irish inmate, a former laborer, had spent his entire savings to buy drinks for several countrymen instead of using the money to book passage for his family to New York. Once penniless, he became in Ely's words a "maniac." What led him to ruin could also do the same to other Irish immigrants, according to Ely, for he considered "their love of company . . . one of their greatest temptations." In another instance he described an Irish woman "sick of fever," who had been a "good mother and wife before her husband deserted her," now languishing near death. The unwritten moral was evident: the Irish were their own worst enemies.[16]

The large number of poor Irish was in part due to the steady stream of immigrants leaving the Emerald Isle for the Americas. As Kirby Miller, Lynn Lees, and others have shown, pre-famine, nineteenth-century Ireland had more than its share of difficulties. Irish nationalists, Protestant and Catholic, bristled under British rule, especially in the aftermath of the failed Rebellion of 1798. The economy also prompted some to leave. Rising English demand for Irish foodstuffs and livestock led landlords to enclose and consolidate their holdings, turning once landed tenant farmers into propertyless laborers. For many people emigration appeared the only recourse. Newspapers played a crucial role, for they printed announcements about ship departures as well as information about new countries. Once in America, immigrants might pen letters to family members, informing them about conditions in the New World.[17] Numbers, however, tell the story better. A leading student of Irish immigration states that close to one million Irish men and women left their homes between 1815 and 1845—many of these to the Americas. Immigrants from the British Isles, the majority of whom were Irish, far surpassed any other ethnic group arriving in the port of New York: from 1820 to 1830 over 81,000 people came ashore compared to a paltry 8,000 Germans, the next largest group. Nor do these figures include those people who had made their way into New York from the maritime provinces of British North America—many of whom merely viewed Nova Scotia and New Foundland from the ship before heading on to Manhattan. Others were dumped outside Manhattan in Connecticut, Long Island, and New Jersey. Despite harsh penalties for such actions, ship captains remained undaunted and in one instance set ashore at Perth Amboy "a very low description of immigrants" from Ireland. Inevitably, these people found their way into the city.[18]

The sheer number of Irish immigrants provides only a partial explanation as to why they comprised so large a percentage of the almshouse residents. Economic status is equally important. Prior to 1820 most of the immigrants were drawn from the small farmer class of northern Ireland—people of middle-class background with sufficient funds to establish themselves in America. There were even some emigrés who had been active in the Rebellion of 1798. Such men as Thomas Addis Emmet, William McNevins, and Robert Adrian achieved comfortable positions in the community, mixing easily with the urban elite and forming the nucleus of an Irish upper class.[19] Poorer Irish immigrants, if few in comparison, were still numerous enough to form an identifiable segment of the almshouse population. By the 1820s more Irish Catholic immigrants arrived; many of them were less well off than their Protestant countrymen. Irish Catholic fishermen, servants, and laborers were sometimes ill-equipped for life in the urban seaport. Lack of marketable skills kept them clustered in low-paying jobs. Indeed, as one observer noted, the Irish could be seen selling fruits and vegetables on a "shattered cider barrel turned on end or . . . sitting on an old cart drawn by a poor crippled nag. They are the hucksters and laborers of the walk." Those not working as carters or hucksters, laborers or porters, might become domestic servants—a position they shared in common with many free blacks. Although wealthy Protestants might harbor anti-Catholic attitudes, they nonetheless relied on Irish domestics as a cheap source of labor.[20]

Even those fortunate enough to secure employment needed to be wary of possible competitors. Licensed native cartmen, for instance, complained vociferously about unlicensed, that is, Irish, carters who consistently underpriced them. In another more ironic case licensed porters, many of whom were Irish, petitioned the city against "unauthorized vagabonds" stealing work away from them. Prejudice was another factor. While political restrictions against Catholics had virtually ended by the early 1800s, nativist sentiment against them occasionally flared, resulting in violent street brawls. For staunch Protestants, the Catholic Irish posed a threat to their political and economic livelihood, for they believed that to countenance Catholicism would be to imperil the very foundations of the new republic. Given such attitudes it is perhaps not surprising that many Irish found economic advancement difficult and social acceptance limited.[21]

The lack of a strong private charitable network also caused many to enter the almshouse. Although the Irish could turn to the Friendly Sons of St. Patrick (1784) and the Catholic Orphans Society (1817), both groups proved unable to satisfy the larger needs of the Irish immigrant community. The Friendly Sons of St. Patrick had more the appearance of a social club than a relief organization; moreover, a largely Protestant contingent of Irish emigrés and Irish-American politicians controlled the society—people who may have felt less willing to assist Irish Catholic laborers, carters, or porters. The organization also possessed "no established funds" for distribution, depending instead upon periodic special collections.[22] The Catholic Church remained handicapped by its small size—it had only two parishes until 1829—and internal squabbles between French and Irish Catholics over the control of individual congregations. Still, the Church did raise $3,000 annually for poor relief. As for the existing Catholic relief agencies, they usually catered to widows and orphans instead of unemployed men with families. Other sources of private charity had additional drawbacks; many of these were monopolized by evangelical Protestants, who sought to reform and support indigent folks. Consequently, Irish Catholics had few alternatives other than some form of public welfare.[23]

Similar factors affected other ethnic groups in varying degrees. The British, that is, the English, Scots, and Welsh, and the Germans, who comprised the second and third largest groups entering the nation, also formed the second and third largest blocs of inmates in the almshouse. Natives of Great Britain generally accounted for 9 or 10 percent of the institution's population, although they did attain a high of 17 percent in 1813. The Germans reached a peak of 7 percent in 1805 before diminishing to a meager 2 percent in 1830 (see Table 14). The share of the inmate population in both groups decreased over time, as the poor Irish came to dominate more fully the space inside the institution. Both groups had private benevolent societies that may have been more successful than the Irish societies in caring for their destitute fellows. In fact, the St. Andrew Society for Scots raised $1,000 in 1800 and $900 in 1801 and 1802—sums of money that presumably kept some needy Scots off

Table 14
British and German Inmates in Manhattan's Almshouse, 1805-1830

	British		German		
Year	N	%	N	%	Total Inmates
1805	63	11	39	7	586
1813	219	17	43	3	1,265
1814	114	9	48	4	1,201
1815	88	7	29	2	1,293
1818	125	8	39	3	1,506
1824	102	7	70	5	1,476
1826	127	9	57	4	1,468
1828	156	10	32	2	1,672
1830	198	11	30	2	1,876

Source: Almshouse Folders, City Clerk's Files, NYMA.

the welfare rolls. A German society founded for the "Encouragement of Emigration" and the "Assistance of Needy Immigrants" in 1784 may have done likewise.[24] Moreover, German and English immigrants apparently suffered from fewer economic disadvantages than the Irish. A greater proportion of them possessed artisan skills well adapted to the New World; indeed, one authority on English emigrés termed them the "invisible immigrants," that is, people who literally blended into the landscape without attracting much notice. Less is known about the early German-American community in Manhattan, but they too may have done better than the Irish. Certainly, they received less critical attention from municipal authorities.[25]

Other ethnic groups managed to remain relative strangers to the almshouse. The French, for example, seldom appeared on public welfare rolls in great numbers, although a noticeable community of them resided in Manhattan. What makes this fact particularly curious is the relative poverty of the many refugees from former French possessions in the West Indies, who had arrived in the city starting in the 1790s. Instead of applying for public assistance, these newcomers by 1808 came under the protective embrace of the Frenchmen's Benevolent Society. This association aided as many as three hundred of its destitute compatriots during certain years. Such efforts produced results: only nine French persons appeared in the almshouse census of 1813, while the Society furnished food, clothing, shelter, and firewood to over one hundred individuals that year, most of them "infirmed, old, [and] widows with children." Normally such persons would have been prime candidates for the almshouse. Two years later the Society acquired $250 from the Common Council to help these same refugees.[26] The Society's ability to acquire public funding, which complemented its private sources of revenue, reveals its skill in applying pressure upon the city government. While several benevolent societies such as the Humane Society regularly received municipal allocations, the French Society seems to have been the only ethnic organization able to command funding on a regular basis. They apparently accomplished this by stressing the benefits of city contributions and by hinting broadly at the unpleasant alternative that might result if funds were not forthcoming. In 1829 a petition from the Society alerted the city fathers to "the large number of steerage passengers," some thirty families in all, who cost them $150 a month to support. It also noted that "owing to the relief granted by the Society to the distressed inhabitants of this city, very few, if any of them, have been admitted, and thereby it saved an increase of expense to the institution." Their underlying message was obvious: the city should advance the money or face the prospect of possibly more expenditures from the public purse when such immigrants had to enter the almshouse.[27]

Some groups could duplicate the success of the French in keeping their people off public welfare. Manhattan's Jewish community made a special effort to assist their fellow religionists, some of whom were recently arrived immigrants. As we have seen, Shearith Israel—the first Jewish synagogue in Manhattan—had played a leading philanthropic role in the eighteenth century, dispensing funds to those in need; it continued this policy into the nineteenth century. Not only could destitute Jews receive gifts of firewood in winter or matzoth before Passover, but members of the congregation might be given yearly pensions. The synagogue, for example, dispensed $200 in 1810 and 1825. One Jewish historian has claimed that the efforts of the temple to assist the less fortunate "went beyond other mutual aid societies," and the evidence would seem to bear this out. There appear to have been only five Jewish inmates in the almshouse during the early decades of the nineteenth century, and at least one of these was a man who had probably not made contact with the Jewish community for assistance, most likely because he was a recent immigrant. Even Christian sources by the 1850s noted that there were no Jewish beggars seen in the streets of the city.[28]

In retrospect, the ability of immigrants to avoid the almshouse reflected their degree of social unity as well as their overall economic standing. Those foreign nationals with well-organized benevolent societies could turn to them first instead of the almshouse; those with weak organizations normally had to go to the city for assistance. Similarly, foreigners with skills and money remained less likely to descend into the depths of poverty than those of marginal economic status. Although people of many nationalities received charity, the Irish, it seems, were prime candidates for public welfare. The impoverished existence from which they fled was duplicated for many in the urban environment of Manhattan. Admittedly, the extent of emigration from the Emerald Isle also contributed to the preponderance of Irish paupers vis-à-vis the less numerous British, German, or French. But this factor would have diminished in importance if Irish immigrants had possessed sufficient funds, skills, or social connections. Their failure in these respects illustrates why they formed the dominant foreign element inside the municipal almshouse.[29]

Domestic poor people present yet another segment of urban lower-class life. Poorhouse officials divided destitute Americans into three categories: those born in Manhattan, those born in New York State excluding the city, and those born in other states of the union; as a group, native-born individuals always retained a numerical edge over their foreign counterparts during the thirty-year period. The domestic poor in each of these geographic subdivisions also displayed an impressive stability, exhibiting relatively minor changes in percentage and rank size (see Table 15). Those born in Manhattan, including the offspring of the foreign poor, had a considerable numerical edge over the other groups, outnumbering them on the order of three to one in certain years. Their dominance was never threatened by the other two, much as the dominance of the Irish over other foreign immigrants stayed unchallenged. The New York State poor and those from other states of the Union, however, did experience a minor shifting of rank. Al-

CONFUSION OF DIALECTS 181

Table 15
The Domestic Poor in Manhattan's Almshouse, 1800-1830

Year	Manhattan (%)	New York State (other than city) (%)	Other States (%)	N
1800	76.3	9.4	14.2	591
1801	74.7	10.5	14.6	615
1802	10.5	14.6	15.0	600
1803	73.8	11.2	14.9	624
1804	75.6	8.9	14.4	603
1805	74.8	10.9	14.2	633
1806	74.0	10.8	15.0	600
1807	73.1	11.4	15.3	656
1808	70.5	15.2	14.2	690
1809	70.4	14.9	14.5	715
1810	71.7	12.6	15.5	709
1811	74.4	12.7	12.8	811
1812	76.6	10.8	12.5	951
1813	75.0	9.3	15.5	831
1814	75.0	10.2	14.6	855
1815	76.4	11.0	12.5	917
1816	75.1	10.2	14.6	1,027
1818	73.5	12.5	13.9	1,060
1824	74.2	10.9	14.8	889
1826	69.9	12.2	17.7	888
1828	70.6	12.0	17.2	960
1830	72.4	12.2	15.3	1,106

Source: Figures for 1800-1816 taken from Raymond A. Mohl, Poverty in New York, 1783-1825 (New York: Oxford University Press, 1971), p. 86; other figures from Almshouse Folders Census located in City Clerk's Files, NYMA. Percentages may not add up to 100 due to rounding.

though the so-called "destitute adventurers from other parts," that is, the out-of-staters, generally held the advantage in size, the gap between them and their rivals could be closed.[30] In fact, figures for 1808 and 1809 reveal the New York State poor population slightly surpassing in size the destitute population from other states. This almost reoccurred in 1811, when the state inmates of the institution registered 103 persons to the other states' total of 104. What reasons, therefore, account for these variations in size as well as for the continued dominance of poor Manhattanites?

One logical explanation for the great numbers of the Manhattan-born inmates would be the density of the population in the seaport city compared to the adjoining areas of the countryside. Over the first decades of the century New York continued to dwarf in population such neaby counties as Westchester, Kings, and Queens; by 1820 it contained almost twice as many inhabitants as the three counties combined. Nor is this surprising. Large urban centers often acted as a kind of sponge that drew people in from nearby regions; they could also prevent sizable secondary urban centers from appearing nearby. The symbiotic commercial relationship between rural crop-producing regions and the urban marketplace was at least partially responsible for these two results, since the countryside could feed the excess number of people in urban areas.[31] Under these conditions the pool of paupers born in the city was much greater than the potential supply of paupers from nearby localities. Indeed, the destitute classes of Manhattan possessed a locomotive effect: the swarms of needy immigrants with children born in the city increased the size of the Manhattan pauper class, while destitute migrants from other parts of the nation added their city-born children as well. Time and again, widowed or single mothers from the countryside would enter the almshouse, sometimes to give birth to children. Physical unions inside the almshouse, legal or otherwise, produced yet another crop of city-born paupers to add to the welfare rolls. As the Reverend Mr. Ely pointed out in 1811: "In some rooms husbands and wives, with children, and even unmarried persons sleep together. Marriage is permitted in this institution, because it cannot be prevented, under existing circumstances to procreate a future race of paupers. These things should not be." Nor did the good Reverend exaggerate: an 1806 account of the inmates listed 15 percent of the children as illegitimate, many of them probably conceived inside the institution.[32]

The large number of Manhattan-born poor persons was also the result of the state poor laws. Until 1824, when all intercounty removal of the needy was halted, the city had the authority, if not always the means, to transport non-resident paupers. How often they did so remains uncertain; different sets of municipal records tell conflicting stories, and the city authorities themselves complained about difficulties in identifying non-residents. Nonetheless, from 1808 to 1811 over four hundred families and persons were transported, people who in other instances might have entered the almshouse.[33] This weapon helped guarantee the numerical majority of the Manhattan-born poor population.

Explaining alterations in the relative size of the state-born poor and the out-of-state poor populations requires more speculation. The city naturally attracted a wide spectrum of laborers and artisans "from various parts of this and neighboring states," according to a report in 1817. William Cobbett was less polite and claimed that "all the disorderly crowd to it."[34] Even so, no civil official attempted to explain why the New York State poor outnumbered the poor from other states in 1808 and 1809. The growth of the former class may well illustrate how such political restrictions on commerce as the Embargo and Non-Intercourse Acts rerouted normal migration patterns from the city. Certainly, working-class individuals had little incentive to stay in a seaport barren of trading ships. It is also a fact that marginally poor laborers and artisans might travel many miles to look for work, seeking out the best price for their services. Moreover, the removal records from Queens county for 1808 and 1809 show a doubling in the number of people transported, with fifteen families or individuals removed in 1809 compared to seven the previous year.[35] This small number may well be an indicator of an even larger group of less destitute people taking to the road.

If economic conditions caused the New York State poor population to forge ahead, why was this pattern not repeated during the depression years after the War of 1812? From 1816 onward the out-of-state poor increased their position in regard to the in-state poor and showed few signs of diminishing.

Several theories offer possible answers. Perhaps this development stems from the desire of people outside the state to try their fortunes in Manhattan; after all, New York State shared borders with New Jersey, Pennsylvania, and Connecticut—three relatively populous areas in comparison to the city's immediate environs. People coming from longer distances may have had less direct knowledge of the urban economy during the depression years than those closer to the city. Improvements in road and water transportation also played a role: more regular shipping service, highlighted by the introduction of coastal steamboats, and better roads tied Manhattan into a wider transportation grid accessible to many people from out of state. The construction of the Erie Canal, in turn, may have spurred in-staters to move north and west more than those from adjoining states near Manhattan.[36]

Scanty evidence from other sources suggests that migrants from different states entered Manhattan more frequently than did their in-state counterparts. Returns from the city watch list of 1800, which recorded the names of city constables and their place of birth, revealed slightly more people from outside New York State than inside on the order of 40 percent to 35 percent. Citizenship records for 1812 and 1813 confirm this again with out-of-staters ahead thirteen to three. Timothy Dwight suggested that New Englanders formed the largest group of migrants into the city, with people from Connecticut especially prominent. Indeed, he believed his fellow Yankees outnumbered the original Anglo-Dutch inhabitants of Manhattan.[37]

While the limited quantitative data and Dwight's observation prohibit any solid generalization, more concrete evidence is available from the removal records of 1808 to 1811, known also as the Vessel Book. Figures for 1808 and 1810 show that 60 and 63 percent of the people removed were sent out of state, presumably to their last known legal residence. This enhances the argument regarding the numerical strength of the out-of-state migrants.[38] Data from the book provides a treasure trove of information, for it details the social characteristics and geographic origins of poor non-residents. The book lists names, marital status, offspring, last legal residence, and occasionally the reasons for removal. Essentially, the book serves as a kind of migration ledger, noting where people had resided before arriving in Manhattan; it also allows us to determine if certain people, single or married, male or female, appeared more frequently. Next to the almshouse censuses themselves, this record furnishes one of the best insights into the identity of the non-resident poor.

As a group transported poor persons included more single men than single women, with such people outnumbering married couples (see Table 16). The great majority were white, comprising about 90 percent of the transported poor, while blacks formed the remaining 10 percent. Among the ranks of these folks could be found sailors, artisans, and laborers—many of them crippled or unable to work. Prostitutes also appeared, such as Betsy Hancock, who had established a brothel on Bedlow Street along with her fourteen- and eighteen-year-old daughters. Street beggars and vagrants were among some of the others.[39] The transported poor resembled the inmates of the almshouse in terms of their diversity. There were those

Table 16
Household Status and Race of the Transported Poor,
New York City, 1808-1811

Status	Whites (%)	Blacks (%)	Total %	N
Single				
Men	93	7	39	167
Women	86	14	32	138
Families				
Two-Parent	91	9	15	64
One-Parent	92	8	14	61
Total				430

Source: Register of Persons Transported or Removed, 1808-1811, Vessel Book, vol. 089, Almshouse Records, NYMA.

who had been struck down by personal misfortune as well as hardened vagrants with no visible signs of support. Official comments about these folk leave little doubt about how the authorities felt toward them, for a prostitute from the bridewell could hardly elicit the same degree of compassion as an aged widow or ill sailor. In fact, the official register suggests that some of the transported poor were well known to the authorities. A city officer listed Alexander Bogard of Philadelphia as "an old offender" when transported in 1809, and Alexander Dyer, known by the alias "Shitting Elleck," had been "fifteen years a vagrant."[40] The reputation of these people was occasionally reinforced in the memory of city officials by their repeated returns to Manhattan after being removed; the city sent Mother Hancock and her two daughters to their last legal settlement in Connecticut no fewer than four times in seven months. Although the Hancock women held the record for most attempted returns, other persons, some of whom were also prostitutes, managed to cross into Manhattan only to be removed a second time. The lure of urban life and perhaps the lure of illicit employment undoubtedly spurred them on. With luck, they might find sanctuary from city constables and marshalls in the dramshops and boarding houses of lower-class neighborhoods.[41]

Whatever their reasons, the itinerary of the migrant poor reveals the extent of Manhattan's attraction to lower-class individuals from both the nearby countryside and less accessible regions. Dividing destitute people between in-state and out-of-state migrants shows a pronounced tendency for people to enter Manhattan from outside of the state—a fact that corresponds with the available, albeit slim, evidence.[42] Although towns in Westchester, Dutchess, Kings, and Queens counties contributed their share of paupers, communities in New Jersey, Connecticut, and Pennsylvania, especially the city of Philadelphia, produced even greater numbers of wayfarers (see Table 17). Whether individuals from these two broad-based groups intended to settle in the city permanently is another matter: some "traveling persons" or "old traveling pauper," as designated by officials, were rootless transients more at home on the road than in any one location; others had every intention of residing in Manhattan.

The degree of geographic mobility was often related to such variables as gender, family size, and age. A recent study of eighteenth-century migration patterns among the destitute of Massachusetts shows that most were young rather than old, with single and one-parent households predominating; these migrants seldom traveled more than ten miles, but they changed locations frequently.

Table 17
Place of Origin of the Transported Poor, New York City, 1808–1811

Place of Origin	N
Out of state	
Pennsylvania	115
New Jersey	99
Connecticut	27
Massachusetts	25
Total	266
In state	
Long Island	53
Albany	26
Westchester	16
Dutchess	11
Total	106

Source: Register of Persons Transported or Removed, 1808–1811, Vessel Book, vol. 089, Almshouse Records, NYMA. I am acting on the assumption that the poor were removed to their last legal residence as stipulated in the state poor laws.

On Long Island during the early nineteenth century migrants were also locally based, moving from town to town. Some, especially immigrants, went across county and state lines. Entries from the Vessel Book suggest that distance traveled was a factor of gender as well. While in-state single women outnumbered men 55 to 45, among the out-of-staters men led women by 119 to 76. Admittedly, some women could and did travel further within New York than men entering from another state; Albany, for example, was a longer trek to Manhattan than was Perth Amboy, New Jersey. Yet many out-of-state men started from Philadelphia, Boston, or New London.[43] What could account for the longer trips of the men?

As we have noted previously, to be a single woman on the road during the early 1800s was to court suspicion. Respectable single women normally remained tied to their families or close relatives until marriage permitted them to leave the local area. While able to move with relative freedom to nearby towns to enjoy social festivities or among the crowded streets of their home cities, most women journeying longer distances traveled with a companion or in a group. When Benjamin Strong, a Manhattan merchant, sent his daughter to Long Island in 1804, he wrote his brother in Brookhaven that a "black woman by the name of Linah goes along who will take charge of her." Other respectable families no doubt adopted the same precautions.[44] Moreover, unlike transient men, who could easily hire themselves out to farmers as casual laborers, single women on the road had fewer opportunities. Farmers usually hired girls from the village or relied on friends and relatives to furnish them with servants; naturally, this limited the number of opportunities for transient women who were strangers to the villagers. Single women who did take to the road without definite job prospects represented the most destitute and perhaps the most desperate class of transients—people with no money and little future. Significantly, transported prostitutes often came from more distant locations: eighteen out of a total of twenty-eight were from out of state and several from in state had come from Albany and other faraway locales. Unable to find employment in the countryside, they may well have turned their sights to the anonymous urban environment of Manhattan.[45]

Curiously, some of the variable affecting white single transients proved less evident among black people of the same description. Whereas single white men outnumbered single white women, black women led men by twenty-six to fifteen. Part of the reason for this disparity may well be due to the nature of the urban economy and the role of black men and women within it. Both sexes suffered from blatant discrimination, yet women could more often secure employment as domestics or hucksters, positions that posed less of a threat to the white male working class. Here, at least, was job security of a sort.[46] Black men fared worse. Not only did they have to compete against white tradesmen and laborers, but they sometimes found themselves denied entry into certain occupations. They were unable to become carters since the municipal government refused to grant them licenses; their jobs as hackney cab drivers came under attack from Irish immigrants, who attempted to monopolize the position for themselves. Prejudice was pervasive. Peter Williams, a leading black cleric, agreed that blacks were better off in rural areas than in the city because of urban white antagonism. This may explain why fewer black men entered Manhattan: the opportunities were simply too few.[47]

The demographic profile of the black community further reflects this fact. While urban centers in America often attracted women, the differences in the sex ratio between black women and men in New York City was substantially greater than that of the white community. The 1813 municipal census shows some wards of Manhattan where black women composed a ratio of 200:100 over black men—a far cry from white women, who never exceeded a ratio of 122:100 of a ward's population.[48] Only in the tenth ward of the city was the sex ratio of blacks and whites virtually identical (see Table 18). The black community, therefore, was very much a female community, if not in actual influence, then in terms of simple numbers.

Differences of gender aside, the number of black people sent to their original residence from Manhattan remains illuminating. The Common Council specificially targeted blacks in 1807 as among those to be forcibly removed from Manhattan if they lacked a legal settlement there. In 1807 the Council appointed several constables of the city "to be employed by the commissioners of the almshouse for the purpose of bringing up for examination all vagrants, negroes, common prostitutes, and other persons likely to become chargeable." Despite the edict, transported blacks formed under 10 percent of the total number removed, a figure that represented roughly their share of the city's population in 1813.[49] For all their bluster, the municipal authorities had succeeded in ex-

Table 18
Sex Ratio of Whites and Blacks in New York City, 1813

Ward	Whites Female:Male	N	Blacks Female:Male	N
First	117:100	6,430	170:100	742
Second	104:100	6,273	233:100	594
Third	108:100	6,291	163:100	784
Fourth	113:100	8,210	156:100	675
Fifth	113:100	11,318	150:100	1,950
Sixth	113:100	9,814	138:100	1,235
Seventh	122:100	9,872	133:100	690
Eighth	100:100	9,090	133:100	295
Ninth	108:100	3,073	117:100	387
Tenth	113:100	9,307	113:100	418

Source: New York City Census of 1813, Census Folder, 1813, City Clerk's Files, NYMA.

pelling relatively few black persons, although they lumped them together indiscriminately with the unrespectable elements of the lower classes, unmindful that many blacks were neither vagrants nor prostitutes. It is possible that black people normally evaded capture, but this appears unlikely since many of them, presumably actual residents, had been incarcerated in the bridewell. In fact, this institution, which housed debtors, prostitutes, and petty criminals, possessed a black inmate population of over 50 percent for many years. Petty offenses often overlooked in whites could be used against blacks. Thus, the authorities had the means to deport black non-residents much as they had the means to incarcerate them in the bridewell; they failed to do so because there was simply no great mass of black migrants coming into the city.[50]

The black community in Manhattan was in every sense a second-class community, victimized by both legal ordinances and social customs. Moreover, the freedom bequeathed to all came at a price, since voting restrictions passed in 1821 effectively disenfranchised almost the entire adult population.[51] Life in the urban environment promised few benefits to black people. Political participation remained limited, economic advancement rare. Not surprisingly, many blacks lived in their own separate neighborhoods, housed in dilapidated structures that afforded scant protection from the elements. Crowded living conditions also made them easy prey for disease: an epidemic that claimed the lives of almost three hundred people in August 1821 confined its "ravages to Bancker Street and its neighborhood" and attacked "chiefly . . . people of color," according to a municipal report. This predominantly black section produced one-half of all black victims in the city, with blacks in general comprising 46 percent of all recorded deaths from the fever, a statistic that caused the city fathers to marvel at the epidemic's destructive power on a group that "formed not a twentieth part of the population of the city." Even an unsympathetic observer could agree several years later that the black population was "generally in a most woeful condition."[52] Lack of jobs, poor housing, and high mortality rates had inflicted their toll.

In terms of relative size the black community was losing its share of the urban population. Although blacks had been 17 percent of the population in 1756, they formed about 10 percent in 1800 and 1810 before declining to under 9 percent in 1820. By 1830 black residents represented less than 7 percent of Manhattan's population. In part, this situation was due to the greater influx of white migrants from the surrounding areas and immigrants from overseas; they simply overwhelmed the black population numerically. So, too, a higher mortality rate among blacks limited their rate of growth compared to whites.[53] By any measurement urban blacks were becoming even more of a minority in the city, losing out to a large native population with a lower death rate and growing numbers of immigrants.

Given these circumstances, one might expect that blacks—among the most despised and economically destitute of all classes—would form a disproportionately large number of inmates inside the almshouse. White critics tended to confirm this impression. Cobbett, among others, considered free black people "a disorderly, improvident set of beings," a burden for the white populace to support. An anonymous Scotsman claimed "not one in ten has behaved with propriety but have become drunken, lascivious, and thievish. I cannot conceive from their lazy lounging conduct how the half of them find sustenance." Complaints to the City Council supplemented this chorus of criticism, noting the "indecent and disorderly conduct of certain blacks" or referring to them as "idle Negroes";

CONFUSION OF DIALECTS 191

other whites complained to the city about black people who had settled as squatters on the public land.[54] Yet the free black community of Manhattan furnished relatively few paupers for the almshouse. Indeed, during certain years their share of the inmate population was lower than their share of the city's population. A class of people who normally received scant sympathy from the white majority had defied the odds in avoiding the poorhouse.

Black success is revealed firsthand in the several censuses of the almshouse. In 1806 black inmates, men, women, and children, comprised just over 5 percent of the almshouse population, although their share of the city's population was probably 10 percent. Admittedly, these percentages are somewhat deceiving, for almost half of the black populace in 1800 remained enslaved, placing dependent blacks at rough parity with the freedmen of the city.[55] Later censuses show more revealing figures. John Stanford, an almshouse preacher, compiled censuses from 1816 to 1826 that showed a decline in the ratio of black paupers to white paupers during most years when slavery as an institution had become almost extinct. Twelve percent of the black community in 1813 and 5.5 percent in 1821 remained enslaved.[56] While freedom of a sort blossomed into reality for all save a few, the number of black paupers remained insignificant. By 1824 only 4 percent of the almshouse inmates were black. In fact, the ratio of black inmates to white inmates was roughly two-thirds the number of blacks to whites in the general population during much of the 1820s. Although blacks were sometimes separated from whites in separate apartments, no evidence shows white authorities consciously trying to exclude poor blacks. They simply came in fewer numbers.[57]

This phenomenon is a tribute to the internal cohesiveness of Manhattan's black community. It managed despite numerous difficulties to assist less fortunate individuals by means of such private benevolent organizations as the Wilberforce Philanthropic Society of New York (1812) and the New York African Society (1808). Lacking white financial assistance, these groups tended their destitute neighbors, especially widows, orphans, and the infirmed. The African Society, for example, possessed sufficient funds to purchase a building at a cost of $1,800 in 1820 to house their organization. The contributions, although collected from a "narrow socio-economic strata throughout the whole city," still made it possible to supply the needs of many unfortunate black people.[58] In effect, these organizations symbolize the unity of the black community in caring for its poor.

Nevertheless, these organizations failed to supply the wants of all the destitute, for their financial resources were limited. Many impoverished black inhabitants then applied for outdoor relief instead of entering the institution, displaying an independent turn of mind. City officials recorded 887 black families and 1,975 white families who received home relief between April 1813 and April 1814; the following term to April 1815 saw 1,233 black families and 2,283 white families acquiring such assistance.[59] While such figures illustrate the extent of poverty among black people, their unduly heavy reliance on outdoor relief suggests a reluctance on the part of black New Yorkers to enter the almshouse. Conceivably, the idea of institutional relief was anathema to those so recently released from the institution of slavery; it meant subjecting oneself to a set of regulations and the commands of a keeper, a situation not all that dissimilar from the one many former slaves had left. Charity from within an institution may have also signified to blacks a loss of autonomy. Given the stated philosophy of the almshouse officials, who sought to rehabilitate poor people through work, this was certainly a legitimate concern for blacks. Better to preserve one's identity in a drafty, overcrowded tenement in the sixth ward than to lose it in an institution. Blacks did not dispute their need for charity, but many preferred to choose for themselves how they received it.[60]

Black people were hardly alone in this regard. The native-born white poor (along with some immigrants presumably) evinced a similar disdain for institutional relief. We have already seen how eighteenth-century poor people disliked incarceration, and later generations of poor folk acted little differently. They attempted to steer clear of the almshouse whenever possible, relying on private benevolent organizations. New York City during the first decades of the nineteenth century possessed a plethora of benevolent societies: there appeared to be one for almost every major artisan group; moreover, particular organizations appealed to particular needs. Caroll Smith-Rosenberg, Raymond Mohl, and others have noted the importance of private charities in Manhattan, many of which were religiously inspired by evangelical Protestants. The Female Reform Society, for example, tried to assist and rehabilitate prostitutes; other societies simply furnished food or firewood. Some organizations targeted separate occupations, such as the Marine Society and Pilots Charitable Society. They provided sailors and their widows and children with funds. Working-class folk, as Mohl has noted, banded together in 1808 to form the Assistance Society. The founders wanted the Society to cover the "deficiencies of other charitable societies." Although convinced that poverty was a byproduct of immoral behavior, the Society's members did attempt to help unemployed working folk, assisting more than 28,000 during its first four years of assistance. Still other artisans might turn to the General Society of Mechanics and Tradesmen, which aided working folk of different occupations.[61]

Not everyone existed solely upon these charities. Some laborers had no artisan affiliation, and they may have found the funds from certain organizations too limited. Such folk might then turn to the city. One means of doing so was to apply to the Charity Committee of the Common Council, which evaluated requests for assistance. Appeals for aid in such cases sometimes revealed a determination to avoid incarceration if at all possible. In 1803 Elizibeth Burnes, a poor widow, petitioned the city for a grant of land to settle upon, after learning that her present residence was not on common land but private property. She also noted that "being far advanced in years the multiplicity of people in the almshouse would be rather irksome," hence her request for a piece of property. Jonathan Seaman in 1815 asked the Common Council for a liquor permit since the loss of his leg made it impossible for him to labor. The alternative of being supported in the almshouse with his wife and three children, he claimed, "would be dispagwiable [sic] to me and expensive to the public."[62] During the economic depression caused by the Embargo Act of 1808 large numbers of unemployed sailors presented a petition to the mayor, asking for work. They did not wish to be "objects of charity," but noted that they soon would be unless "there is some method taken for our support. We are for the most part hale, robust, and hearty men and would choose some kind of employment than the poorhouse for a livelihood." This statement is significant not so much because the sailors preferred work to charity but because they complained about the possibility of incarceration. Presumably, they had fewer objections to outdoor relief.[63]

Assistance outside the almshouse could be obtained in other ways, too. People could go directly to the institution and receive small sums of money; officials might also visit the homes of the poor and disperse funds. Whether these poor folks could always refuse admission into the almshouse and always receive assistance at home is uncertain. According to a visitor to the almshouse in 1811, "Those who can get along with some aid short of an entire subsistence are left at home and called outdoor poor. Those, who have very little or no reliance, but on the public bounty, are transferred to the building." And yet a degree of ambiguity seems to have existed; the condition of people assisted at home sometimes resembled the condition of those in the almshouse. Sick and handicapped persons could be found on the welfare rolls inside and outside the almshouse. Perhaps poor relief administrators themselves determined how such persons could be supported. And welfare officials with ties to poorer neighborhoods—in particular, city aldermen, who sometimes disbursed alms—might have been understandably reluctant to commit their constituents. In this regard, the welfare system possessed a degree of flexibility, and some poor folk might have been quick to take advantage of it.[64]

The identity of the urban dependent poor population thus hinged upon a number of factors relating to the external dynamic of the urban economy and the internal cohesiveness of different racial and ethnic groups. Immigrants anchored at the bottom of the social structure, such as the Irish, formed a large share of the inmate population and comprised 25 percent of all paupers during most of the 1820s; the more affluent English and German immigrants ranked second and third respectively behind the Irish, while the French and the Jews were among the least visible of the poor. Economic rank and numerical strength helped to define the ethnic proportion of the almshouse inmates. So, too, the ability of various immigrants to support fellow countrymen determined whether or not they ended in the poorhouse. Despite possessing several benevolent organizations, the Irish proved simply too numerous for their fellows or their church to handle. Other groups were better served in this respect.

The number of native-born poor persons continued to remain high so long as the children of immigrant paupers born in Manhattan were counted as natives. Without them, native poor persons would have figured less prominently in the census tallies. The same was true of Manhattan-born poor persons, who outnumbered their in-state and out-of-state counterparts, since all offspring born in New York City were always identified as city dependents. Thus, the identity and the number of destitute people was sometimes the result of an administrative mechanism that did not always reflect reality. Destitute people, it seems, could also decide if they wanted to be admitted into the almshouse. Individuals who went to private benevolent organizations demonstrated their independence of the almshouse. While many people, black and white, displayed little desire for institutional relief, they had few qualms over accepting outdoor charity. They consciously made this choice. And this choice, in part, determined the identity of the dependent poor of New York City.

Conclusion

The evolution of poor relief in New York City and its rural environs followed a complex course of development during the eighteenth and early nineteenth centuries. As we have seen, the institutionalization process proceeded fitfully, especially within the country towns of Queens, Suffolk, and Westchester. Rural communities governed by local concerns adopted different mechanisms of relief to suit their needs: towns could alternate between pauper auctions and almshouses, while sometimes retaining home relief as an option. It was not unusual for a town to build an almshouse, abandon it, and construct another one at some later date. In Manhattan, however, the path to institutional relief remained relatively straightforward, as the city erected new and more elaborate structures to lodge poor persons. Yet changes of a sort did occur. Over time, the Manhattan almshouse went from a private house rented by the city to a specifically designed structure with numerous rules and harsh penalties. Economy and discipline became as important as charity within the later almshouses.

The chronological development of poor relief also tells us something about the responsiveness of urban and rural environments to poverty. Historians, traditionally, consider urban municipalities more receptive to change; it is cities where new ideas and new ways of doing things often first appear. Historians could point to the New York City almshouses of 1700 and 1735 as clear proof of an urban reform impulse, contrasting it with the supposed provincialism of the countryside, where home relief of indigent people was the norm. Some have even gone so far as to imply that rural society

CONCLUSION 197

did not accept the poorhouse until the Age of Jackson. Yet rural society did not lag that far behind Manhattan in turning to new modes of assistance. To be sure, Manhattan had the earliest poorhouse, but by the 1730s and 1740s eastern Long Island communities considered the erection of workhouses. During the Revolutionary period many towns and villages had adopted such mechanisms as poorhouses or pauper auctions. Such actions dispel the myth of rural provincialism at least in matters of poor relief.

This evidence suggests that we must re-evaluate certain assumptions regarding the cultural ethos of both urban and rural environments. Manhattan's early reliance on institutional relief in the 1730s did not necessarily symbolize the emergence of a progressive urban *mentalité*—if such a murky term can be used. Instead, the genesis of the Manhattan almshouse was due to the city's lack of social cohesion and the widening economic chasm separating rich and poor, both of which were made worse by the steady arrival of impoverished immigrants. Internal developments such as these were responsible for forcing the hand of the city fathers. When similar problems became evident in the countryside during the middle of the eighteenth century, villagers adopted like measures in regard to the poor. The appearance of transients and the dissolution of social unity prompted the freeholders to act quickly. Although the pauper auction may have represented a halfway stage between home relief and institutional relief, it was nonetheless an important social development. Like the almshouse, the public sale of indigent persons to the lowest bidder effectively segregated poor people from their own society, in effect transforming them into marketable commodities. The willingness of the villagers to employ such radical measures attests to their own propensity for change.

The urban-rural response to poverty was thus the result of conditions that emanated from within the two environments. The dynamics of community life in Manhattan and its rural environs influenced the particular mechanism of poor relief. Such factors, in turn, also explain why city and countryside sometimes followed different policies toward destitute people during the early national period. It was not necessarily the case of a cosmopolitan urban environment distinguishing itself from the rustic, provincial countryside—far from it. The city continued to rely on institutional relief to monitor the poor in a largely futile attempt to halt the spiraling cost of public welfare. The countryside, which witnessed no dramatic upsurge in the poor rates during the 1790s and the early 1800s, was able to abolish the poorhouse in favor of the pauper auction, a decision that reflected a pragmatic response to altered conditions. No pressing need existed for institutionalizing destitute persons when other methods proved equally effective. When poor relief expenditures rose sharply during the Panic of 1819, most communities abolished the pauper auction and turned to the poorhouse.

The destitute, of course, were the people most affected by such developments. As we have seen, this group of inarticulate individuals—white, black, and native American—normally eked out a modest subsistence as laborers, servants, sailors, and fishermen; few had much hope of advancement. Yet it would be wrong to characterize them as a class of people with few social distinctions. Some of them—single white men, in particular—were more mobile than others, willing to travel longer distances across counties and states to acquire employment. These footloose laborers became travelers of the road, transients who seldom settled long in one place or worked exclusively for one employer. By contrast, working-class black people seem to have moved less often and over shorter distances. Both urban and rural blacks remained stationary during the early national period, perhaps because of social ties to their local neighborhoods. Whatever the reasons, the black and white poor populations could often be distinguished by their relative degree of geographic mobility.

The destitute also responded differently toward charity. Irish immigrants crowded the halls and apartments of the Manhattan almshouse as early as the 1790s. Long before the Great Famine of the 1840s, Irish immigrants comprised a substantial number of the institutionalized poor, often representing a quarter of the inmate population. Too few charitable societies and a still maturing Catholic Church help to explain why the Irish entered the institution in such numbers. They had no other alternative. Other groups such as the French and the Jews compiled an extraordinary record in avoiding incarceration; they could depend upon private benevolence from benevolent societies or religious organizations. Similarly, Manhattan's black community stayed underrepresented in the almshouse. While many urban blacks remained anchored at the bottom of the social structure, they preferred to rely on outdoor relief from city officials or turn to their own societies. The almshouse environment held little attraction for them. Poor people, moreover, evinced a keen interest in the operation of public welfare, making their wants known to officials while attempting at times to circumvent the rules of the almshouse. Although we have less evidence of this in the countryside, some of the rural poor together with friends and neighbors attempted to manipulate the pauper auction to their own advantage, eventually unleashing the wrath of the more well-to-do classes. On other occasions when rural poor people were commanded to enter the almshouse they refused. Quite clearly, they had a sense of themselves as individuals in these matters.

Poverty and poor relief presented a challenge to both officials and poor people in early American society. Local communities attempted as best they could to assist their destitute neighbors, balancing compassion with economy, benevolence with discipline. By the 1820s the charitable aspects of public welfare became less apparent, although they were never completely absent. Poor people, if less numerous in the countryside, still continued to crowd into the city, often receiving relief at home or in the almshouse. Did early American society find any solutions to poverty? Clearly, it did not, aside from some stopgap measures. What it did was to deal with a situation that required increasing sums of revenue and that needed to be addressed. As for the poor people themselves, they remained a class apart from middle-class America, in effect, a class of invisible citizens lodged in almshouses or set off in slums. Yet they were not completely forgotten. The story of poverty and poor relief in early America is only one chapter in a still unfolding narrative—a narrative that late twentieth-century America is no closer to concluding.

Appendices

Appendix A
Population of Manhattan and Nearby Counties, 1703-1790

Year	Manhattan	Queens	Suffolk	Westchester
1703	4,375	4,394	3,346	1,946
1723	7,248	7,191	6,241	4,409
1731	8,622	7,995	7,675	6,023
1756	13,040	10,786	10,290	13,257
1771	21,163	10,980	13,128	21,747
1786	23,614	13,084	13,793	20,554
1790	33,171	16,014	16,440	23,941

Source: Evarts B. Greene and Virginia D. Harrington, *American Population Before the Federal Census of 1790* (New York: Columbia University Press, 1932; reprint ed., Gloucester, Mass.: Peter Smith, 1966), pp. 95-97, 101-102, 104-105.

APPENDICES

Appendix B
County and Selected Township Populations of Queens, Suffolk, and Westchester, 1790-1830

Community	1790	1800	1810	1820	1830
Queens	16,014	16,893	19,336	21,519	22,460
Jamaica	1,675	1,661	2,110	2,292	2,376
Newtown	2,111	2,312	2,437	2,158	2,610
North Hempstead	2,696	2,413	2,750	3,207	3,091
Oyster Bay	4,097	4,548	4,725	5,518	5,349
South Hempstead	3,829	4,141	5,084	5,939	6,215
Suffolk	16,440	19,464	21,113	24,272	26,780
Brookhaven	3,224	4,042	4,176	5,218	6,095
Huntington	3,260	3,894	4,424	4,935	5,583
Islip	609	958	885	1,156	1,653
Smithtown	1,022	1,413	1,592	1,874	1,686
Westchester	24,003	27,347	30,272	32,638	36,456
Bedford	2,470	2,404	2,374	2,432	2,750
East Chester	740	738	1,039	1,021	1,030
New Castle	—	1,468	1,291	1,368	1,336
Rye	986	1,074	1,278	1,342	1,402

Source: Census figures derived from tables in New York State Census of 1865, Microfilm Collection, SUNY-Stony Brook.

Notes

ABBREVIATIONS

HHO	Huntington Historian's Office, Huntington, N.Y.
ICS	Institute of Colonial Studies, Microfilm Collection, SUNY-Stony Brook
NYHS	New York Historical Society, New York City
NYMA	New York Municipal Archives, New York City
NYPL	New York Public Library, New York City
PRP	Papers Relating to the Poor, Brookhaven Town Clerk's Office, Patchogue, N.Y.
SPG	Society for the Propagation of the Gospel
SUNY	State University of New York

INTRODUCTION

1. Michael G. St. John Crevecoeur, *Letters from an American Farmer* (Gloucester, Mass.: Peter Smith, 1968); David M. Potter, *People of Plenty: Economic Abundance and the American Character* (Chicago: University of Chicago Press, 1954); James T. Lemon, *The Best Poor Man's Country: A Geographic Study of Early Southeastern Pennsylvania* (Baltimore: Johns Hopkins University Press, 1972).

2. Michael B. Katz, *Poverty and Policy in American History* (New York: Academic Press, 1983); Walter I. Trattner, *From Poor Law to Welfare State: A History of Social Welfare in America* (New York: Free Press, 1974). For a look at the historiography of public welfare see Clarke A. Chambers, "Toward a Redefinition of Welfare History," *Journal of American History* 73 (September 1986): 407-433.

3. Gary Nash, "Urban Wealth and Poverty in Pre-Revolutionary America," *Journal of Interdisciplinary History* 6 (Spring 1976): 545-584; Edward Pessen, *Riches, Class, and Power Before the Civil War* (Lexington, Mass.: D. C. Heath, 1973); James A. Henretta, "Economic Development and Social Structure in Colonial Boston," *William and Mary Quarterly* 22 (January 1965): 75-92.

4. David J. Rothman, *The Discovery of the Asylum: Social Order and Disorder in the New Republic* (Boston: Little, Brown, and Co., 1971).

5. Gary Nash, *The Urban Crucible: Social Change, Political Conscious-*

NOTES TO INTRODUCTION

ness, and the Origins of the American Revolution (Cambridge, Mass.: Harvard University Press, 1979); John K. Alexander, *Render Them Submissive: Responses to Poverty in Philadelphia, 1760-1800* (Amherst: University of Massachusetts Press, 1980); Raymond A. Mohl, *Poverty in New York, 1783-1825* (New York: Oxford University Press, 1971).

6. For rural poor relief consult Virginia Bernhard, "Poverty and the Social Order in Seventeenth-Century Virginia," *Virginia Magazine of History and Biography* 85 (April 1977): 141-155; Douglas L. Jones, "The Strolling Poor: Transiency in Eighteenth-Century Massachusetts," *Journal of Social History* 8 (Spring 1975): 28-54; Charles R. Lee, "Public Poor Relief and the Massachusetts Community, 1620-1715," *New England Quarterly* 55 (December 1982): 564-585. One community study that does deal with poor relief is Lynne Withey, *Urban Growth in Colonial Rhode Island: Newport and Providence in the Eighteenth Century* (Albany: SUNY Press, 1984), pp. 52-67.

7. Katz, *Poverty and Policy*, p. 59.

8. Mohl, *Poverty in New York*, p. 116.

CHAPTER I

1. Charles Lodwick to Francis Lodwick and Mr. Hooker, 20 May 1692, New York, in *Collections of the NYHS* (2nd ser.; New York: NYHS, 1848-1849), 2: 243-250, passim. For additional information on Lodwick see Robert C. Ritchie, *The Duke's Province: A Study of New York Politics and Society, 1664-1691* (Chapel Hill: University of North Carolina Press, 1977), pp. 126, 213, 226-227.

2. Daniel Denton, *A Brief Description of New York, 1670* (Ann Arbor, Mich.: University Microfilms, 1966), pp. 1-21, passim. For information on Denton see Cornell Jaray, ed., *Historical Chronicles of New Amsterdam, Colonial New York, and Early Long Island* (2 vols., 2nd ser.; Port Washington, N.Y.: Ira J. Friedman, 1968), 2:15-16.

3. Sarah Kemble Knight, *Private Journal of Sarah Kemble Knight, 1704* (reprint ed.; Norwich, Conn.: Academy Press, 1901), pp. 65-67.

4. For information on the physical geography of lower New York consult John H. Thompson, ed., *Geography of New York State* (Syracuse, N.Y.: Syracuse University Press, 1966).

5. Father Isaac Jogues, "Novum Belgium, 1646," in J. Franklin Jameson, ed., *Narratives of New Netherland* (New York: Charles Scribner's Sons, 1909), pp. 259-260. For additional information on Manhattan's ethnic and religious divisions see Joyce D. Goodfriend, "Too Great a Mixture of Nations: The Development of New York City Society in the Seventeenth Century," Ph.D. diss., UCLA, 1975.

NOTES TO CHAPTER I 205

6. Jogues, "Novum Belgium," p. 259; E. B. O'Callaghan, *History of New Netherland* (2 vols., reprint ed.; Spartanburg, S.C.: Reprint Co., 1966), 1: 348-349; Andrew Van Donck, "Representation of New Netherlands, 1649," in Jameson, ed., *Narratives of New Netherland*, pp. 293-297; Michael Kammen, *Colonial New York: A History* (New York: Charles Scribner's Sons, 1975), pp. 48-72, passim; Philip L. White, "Municipal Government Comes to Manhattan," *NYHS Quarterly* 37 (April 1953): 146-147; Goodfriend, "Too Great a Mixture of Nations," p. 19.

7. Kammen, *Colonial New York*, chaps. 2 and 3, passim.

8. For the settlement of Long Island see Nathaniel S. Prime, *A History of Long Island from Its First Settlement by Europeans to the Year 1845* (New York: Robert Carter, 1845).

9. Ibid., pp. 78, 100.

10. O'Callaghan, *History of New Netherland*, 2: 282, 350-352.

11. Kammen, *Colonial New York*, p. 52.

12. O'Callaghan, *History of New Netherland*, 2: 282-283, 312-314. Also see Thomas H. Edsall, "Kingsbridge," chapt. 19 in J. Thomas Schaft, ed., *The History of Westchester County* (2 vols.; Philadelphia: L. E. Preston and Co., 1886), 1: 745; Alvah P. French, ed., *History of Westchester County* (2 vols.; New York: Lewis Historical Publishing Co., 1925), 1: 167-168.

13. To trace these events in more detail see Ritchie, *Duke's Province*, pp. 167-177.

14. "Governor Dongan's Report on the State of the Province, 22 February 1687," in E. B. O'Callaghan and Berthold Fernow, eds., and John Brodhead, comp., *Documents Relative to the Colonial History of the State of New York* (15 vols.; Albany, N.Y.: Weed, Parson, and Co., 1856-1887), 3: 161.

15. Sung Bok Kim, *Landlord and Tenant in Colonial New York: Manorial Society, 1664-1775* (Chapel Hill: Institute of Early American History and Culture, University of North Carolina Press, 1978), pp. 69-70; Kenneth Scott and Susan E. Klaffry, *A History of the Joseph Lloyd Manor House* (Setauket, N.Y.: Society for the Preservation of Long Island Antiquities, 1976), pp. 10-11; Patricia U. Bonomi, *A Factious People: Politics and Society in Colonial New York* (New York: Columbia University Press, 1971), pp. 30-31.

16. Jean B. Peyer, "Jamaica, Long Island, 1656-1776: A Study of the Roots of American Urbanism," Ph.D. diss., CUNY, 1974, pp. 87-88; Prime, *History of Long Island*, pp. 240-241; "Smithtown Estimations, 28 September 1683," in E. B. O'Callaghan, ed., *Documentary History of the State of New York* (4 vols.; Albany, N.Y.: Weed, Parson, and Co., 1850-1851), 2: 308.

17. For settlements in these regions see Prime, *History of Long Island*; Benjamin F. Thompson, *History of Long Island* (3 vols., 3rd ed., reprint

ed.; Port Washington, N.Y.: Ira J. Friedman, 1962); Schaft, ed., *History of Westchester County*; Robert Bolton, Jr., *A History of the Several Towns, Manors, and Patents of the County of Westchester from Its First Settlement to the Present Time* (2 vols.; New York: A. S. Gould, 1848).

18. Theresa H. Bristol, "Westchester County, New York, Miscellanea," *New York Historical and Genealogical Record* 49 (January 1928): 66-88; Evarts B. Greene and Virginia D. Harrington, *American Population Before the Federal Census of 1790* (New York: Columbia University Press, 1932), pp. 92-94.

19. "A List of the Inhabitants of the Town of Southampton . . . 1698," in O'Callaghan, ed., *Documentary History*, 1: 437-447; "An Exact List of All the Inhabitants' Names Within the Town of Flushing . . . 1698," in ibid., 1: 432-437; "Population of Easthampton, 1687," in ibid., 3: 219; Greene and Harrington, *American Population*, p. 92.

20. Mr. John Sharpe to Secretary, SPG, 24 November 1705, New York, SPG Letter Books, ser. A, vol. 2, 129, Microfilm Collection, SUNY-Stony Brook; "An Exact List of All the Inhabitants Within the Town of Flushing, 1698," 1: 432-437; Peyer, "Jamaica, Long Island," pp. 214-215, 228; Jessica Kross, *The Evolution of an American Town: Newtown, New York, 1642-1775* (Philadelphia: Temple University Press, 1983), pp. 110-111; Bonomi, *Factious People*, p. 24.

21. John Miller, *New York Considered and Improved, 1695*, with an intro. by Hugo Paltsits (New York: Burt Franklin, 1970), pp. 54-55; Kross, *Evolution of an American Town*, pp. 111-113.

22. French, *History of Westchester*, 1: 252, 263; John W. Pratt, *Religion, Politics, and Diversity: The Church-State Theme in New York* (Ithaca, N.Y.: Cornell University Press, 1967), pp. 40-44; quotation may be found in Robert Bolton, *History of the Protestant Episcopal Church in the County of Westchester* (New York: Stanford and Swords, 1855), p. 181. For a look at the Dutch consult Gerald F. De Jong, *The Dutch in America, 1609-1974* (Boston: Twayne Publishers, 1975).

23. Rufus M. Jones, *The Quakers in the American Colonies* (London: MacMillan and Co., 1911), pp. 230-238.

24. Pratt, *Religion, Politics, and Diversity*, pp. 26-48; Miller, *New York Considered and Improved*, p. 55; Heathcote quotation is from Reverend William S. Coffey, "Colonial Period," chapter 5 in Schaft, ed., *History of Westchester County*, 1: 164.

25. Arthur E. Peterson, *New York as an Eighteenth-Century Municipality Prior to 1731*, (New York: Longmans, Green, and Co., 1917), pp. 12-15; Ritchie, *Duke's Province*, pp. 40-41.

26. Thomas J. Archdeacon, *New York City, 1664-1710: Conquest and Change* (Ithaca, N.Y.: Cornell University Press, 1976), p. 78.

27. Quoted in Carl T. Bridenbaugh, *Cities in the Wilderness: The First*

Century of Urban Life in America, 1625-1742 (New York: Oxford University Press, 1938), p. 148, also p. 147 for Manhattan's leasing policy; Greene and Harrington, *American Population*, p. 93.

28. Bridenbaugh, *Cities in the Wilderness*, pp. 141, 217-218; David T. Valentine, *History of the City of New York* (New York: G. P. Putnam and Co., 1853), p. 216; Herbert Osgood et al., eds., *Minutes of the Common Council of the City of New York* (8 vols.; New York: Dodd, Mead, and Co., 1905), 2: 23.

29. "Governor Dongan's Report, 22 February 1687," 3: 399; Goodfriend, "Too Great a Mixture of Nations," pp. 90-93; Greene and Harrington, *American Population*, p. 92.

30. "Representation of Messrs. Brooke and Nicolls to Board of Trade, 26 August 1696," in O'Callaghan and Fernow, eds., *Documents Relative to the State of New York*, 4:181-182; Goodfriend, "Too Great a Mixture of Nations," pp. 90-91; Jon Butler, *The Huguenots in America: A Refugee People in New World Society* (Cambridge, Mass.: Harvard University Press, 1983), pp. 147-148.

31. Greene and Harrington, *American Population*, p. 92; Goodfriend, "Too Great a Mixture of Nations," pp. 24, 36; Valentine, *History of the City of New York*, pp. 221-224; Gary Nash, *The Urban Crucible: Social Change, Political Consciousness, and the Origins of the American Revolution* (Cambridge, Mass.: Harvard University Press, 1979), p. 14.

32. Archdeacon, *New York City, 1664-1710*, pp. 78-96; Butler, *Huguenots in America*, p. 158; Hyman B. Grinstein, *The Rise of the Jewish Community of New York, 1654-1860* (reprint ed.; Philadelphia: Porcupine Press, 1976); Kenneth Scott, "The New York Slave Insurrection of 1712," *NYHS Quarterly* 45 (January 1961): 43-74.

33. Quoted in Gabriel P. Disoway, *The Earliest Churches of New York* (New York: J. G. Gregory, 1865), p. 45.

34. Osgood et al., eds., *Minutes of the Common Council*, 1: 169; Disoway, *Earliest Churches*, pp. 19-131, passim; Miller, *New York Considered and Improved*, p. 54.

35. "An Address of the Governor and Council to the King, 6 August 1691," in O'Callaghan and Fernow, eds., *Documents Relative to the State of New York*, 3: 797; *A Maritime History of New York*, with an intro. by Fiorello H. LaGuardia (Garden City, N.Y.: Doubleday, 1941), p. 41; Kammen, *Colonial New York*, p. 106.

36. "Answers of Governor Andros to Inquiries About New York, 6 April 1678," in O'Callaghan and Fernow, Eds., *Documents Relative to the State of New York*, 2: 261; "Governor Dongan's Report, 22 February 1687," 3: 398; Nash, *Urban Crucible*, p. 66; Archdeacon, *New York City, 1664-1710*, p. 70; Kammen, *Colonial New York*, pp. 151-152.

37. *Knight, Journal*, pp. 63-64; Miller, *New York Considered and Im-*

NOTES TO CHAPTER I

proved, p. 45; Archdeacon, *New York City, 1664-1710*, pp. 60-67; Charles Wolley, "A Two-Year Journal in New York, 1679-1680," in Jaray, ed., *Historical Chronicles of New Amsterdam* (1st ser.; Port Washington, N.Y.: Ira J. Friedman, 1968), 1: 35.

38. Nash, *Urban Crucible*, pp. 66-70; Valentine, *History of the City of New York*, pp. 225-226; *Maritime History of New York*, p. 49; James G. Lydon, *Pirates, Privateers, and Profits*, with an intro. by Richard B. Morris (Upper Saddle River, N.J.: Gregg Press, 1970), pp. 36-81, passim; "Governor Fletcher to Lords of Trade, 30 May 1696," in O'Callaghan and Fernow, eds., *Documents Relative to the State of New York*, 4: 151; "Earl of Bellomont to Lords of Trade, 8 May 1698," in O'Callaghan and Fernow, eds., *Documents Relative to the State of New York*, 4: 304-306.

39. Archdeacon, *New York City, 1664-1710*, p. 130; *Maritime History of New York*, p. 49.

40. Nash, *Urban Crucible*, pp. 65-66.

41. See Percy W. Bidwell and John I. Falconer, *The History of Agriculture in the Northern United States, 1620-1860* (New York: Peter Smith, 1941), for an overview of the subject. For a more speculative description of rural society see James A. Henretta, "Families and Farms: Mentalité in Pre-Industrial America," *William and Mary Quarterly* 35 (January 1978): 3-32.

42. Quoted in Bolton, *History of the Protestant Episcopal Church*, p. 60; Bettye Hobbs Pruitt, "Self-Sufficiency and the Agricultural Economy of Eighteenth-Century Massachusetts," *William and Mary Quarterly* 41 (July 1984): 333-364.

43. "Assessment Roll of Westchester and Eastchester, 1675," in O'Callaghan and Fernow, eds., *Documents Relative to the State of New York*, 13: 488; Kross, *Evolution of an American Town*, p. 93.

44. *Landlord and Tenant*, pp. 143, 146; *Papers of the Lloyd Family, 1654-1826* (2 vols.; New York: NYHS, 1926-1927), 1: 206-207.

45. Edsall, "Kingsbridge," 1: 746-747; Wolley, "Two-Year Journal in New York," p. 34; Kross, *Evolution of an American Town*, p. 40; Reverend William Berrian, *An Historical Sketch of Trinity Church, New York* (New York: Stanford and Swords, 1847), p. 18.

46. William S. Pelletreau, ed., *Records of the Town of Southampton, Long Island* (6 vols.; Sag Harbor, N.Y.: John Hunt, 1874-1915), 2: 59-60; "Address of the Governor and Council, 6 August 1691," 3: 797-798.

47. "Lord Cornbury to the Lords of Trade, 10 August 1706," in O'Callaghan and Fernow, eds., *Documents Relative to the State of New York*, 4: 1180; Kross, *Evolution of an American Town*, pp. 9-10.

48. Quoted in Bolton, *History of the Protestant Episcopal Church*, p. 247.

49. "Lord Cornbury to the Lords of Trade, 1 July 1708," in O'Callaghan

and Fernow, eds., *Documents Relative to the State of New York*, 5: 54-60.

50. Archdeacon, *New York City, 1664-1710*, pp. 58-61, 70-75.

51. Ibid., p. 39; Valentine, *History of the City of New York*, pp. 232-236, passim; Mary L. Booth, *History of the City of New York* (New York: W. R. C. Clark, 1867), pp. 171-173.

52. Butler, *Huguenots in America*, p. 157; Archdeacon, *New York City, 1664-1710*, p. 68.

53. Wayne Andrews, ed., "A Glance at New York in 1697: The Travel Diary of Dr. Benjamin Bullivant," *NYHS Quarterly* 40 (January 1956): 55-73; Miller, *New York Considered and Improved*, p. 40; Knight, *Journal*, p. 63.

54. Goodfriend, "Too Great a Mixture of Nations," p. 137.

55. Ibid., p. 158; Archdeacon, *New York City, 1664-1710*, p. 148; James A. Henretta, "Economic Development and Social Structure in Colonial Boston," *William and Mary Quarterly* 22 (January 1965): 75-92. On the topic of social structure in general see Jackson T. Main, *The Social Structure of Revolutionary America* (Princeton, N.J.: Princeton University Press, 1965).

56. Nash, *Urban Crucible*, p. 71.

57. "Population of Easthampton, 1687," 3: 219.

58. Quoted in French, *History of Westchester*, 2: 679-680. For Jamaica see Ritchie, *Duke's Province*, p. 131.

59. Peyer, "Jamaica, Long Island," p. 86; Bernice Marshall, *Colonial Hempstead: Long Island Life Under the Dutch and English* (2nd ed., reprint ed.; Port Washington, N.Y.: Ira J. Friedman, 1962), pp. 20-21; Kross, *Evolution of an American Town*, pp. 60-67.

60. Jackson T. Main, *Society and Economy in Colonial Connecticut* (Princeton, N.J.: Princeton University Press, 1985), pp. 64, 181-187, 200-205.

61. Ibid., pp. 38-39; Ritchie, *Duke's Province*, p. 130.

62. "Assessment Roll of Westchester and Eastchester, 1675," 3: 489; "Account of What Estate the Inhabitants of Westchester Have Given Be Rated This Year, 1683," in O'Callaghan and Fernow, eds., *Documents Relative to the State of New York*, 13:574; "Smithtown Estimations, Sept. 28, 1683," 2: 308, "Valuacion of the Rateable Estate Belonging to Brookhaven, Anno 1683," 2: 308-309, and "Flushing Tax List, 1683," 2: 263-264, in Callaghan, ed., *Documentary History*.

63. "A List of the Ratable Estate of ye Town of Huntington Taken in 1683," in O'Callaghan, ed., *Documentary History*, 2: 307; "Account of What Estate the Inhabitants of Westchester Have Given, 1683," 13: 574; Ritchie, *Duke's Province*, p. 136; *Records of the Town of Southampton*, 2: 360-364.

64. "Earl of Bellomont to the Lords of Trade, 12 May 1699," in

O'Callaghan and Fernow, eds., *Documents Relative to the State of New York*, 4: 511.

CHAPTER II

1. "Governor Dongan's Report on the State of the Province, n.d.," in E. B. O'Callaghan, ed., *Documentary History of the State of New York* (4 vols.; Albany, N.Y.: Weed, Parson, and Co., 1850-1851), 1: 415. For a description of seventeenth-century poor relief consult Bryan J. McEntegart, "How Seventeenth Century New York Cared for Its Poor," *Thought* 1 (March 1927): 588-612 and 2 (1927): 403-429.

2. See Robert E. Cray, Jr., "Poverty and Poor Relief: New York City and Its Rural Environs, 1700-1830," Ph.D. diss., SUNY-Stony Brook, 1984, chap. 1, for an overview of changes in the poor relief system.

3. McEntegart, "How Seventeenth-Century New York Cared for Its Poor," pp. 404-411, passim; *The Colonial Laws of the State of New York from the Year 1664 to the Revolution* (5 vols.; Albany, N.Y.: J. B. Lyon, 1894), 1: 131-132; David M. Schneider, "The Patchwork of Relief in Provincial New York, 1664-1775," *Social Service Review* 12 (December 1938): 469-494. Also see E. M. Leonard, *The Early History of English Poor Relief* (Cambridge, Eng.: Cambridge University Press, 1900).

4. *Colonial Laws of New York*, 1: 238, 348-349, 456; David M. Schneider, *The History of Public Welfare in New York State, 1609-1866* (Chicago: University of Chicago Press, 1938), pp. 37-42, 68-69; John W. Pratt, *Religion, Politics, and Diversity: The Church-State Theme in New York* (Ithaca, N.Y.: Cornell University Press, 1967), pp. 40-41. Also see Hyman B. Grinstein, *The Rise of the Jewish Community in New York, 1654-1860* (reprint ed.; Philadelphia: Porcupine Press, 1976), pp. 131-136; John Cox, *Quakerism in the City of New York, 1657-1930* (New York: Privately printed, 1930), pp. 42-43.

5. Herbert Osgood, et al., eds., *Minutes of the Common Council of the City of New York* (8 vols.; New York: Dodd, Mead, and Co., 1905), 1: 205, 385; McEntegart, "How Seventeenth-Century New York Cared for Its Poor," pp. 421-422; Steven J. Ross, "Objects of Charity: Poor Relief, Poverty, and the Rise of the Almshouse in Early Eighteenth-Century New York City," p. 10, paper to be published in Conrad Wright and William Pencak, eds., *New Approaches to Colonial and Revolutionary New York* (Charlottesville: University Press of Virginia, 1988). I am grateful to Professor Ross for allowing me to cite his work.

6. For accounts of Dutch charity see Edward T. Corwin, ed., *Ecclesiastical Records of the State of New York* (7 vols.; Albany, N.Y.: J. B. Lyon, 1901-1916), 1: 387, 621-622; Ross, "Objects of Charity," pp. 10-11; Schneider,

NOTES TO CHAPTER II 211

History of Public Welfare, pp. 37-42, passim. Early poor relief lists seem to show few Dutch persons as objects of charity. See, for example, the 1713 pauper list in Arthur Everett Peterson, *New York as an Eighteenth-Century Municipality Prior to 1731*, (New York: Longmans, Green, and Co., 1917), pp. 188-189.

7. Grinstein, *Rise of the Jewish Community*, p. 150 n. 1; Cox, *Quakerism in the City of New York*, pp. 42-43.

8. John Miller, *New York Considered and Improved, 1695*, with an intro. by Hugo Paltsits (New York: Burt Franklin, 1970), p. 40; Jon Butler, *The Huguenots in America: A Refugee People in New World Society* (Cambridge, Mass.: Harvard University Press, 1983), p. 183.

9. McEntegert, "How Seventeenth-Century New York Cared for Its Poor," pp. 415, 424-425. For a discussion of charity as a Christian act see Christine L. Heyrman, "A Model of Christian Charity: The Rich and the Poor in New England, 1630-1730," Ph.D. diss., Yale University, 1977). Also see David J. Rothman, *The Discovery of the Asylum: Social Order and Disorder in the New Republic* (Boston: Little, Brown, and Co., 1971), pp. 6-12, passim; Stephen Foster, *Their Solitary Way: The Puritan Social Ethic in the First Century of Settlement in New England* (New Haven, Conn.: Yale University Press, 1971), pp. 128-134, passim.

10. Kenneth Scott, "The Churchwardens and the Poor in New York City, 1693-1747," *New York Genealogical and Biographical Record* 99-102 (1968-1971): 157-164, passim.

11. *Colonial Laws of New York*, 2: 56-61. It is also possible that New Yorkers were more concerned about itinerant tradesmen coming into Manhattan doing business and departing without paying taxes; see Ross, "Objects of Charity," p. 16.

12. Ross, "Objects of Charity," p. 16.

13. Raymond A. Mohl, *Poverty in New York, 1783-1825* (New York: Oxford University Press, 1971), p. 42; *Colonial Laws of New York*, 1: 507.

14. Minutes of the Justices, Churchwardens, and Vestrymen, 1694-1747, 2 vols., transcript by George H. Moore, Manuscript Room, NYPL, 1: 241; Mohl, *Poverty in New York*, p. 42; Ross, "Objects of Charity," p. 21.

15. Minutes of the Justices, 1: 237, 259-260; Ross, "Objects of Charity," pp. 21-23; Rothman, *Discovery of the Asylum*, pp. 36-38.

16. Osgood et al., eds., *Minutes of the Common Council*, 3: 59-60; Mohl, *Poverty in New York*, p. 43.

17. Osgood et al., eds., *Minutes of the Common Council*, 2: 336; Ross, "Objects of Charity," p. 32; Minutes of the Justices, 2: 188. For the British system of badging see Leonard, *Early History of English Poor Relief*, p. 25; J. R. Poynter, *Society and Pauperism: English Ideas of Poor Relief, 1795-1834* (London: Routledge and Kegan Paul, 1969), p. 13.

18. Mary Lou Lustig, *Robert Hunter, 1664-1734: New York Augus-*

tan Statesman (Syracuse, N.Y.: Syracuse University Press, 1983), pp. 60-67; Walter Allen Knittle, *Early Eighteenth-Century Palatine Emigration* (reprint ed.; Baltimore: Genealogical Publishing Co., 1965), pp. 128-131, 147-148; Schneider, *History of Public Welfare*, pp. 56-58; Osgood et al., eds., *Minutes of the Common Council*, 2: 408-409. Also see H. T. Dickinson, "The Poor Palatines and the Parties," *English Historical Review* 82 (July 1967): 464-485, for the English background.

19. "Petition of Peter William Romers, 5 September 1711," in O'Callaghan, ed., *Documentary History*, 3: 342; Lustig, *Robert Hunter*, pp. 67-69.

20. Corwin, ed., *Ecclesiastical Records*, 3: 2168-2170; "Order for Apprenticing the Palatine Children, 20 June 1710," in O'Callaghan, ed., *Documentary History*, 3: 334; "Names of Palatine Children Apprenticed by Governor Hunter, 1710-1714," in O'Callaghan, ed., *Documentary History*, 3: 341-342. For apprenticeship procedures in Manhattan consult Peterson, *New York as an Eighteenth-Century Municipality*, 1: 69-74.

21. "Names of Palatine Children Apprenticed," 3: 341-342.

22. Scott, "Churchwardens and the Poor," 102 (July 1971): 153.

23. Gary Nash, *The Urban Crucible: Social Change, Political Consciousness, and the Origins of the American Revolution* (Cambridge, Mass.: Harvard University Press, 1979), pp. 123-125.

24. *New York Gazette*, 18 February 1734; Osgood et al., eds., *Minutes of the Common Council*, 4: 240-241; Mohl, *Poverty in New York*, pp. 43-44; Ross, "Objects of Charity," pp. 27-31.

25. Osgood et al., eds., *Minutes of the Common Council*, 4: 307-311.

26. Minutes of the Justices, 2: 281-283, 347-348, 361-362.

27. On ethnic divisions see Thomas J. Archdeacon, *New York City, 1664-1710: Conquest and Change* (Ithaca, N.Y.: Cornell University Press, 1976); Bruce M. Wilkenfeld, "New York City Neighborhoods, 1730," *New York History* 57 (January 1976): 165-182.

28. Nash, *Urban Crucible*, p. 127.

29. Ross, "Objects of Charity," pp. 37-38; Stephen E. Wiberly, "Four Cities: Public Poor Relief in Urban America," Ph.D. diss., Yale University, 1975, p. 193 n. 10; Minutes of the Justices, 2: 348-349, 368, 378, 388.

30. See Peterson, *New York as an Eighteenth-Century Municipality*, pp. 188-189.

31. Ross, "Objects of Charity," pp. 18, tables 4-5, pp. 21, table 6.

32. Osgood et al., eds., *Minutes of the Common Council*, 1: 211-212. A brief list of works dealing with the inarticulate and crowd actions include Jesse Lemisch, "Jack Tar in the Streets: Merchant Seamen in the Politics of Revolutionary America," *William and Mary Quarterly* 25 (July 1968): 371-407; Jesse Lemisch, "Listening to the Inarticulate: William Widger's Dream and the Loyalties of the American Revolutionary Seamen in British

Prisons," *Journal of Social History* 2 (1969-1970): 1-27; George Rude, *The Crowd in History: A Study of Popular Disturbances in France and England, 1730-1848* (New York: John Wiley and Sons, 1964); Edward Countryman, *A People in Revolution: The American Revolution and Political Society in New York, 1760-1790* (Baltimore: Johns Hopkins University Press, 1981).

33. Minutes of the Justices, 2: 373-374.

34. Ibid., 2: 410.

35. Wiberly, "Four Cities," pp. 70-72; "A Guide to the Vestry: Of an Essay Endeavoring to Show the Duty and Power of the Vestrymen of the City and County of New York" (New York, 1747), Evans, American Imprint Series, no. 5960, pp. i, 27-28.

36. Rothman, *Discovery of the Asylum*, pp. 42-43.

37. Charles R. Street, ed., *Huntington Town Records* (3 vols.; Huntington, N.Y.: Town of Huntington, 1887-1889), 1: 354; *Records of the Town of East Hampton* (5 vols.; Sag Harbor, N.Y.: John H. Hunt, 1887-1905), 2: 383, 447, 452, 458-459; East Hampton Town Account of 1700, East Hampton Town Records, Microfilm Collection, East Hampton Free Library, East Hampton, N.Y. Neither the vestry nor the churchwarden records for Rye or Hempstead go back to the seventeenth century. Also see Jessica Kross, *The Evolution of an American Town: Newtown, New York, 1642-1775* (Philadelphia: Temple University Press, 1983), pp. 100-102.

38. Hempstead Town Records, MS vol. 5, 1709-1843, Town Clerk's Office, Hempstead, N.Y., pp. 27-31; Proceedings of the Vestry and Churchwardens of the Parish of Rye, 1710-1795, Microfilm Collection, SUNY-Stony Brook, pp. 74-75; *Records of the Town of Brookhaven*, bk. C: *1687-1789* (New York: Derrydale Press, 1931), pp. 417-418.

39. Robert Bolton, Jr., *A History of the Several Towns, Manors, and Patents of the County of Westchester from Its First Settlement to the Present Time* (2 vols.; New York: A. S. Gould, 1848), 2: 206-208. The figures cited are estimates, for the printed records do not allow for precise determination since poor rates were lumped together with other charges. Thus, they represent a ceiling; the actual poor rates could have been even lower. For the Rye figures see table 1, Proceedings of the Vestry of Rye, pp. 74-75. See also Hempstead Town Records, MS vol. 5, pp. 27-31, passim.

40. Proceedings of the Vestry of Rye, pp. 82-87; Brookhaven Town Records, ICS, reel AA-980; Rothman, *Discovery of the Asylum*, pp. 30-35; Albert Deutsche, "The Sick Poor in Colonial Times," *American Historical Review* 44 (April 1941): 566-567.

41. *NYHS Collections*, vol. 24 (New York: NYHS, 1893), p. 143; *NYHS Collections*, vol. 27 (New York: NYHS, 1896), pp. 326-327. Also see David E. Narrett, "Preparation for Death and Provision for the Living: Notes

on New York Wills (1665-1760)," *New York History* 57 (October 1976): 417-437.

42. Langdon G. Wright, "In Search of Peace and Harmony: New York Communities in the Seventeenth Century," *New York History* 61 (January 1980): 5-21; Michael Zuckerman, *Peaceable Kingdoms: New England Towns in the Eighteenth Century* (New York: Alfred A. Knopf, 1970).

43. "Records for the Year 1697 to the Year 1818 of the Dutch Reform Church of the Manor of Philipsburgh," bk. 6, trans. Jacob Brinkerhoff, 1876, First Reform Church of North Tarrytown, Tarrytown, N.Y., pp. 346-354, passim; Henry Onderdonk, Jr., *History of the First Reformed Dutch Church of Jamaica, Long Island* (Jamaica, N.Y.: The Consistory, 1884), pp. 5, 20-21, 56-57; Bolton, *History of Westchester*, p. 206.

44. McEntegert, "How Seventeenth-Century New York Cared for Its Poor," pp. 414-415.

45. Town Accounts Folder, HHO.

46. *Records of the Town of East Chester* (6 vols.; East Chester, N.Y.: East Chester Historical Society, 1964), 1: 7, 25; Jean B. Peyer, "Jamaica, Long Island, 1656-1776: A Study of the Roots of American Urbanism," Ph.D. diss., CUNY, 1974, p. 86; *Records of the Town of East Hampton*, 2: 412.

47. *Records of the Town of Brookhaven*, bk. C, pp. 52-53, 55, 57; Proceedings of the Vestry of Rye, p. 54; Suffolk County Book of Quotes, 1746-1826, ICS, reel A-006.

48. *Records of the Town of Brookhaven*, bk. C, p. 224; Proceedings of the Vestry of Rye, pp. 54-55.

49. John A. Fairlie, *Local Government in Counties, Towns, and Villages* (New York: Century Co., 1909), pp. 27-28.

50. Proceedings of the Vestry of Rye, pp. 18, 46.

51. Reverend Thomas to Secretary, SPG, n.d., Hempstead, SPG Letter Books, ser. A, vol. 13, Microfilm Collection, SUNY-Stony Brook, pp. 447-448.

52. "Papers Relating to Churches in Queens County," in O'Callaghan, ed., *Documentary History*, 3: 179.

53. Ross, "Objects of Charity," p. 19. Rothman, *Discovery of the Asylum*, pp. 32-34, suggests that rural villagers adopted a pragmatic attitude toward the boarding process.

54. Data taken from Table 2.

55. Hempstead Town Records, MS vol. 5, pp. 65, 68, 84; *Records of the Town of Brookhaven*, bk. C, pp. 266, 271-272, 277; Proceedings of the Vestry of Rye, pp. 82-87; *Southold Town Records*, vol. 3: *1683-1856* (Southold, N.Y.: Town of Southold, 1983), pp. 20-24.

56. Hempstead Town Records, MS vol. 5, passim; Proceedings of the Vestry of Rye, p. 163; Town Accounts Folder, HHO.

NOTES TO CHAPTER II

57. Rothman, *Discovery of the Asylum*, pp. 32-34; Ross, "Objects of Charity," p. 19; *Records of the Town of Brookhaven*, bk. C, pp. 248, 254; Hempstead Town Records, MS vol. 5, pp. 65, 76.

58. Hempstead Town Records, MS vol. 5, pp. 45, 47; Proceedings of the Vestry of Rye, p. 112.

59. *Records of the Town of East Chester*, 6: 3; Proceedings of the Vestry of Rye, p. 80; Town Accounts Folder, HHO.

60. Hempstead Town Records, MS vol. 5, pp. 65, 98. This would tie in with Ross's findings regarding the economic motivation of urban keepers. For further evidence of this see Alan Watson, "Public Poor Relief in Colonial North Carolina," *North Carolina Historical Review* 54 (October 1977): 347-366, passim.

61. Proceedings of the Vestry of Rye, pp. 108, 131-149, passim; Town Accounts Folder, HHO; Hempstead Town Records, MS vol. 5, passim; *Records of the Town of Brookhaven*, bk. C, p. 274. For further information on widows and poor females see Eugenie Andress Leonard, *The Dear Bought Heritage* (Philadelphia: University of Pennsylvania Press, 1965), pp. 480-483; Mary Beth Norton, *Liberty's Daughters: The Revolutionary Experience of American Women, 1750-1800* (Boston: Little, Brown, and Co., 1980), pp. 132-134, 146-147, passim; Alexander Keyssar, "Widowhood in Eighteenth-Century Massachusetts: A Problem in the History of the Family," *Perspectives in American History* 8 (1974): 83-117; Mimi Abramovitz, "The Family Ethic: The Female Pauper and Public Aid, pre-1900," *Social Service Review* 59 (March 1985): 124-125.

62. The 1741 and 1749 tax lists appear in *Records of the Town of Brookhaven Up to 1880* (Patchogue, N.Y.: Office of the Advance, 1880), pp. 152-154, 161-164. The names of the various keepers were drawn from *Records of the Town of Brookhaven*, bk. C.

63. The names of the keepers in the Proceedings of the Vestry of Rye were compared with the names in the 1763 List of Freeholders in E. Marie Becker, "The 801 Westchester County Freeholders of 1763," *NYHS Quarterly* 25 (July 1951): 283-321.

64. Hempstead Town Records, MS vol. 5, pp. 42, 62; *Records of the Town of Brookhaven*, bk. C, p. 215; Proceedings of the Vestry of Rye, p. 51; Brookhaven Town Records, ICS, reel AA-980.

65. See Table 2 for data; Rothman, *Discovery of the Asylum*, p. 341; Watson, "Public Poor Relief in Colonial North Carolina," p. 349.

66. For work on wealth and the life cycle see Jackson T. Main, "Standards of Living and the Life Cycle in Colonial Connecticut," *Journal of Economic History* 43 (March 1983): 159-165.

67. Suffolk County Court of Sessions Records, ICS, reel EJ-869; Douglas L. Jones, "The Strolling Poor: Transiency in Eighteenth-Century Massachusetts," *Journal of Social History* 8 (Spring 1975): 28-54.

CHAPTER III

1. Charles R. Street, ed., *Huntington Town Records* (3 vols.; Huntington, N.Y.: Town of Huntington, 1887-1889), 2: 435; *The Colonial Laws of the State of New York from the Year 1664 to the Revolution* (5 vols.; Albany, N.Y.: J. B. Lyon, 1894), 3: 674-675.
2. See Chapter II for information in this regard.
3. Peter Kalm, *Peter Kalm's Travels in North America*, ed. Adolph B. Benson (2 vols.; New York: Dover Press, 1966), 1: 131; Dr. Alexander Hamilton, *The Itinerarium of Doctor Alexander Hamilton, 1744*, ed. Carl T. Bridenbaugh (Chapel Hill: Institute of Early American History, University of North Carolina Press, 1948), pp. 43-44; Patrick M'Roberts, *Tour Through Part of the Northern Province of America, 1774-1775*, ed. Carl T. Bridenbaugh (reprint ed.; New York: Arno Press, 1965), pp. 1-5, 9; Reverend Andrew Burnaby, *Travels Through the Middle Settlements of North America, 1759-1760* (3rd ed.; London: T. Payne, 1798), pp. 81-82.
4. Kalm, *Travels in North America*, 1: 126; Gary Nash, *The Urban Crucible: Social Change, Political Consciousness, and the Origins of the American Revolution* (Cambridge, Mass.: Harvard University Press, 1979), pp. 176-177. Quote from the *Independent Reflector* is taken from Thomas F. Devoe, *The Market Book* (2 vols.; New York: The Author, 1862), 1: 112.
5. Quoted in Devoe, *Market Book*, 1: 134.
6. An example of one such unfortunate family can be found in the 14 December 1752 issue of the *Independent Reflector*. A widow writing a letter to the paper related how her husband's death left her "in the greatest poverty" with only her eldest son, a boy of twelve, supporting them from the sale of oysters. Quoted in William Livingston et al., *The Independent Reflector, or Weekly Essays on Sundry Important Subjects More Particularly Adapted to the Province of New York, by William Livingston and Others*, ed. Milton M. Klein (Cambridge, Mass.: Belknap Press of Harvard University Press, 1963), p. 63.
7. A Guide to the Vestry: Of an Essay Endeavoring to Show the Duty and Power of the Vestrymen of the City and County of New York" (New York, 1747), Evans, American Imprint Series, no. 5960, pp. i, 7-8.
8. Ibid., p. 7.
9. Ibid., pp. i, 18, 26-27, 29-31.
10. Herbert Osgood et al., eds., *Minutes of the Common Council of the City of New York* (8 vols.; New York: Dodd, Mead, and Co., 1905), 5: 171, 187, 193, 300, 386, 396, 6: 246, 7: 43, 55, 185, 197.
11. Ibid., 4: 307, 310-311, 324; 6: 385.
12. "Petition of Tobias Van Sandt," 1 January 1769, City Clerk's Files, NYMA; Osgood et al., eds., *Minutes of the Common Council*, 3: 232-233, 281-282, 340; 4: 245, 480; 5: 289.

13. Osgood et al., eds., *Minutes of the Common Council*, 6: 12-13, 158.
14. For an attempt to transport the poor see Robert E. Cray, Jr., "Poverty and Poor Relief: New York City and Its Rural Environs, 1700-1830," Ph.D. diss., SUNY-Stony Brook, 1984, pp. 129-130, 135-137.
15. Quoted in Livingston et al., *Independent Reflector*, p. 85.
16. Nash, *Urban Crucible*, pp. 254-263; Gary Nash, "Urban Wealth and Poverty in Pre-Revolutionary America," *Journal of Interdisciplinary History* 6 (Spring 1976): 545-584, passim. Also see Sharon V. Salinger, "Artisans, Journeymen, and the Transformation of Labor in Late Eighteenth-Century Philadelphia," *William and Mary Quarterly* 40 (January 1983): 62-84.
17. Henry DeForesset, *The New York Almanac, 1747* (New York: DeForesset, 1747), entry for January 1747; Nash, *Urban Crucible*, p. 402, table 10.
18. "An Account of Goods Furnished and Cash Paid Out as Churchwardens and Overseers of the Poor, 1775," City Clerk's Files, NYMA; Nash, *Urban Crucible*, pp. 127, 402, table 10; Raymond A. Mohl, *Poverty in New York, 1783-1825* (New York: Oxford University Press, 1971), pp. 45, 50, 81-82; Carl T. Bridenbaugh, *Cities in Revolt: Urban Life in America, 1743-1775* (New York: Alfred A. Knopf, 1955), pp. 324-325.
19. *New York Mercury*, 20 November 1752; *New York Gazette*, 20 January 1760.
20. "The Committee Appointed by the Inhabitants of the City of New York . . . to Encourage Frugality and Employ the Poor, 29 December 1768," Evans, American Imprint Series, no. 11008; Mohl, *Poverty in New York*, pp. 49-50. In 1747 the vestrymen noted that taxes for the poor would be higher "if every different persuasion of religion did not help some of their own poor, as they do now." See "A Guide to the Vestry," p. 24.
21. Peter Force, ed., *American Archives: A Documentary History* (9 vols., 4th ser.; Washington, D.C.: M. St. Clair Clark and Peter Force, 1837-1854), 4: 1105, 1071-1072; 6: 627; *Journal of the Provincial Congress, Provincial Convention, Committee of Safety, and Council of Safety of the State of New York* (2 vols.; Albany, N.Y.: T. Weed, 1847), 1: 578; Mohl, *Poverty in New York*, p. 50.
22. *New York in the Revolution as Colony and State* (2 vols.; Albany, N.Y.: J. B. Lyon, 1904), 2: 118-119; Force, ed., *American Archives* (5th ser.), 3: 218; David M. Schneider, *The History of Public Welfare in New York State, 1609-1866* (Chicago: University of Chicago Press, 1938), pp. 100-102.
23. Force, ed., *American Archives* (5th ser.), 2: 1272-1273; *Journal of the Provincial Congress*, 1: 767; Schneider, *History of Public Welfare*, pp. 102-103.
24. Oscar Theodore Barck, *New York City During the War for Inde-

218   NOTES TO CHAPTER III

pendence (New York: Columbia University Press, 1931), pp. 84-85, 90-93; Schneider, *History of Public Welfare,* pp. 106-108.

25. Mohl, *Poverty in New York,* pp. 52-60; *Ordinances, Rules, and Bylaws of the Almshouse, 1784* (New York: City of New York, 1785), Broadside Collections, NYHS. For a more extended discussion of the poor laws during the early national period and afterward see Martha Branscombe, *The Courts and the Poor Laws in New York State, 1784-1929* (Chicago: University of Chicago Press, 1943).

26. *Minutes of the Common Council of the City of New York, 1784-1831* (21 vols.; New York: City of New York, 1917), 1: 35, 48-49, 128, 302, 314; Sidney I. Pomerantz, *New York, an American City, 1783-1803: A Study of Urban Life* (New York: Columbia University Press, 1938), pp. 24-25.

27. *Minutes of the Common Council,* 1: 115, 185, 267.

28. Ibid., pp. 263, 287-288, 363; Minutes of the Commissioners of the Almshouse and Bridewell, 1791-1797, Manuscript Room, NYPL, pp. 85, 212, 224. For attempts by the poor to redefine the philosophy of institutions to meet their own needs rather than those of their keepers see Michael B. Katz, *Poverty and Policy in American History* (New York: Academic Press, 1983).

29. For the use of alcohol in the almshouse see Minutes of the Justices, Churchwardens, and Vestrymen, 1694-1747, 2 vols., transcript by George H. Moore, Manuscript Room, NYPL, 2: 280-282; "Account for Liquor Given to Poor Men, 9 November 1770," City Clerk's Files, NYMA; *Bylaws of the Almshouse, 1784.* On drinking in early America see William J. Rorabaugh, *The Alcoholic Republic: An American Tradition* (New York: Oxford University Press, 1979), pp. 6-10.

30. Minutes of the Commissioners of the Almshouse and Bridewell, NYPL, p. 74.

31. Ibid., pp. 258-259.

32. On apprenticeship procedures in general and those in Manhattan in particular consult the following: Arthur Everett Peterson, *New York as an Eighteenth-Century Municipality Prior to 1731* (New York: Longmans, Green, and Co., 1917), pp. 69-74; Marcus W. Jeregan, *Laboring and Dependent Classes in Colonial America, 1607-1783* (Chicago: University of Chicago Press, 1931); Robert E. Seybolt, *Apprenticeship and Apprenticeship Education in Colonial New England and New York* (New York: Teacher's College, Columbia University Press, 1917). A more descriptive overview is furnished by William J. Rorabaugh, *The Craft Apprentice: From Franklin to the Machine Age in America* (New York: Oxford University Press, 1986).

33. Minutes of the Commissioners of the Almshouse and Bridewell, NYPL, pp. 46, 51, 80-81, 165. Also see Nash, *Urban Crucible,* pp.

NOTES TO CHAPTER III

184-185; Priscilla Ferguson Clement, *Welfare and the Poor in the Nineteenth-Century City: Philadelphia, 1800-1850* (Rutherford, N.J.: Fairleigh Dickinson University Press, 1985), pp. 127-128.

34. Apprenticeship of Isaac Van Dyck to Walter McBride, 8 October 1792, New York City Apprentice Records, 1792-1794, NYHS; Seybolt, *Apprenticeship Education*, p. 6; Samuel McKee, *Labor in Colonial New York* (reprint ed.; Port Washington, N.Y.: Ira J. Friedman, 1963), p. 76.

35. Minutes of the Commissioners of the Almshouse and Bridewell, NYPL, pp. 48, 75, 80-81.

36. Ibid., p. 24.

37. Reverend James Wetmore to Secretary, SPG, 20 February 1728, Rye, SPG Letter Books, ser. A, vol. 20, Microfilm Collection, SUNY-Stony Brook, p. 214; Chester J. Miller, "The Early History of Huntington, New York, 1653-1783," M.A. thesis, Pennsylvania State College, 1931; Bernice Marshall, *Colonial Hempstead: Long Island Life Under the Dutch and English* (2nd ed., reprint ed.; Port Washington, N.Y.: Ira J. Friedman, 1962), pp. 167-169; Beatrice Diamond, *An Episode in American Journalism: A History of David Frothingham and His Long Island Herald* (Port Washington, N.Y.: Kennikat Press, 1964), p. 44; Benjamin F. Thompson, *A History of Long Island* (3 vols., 3rd ed., reprint ed.; Port Washington, N.Y.: Ira J. Friedman, 1962), 2: 176-177.

38. Thomas Edsall, "Kingsbridge," chap. 19 in J. Thomas Schaft, ed., *The History of Westchester County* (2 vols.; Philadelphia: L. E. Preston and Co., 1886), 1: 749; Charles W. Baird, *The History of Rye: Chronicle of a Border Town* (New York: Anson D. F. Randolph and Co., 1871), pp. 77-79; Ralph H. Gabriel, *The Evolution of Long Island: A Study of Land and Sea* (New Haven, Conn.: Yale University Press, 1921), pp. 146, 176.

39. For a discussion of commercial farming regions in the northeast see Jackson T. Main, *The Social Structure of Revolutionary America* (Princeton, N.J.: Princeton University Press, 1965), pp. 28-30; Jackson T. Main, *Society and Economy in Colonial Connecticut* (Princeton, N.J.: Princeton University Press, 1985), passim; James T. Lemon, *The Best Poor Man's Country: A Geographic Study of Early Southeastern Pennsylvania* (Baltimore: Johns Hopkins University Press, 1972); Max Schumacher, *The Northern Farmer and His Market During the Colonial Period* (New York: Arno Press, 1975).

40. Michael Kammen, *Colonial New York: A History* (New York: Charles Scribner's Sons, 1975), pp. 288, 297.

41. David L. Gardiner, *Chronicles of the Town of Easthampton* (New York: Brown and Co., 1871), pp. 90-91; Nathaniel S. Prime, *A History of Long Island from Its First Settlement by Europeans to the Year 1845* (New York: Robert Carter, 1845), pp. 42-44.

42. *Southold Town Records*, vol. 3: *1683-1856* (Southold, N.Y.: Town of Southold, 1983), pp. 183-184, 190, 192-193, 198, 211; Southold Town Records, ICS, reel S-128; Gardiner, *Chronicles of the Town of Easthampton*, p. 86; *East Hampton Trustees Journal* (7 vols.; East Hampton, N.Y.: No pub., 1926-1927), 1: 60-64, 104-105.

43. For evidence on the early social structure of rural communities see Chapter I. See also Michael Zuckerman, *Peaceable Kingdoms: New England Towns in the Eighteenth Century* (New York: Alfred A. Knopf, 1970); Street, ed., *Huntington Town Records*, 2: 322-323, 326-327; Transcript Minutes of the Town Board of Rye, 5 vols., Microfilm Collection of the New York State Library, Albany, 1: 3-4; Langdon G. Wright, "In Search of Peace and Harmony: New York Communities in the Seventeenth Century," *New York History* 61 (January 1980): 5-21.

44. Martha B. Flint, *Long Island Before the Revolution* (reprint ed.; Port Washington, N.Y.: Ira J. Friedman, 1967), pp. 336-337; Baird, *History of Rye*, pp. 50, 87, 214; Kammen, *Colonial New York*, p. 295. In Huntington major grants and land sales became rarer by the 1760s. The period between 1720 and 1740 saw several land grants distributed among the townsfolk, perhaps reflecting the fear of the community that land was becoming scarce. See Street, ed., *Huntington Town Records*, 2: 349-350, 369-370, 382-383.

45. Benjamin D. Hicks, ed., *The Records of North and South Hempstead* (8 vols.; Jamaica, N.Y.: Long Island Farmer Print, 1896-1904), 3: 264-266; 4: 23-24, 84, 144, 214, 352; Marshall, *Colonial Hempstead*, pp. 141-144.

46. Tax List of 1764, Tax List Folder, HHO; the New Rochelle Tax List of 1767 appears in James Pitcher's Account Book, Microfilm Collection, NYHS. In Islip in 1757 the top 10 percent controlled one-half of the assessed wealth. See the Islip Tax List, 1757, East Hampton Free Library, East Hampton, N.Y. For a more general portrait of economic stratification see Main, *Social Structure of Revolutionary America*, pp. 7-43, passim; Edward Countryman, *A People in Revolution: The American Revolution and Political Society in New York, 1760-1790* (Baltimore: Johns Hopkins University Press, 1981), pp. 25-26.

47. Robert Bolton, Jr., *A History of the Several Towns, Manors, and Patents of the County of Westchester from Its First Settlement to the Present Time* (2 vols.; New York: A. S. Gould, 1848), 2: 293.

48. Street, ed., *Huntington Town Records*, 2: 436, 439, 484; Transcript Minutes of the Town Board of Rye, 2: 118, 133; Hicks, ed., *Records of North and South Hempstead*, 4: 261. An earlier warning about poachers in Hempstead in 1753 blamed both strangers and "some of the inhabitants" for going into the bays to raid the clam beds (p. 195).

49. Quoted in Jessica Kross, *The Evolution of an American Town:*

NOTES TO CHAPTER III 221

Newtown, New York, 1642-1775 (Philadelphia: Temple University Press, 1983), p. 237.

50. Such artisans were in general poorly paid and seldom acquired much wealth or real estate (Main, *Social Structure of Revolutionary America*, pp. 77-80).

51. Social and economic ties between Suffolk and New England can be examined in Joshua Hempstead, *Diary of Joshua Hempstead, September 1711 to November 1758* (New London, Conn.: New London Historical Society, 1901), pp. 158, 166-167, 319, 546, 559.

52. For the unfortunate Acadians see James Riker, Jr., *The Annals of Newtown in Queens County* (New York: D. Fanshaw, 1852), pp. 163-168, passim; Marshall, *Colonial Hempstead*, pp. 104-105.

53. Proceedings of the Vestry and Churchwardens of the Parish of Rye, 1710-1795, Microfilm Collection, SUNY-Stony Brook, pp. 186, 210; *Records of the Town of Brookhaven*, bk. C: *1687-1789* (New York: Derrydale Press, 1931), p. 119; Hempstead Town Records, MS vol. 5, 1709-1843, Town Clerk's Office, Hempstead, N.Y., pp. 67, 88, 97, 104, 105.

54. *Colonial Laws of New York*, 5: 533-534. Also see Robert E. Cray, Jr., "White Welfare and Black Strategies: The Dynamics of Race and Poor Relief in Early New York, 1700-1825," *Slavery and Abolition* 7 (December 1986): 273-289.

55. Marshall, *Colonial Hempstead*, p. 51; Hempstead Town Records, MS vol. 5, pp. 105, 109; *Records of the Town of East Hampton* (5 vols.; Sag Harbor, N.Y.: John H. Hunt, 1887-1905), 2: 99-100; William S. Pelletreau, ed., *Records of the Town of Smithtown* (Smithtown, N.Y.: Town of Smithtown, 1898), pp. 107-108; Town Accounts Folder, 1769, HHO; *Records of the Town of Brookhaven*, bk. C, p. 236; Reverend James Wetmore to the Secretary, SPG, 11 May 1724, Brookhaven, SPG Letter Books, ser. A, vol. 18, pp. 173-174.

56. For the relative religious calm in Hempstead see Leonard Cutting to the Secretary, SPG, 7 January 1768, Hempstead, SPG Letter Books, ser. B, vol. 3., no. 143.

57. Timothy Wetmore to the Secretary, SPG, 6 May 1761, Rye, SPG Letter Books, ser. B, vol. 3., no. 215.

58. Baird, *History of Rye*, p. 530. One of the Wetmores served as supervisor in 1764 and 1768. John Thomas and John Thomas, Jr., held the office from 1765 to 1767 and from 1769 to 1770. See Transcript Minutes of the Town Board of Rye, 2: 133-134.

59. Quoted in Charles W. Turner, *Annals of St. John's Church, Huntington* (Huntington, N.Y.: Stiles Printing House, 1895), p. 19; Street, ed., *Huntington Town Records*, 2: 512; Moses Scudder, *Records of the First Church in Huntington, Long Island, 1723-1779* (Huntington, N.Y.: Moses Scudder, 1899), pp. 120-129.

60. *Colonial Laws of New York,* 5: 513.
61. Information derived from Hempstead Town Records, MS vol. 5, pp. 55, 88-89; Town Accounts Folder, HHO. Data drawn from Table 3.
62. Hicks, ed., *Records of North and South Hempstead,* 5: 243, 346; Marshall, *Colonial Hempstead,* pp. 121-122; Hempstead Town Records, MS vol. 5, pp. 65, 88, 97, 104-105.
63. Hempstead Town Records, MS vol. 5, p. 109.
64. Proceedings of the Vestry of Rye, pp. 193, 214, 221-222. For additional information on the pauper auction as a system of relief see Benjamin J. Klebaner, "Pauper Auctions: The New England Method of Poor Relief," *Essex Institute Historical Collections* 91 (April 1955): 195-210.
65. MS vol. of Huntington Town Meetings, 1784-1840, HHO, pp. 3, 13, 16, 40-41; Town Accounts Folder, HHO. For conditions during the Revolutionary War see Eleanor S. Dennis, "The Town of Huntington During the War of Independence: A Political-Social Study," M.A. thesis, Long Island University, 1962.
66. Bolton, *History of Westchester,* 1: xii-xiii. For an example of smallpox see J. W. Keeler, "Lewisboro," chap. 9 in Schaft, ed., *History of Westchester County,* 2: 541.
67. *Records of the Town of Brookhaven,* bk. C, pp. 343, 348, 401, 404-405.
68. *Bedford Historical Records* (5 vols.; Bedford Hills, N.Y.: Town of Bedford, 1966-1976), 5: 4-10, passim.
69. For the poor relief policies of these towns see Pelletreau, ed., *Records of the Town of Smithtown,* pp. 216-217; John Cox, ed., *Oyster Bay Town Records* (8 vols.; New York: Tobias Wright, 1931), 7: 176; Kross, *Evolution of an American Town,* p. 100; Arthur C. Downs, ed., *Riverhead Town Records, 1792-1886* (Huntington, N.Y.: Long Islander, 1967), pp. 6-9; Town of Islip, Town Board Minutes Resolutions, 1720-1850, Microfilm Collection, SUNY-Stony Brook, reel 33, 1783; C. M. Woolsey, *The History of the Town of Marlborough, Ulster County* (Albany, N.Y.: J. B. Lyon, 1908), pp. 205-208.
70. Stephanie G. Wolf, *Urban Village: Population, Community, and Family Structure in Germantown, Pennsylvania, 1683-1800* (Princeton, N.J.: Princeton University Press, 1976), pp. 124-125; Anne Baxter Webb, "On the Eve of Revolution: Northampton, Massachusetts, 1750-1775," Ph.D. diss., University of Minnesota, 1976, pp. 183-184; Arthur Chase, *History of Ware, Massachusetts* (Cambridge, Eng.: Cambridge University Press, 1911), pp. 124-125; Samuel Sewall, *History of Woburn, Middlesex County* (Boston: Wiggins and Lunt, 1868), pp. 153-154; Bruce C. Daniels, *The Connecticut Town: Growth and Development, 1635-1790* (Middletown, Conn.: Wesleyan University Press, 1979), p. 162; Lynne Withey, *Urban Growth in Colonial Rhode Island: Newport and Providence in the Eighteenth Century* (Albany: SUNY Press, 1984), p. 61.

71. David J. Rothman, *The Discovery of the Asylum: Social Order and Disorder in the New Republic* (Boston: Little, Brown, and Co., 1971), p. 180.

CHAPTER IV

1. *Minutes of the Common Council of the City of New York, 1784-1831* (21 vols.; New York: City of New York, 1917), 2: 60.

2. Minutes of the Commissioners of the Almshouse and Bridewell, 1791-1797, Manuscript Room, NYPL, p. 150; Thomas E. V. Smith, *The City of New York in the Year of Washington's Inauguration, 1789* (New York: Anson D. F. Randolph and Co., 1889), p. 14; *Minutes of the Common Council*, 2: 126.

3. *Historical Records, North Castle/New Castle: Colonial History and Minutes of the Town Meetings* (2 vols.; Armonk and Chappaqua, N.Y.: Towns of North Castle and New Castle, 1975, 1977), 2: 84; Benjamin D. Hicks, ed., *The Records of North and South Hempstead* (8 vols.; Jamaica, N.Y.: Long Island Farmer Print, 1896-1904), 6:358.

4. Walter B. Smith and Arthur H. Cole, *Fluctuations in American Business, 1790-1860* (Cambridge, Mass.: Harvard University Press, 1935), pp. 12-16.

5. David M. Schneider, *The History of Public Welfare in New York State, 1609-1866* (Chicago: University of Chicago Press, 1938), pp. 115-125, passim.

6. E. P. Thompson, "The Moral Economy of the English Crowd in the Eighteenth Century," *Past and Present* 50 (February 1971): 76-135, remains the classic work in this regard. For changes in New York City see Howard Rock, *Artisans of the New Republic: The Tradesmen of New York City in the Age of Jefferson* (New York: New York University Press, 1979); Sean Wilentz, *Chants Democratic: New York City and the Rise of the American Working Class, 1788-1850* (New York: Oxford University Press, 1984).

7. See "Report of the Secretary of State in 1824 on the Relief and Settlement of the Poor," in David J. Rothman, ed., *Poverty U.S.A.* (New York: Arno Press, 1971), for a discussion of the various methods of relief. Also useful is Martha Branscombe, *The Courts and the Poor Laws in New York State, 1784-1929* (Chicago: University of Chicago Press, 1943), who notes there was "no consistent policy" among the villagers during the period (p. 20).

8. *Minutes of the Common Council*, 2: 121; Sidney I. Pomerantz, *New York, an American City, 1783-1803: A Study of Urban Life* (New York: Columbia University Press, 1938), pp. 362-365, passim.

9. *Minutes of the Common Council*, 2: 167.

10. There was no discussion of moving the almshouse further north of the city line at this time.

11. Everett S. Lee and Michael Lalli, "Population," in David T. Gilchrist, ed., *The Growth of Seaport Cities* (Charlottesville: University Press of Virginia, 1967), pp. 30-33; Pomerantz, *New York, an American City*, p. 159.

12. Bruce M. Wilkenfeld, "The Social and Economic Structure of the City of New York, 1695-1796," Ph.D. diss., Columbia University, 1973. The top 10 percent now controlled 61 percent of the assessed wealth and the bottom 10 percent under 1 percent (pp. 192-195).

13. Ibid., p. 197. Also see Christine Stansell, *City of Women: Sex and Class in New York* (New York: Alfred A. Knopf, 1986), pp. 3-12, for an insightful look at the causes of poverty during this period.

14. Alvin Harlow, *Old Bowery Days: The Chronicles of a Famous Street* (New York: D. Appleton and Co., 1941), pp. 90-91. Also see Carol Gronemen Pernicorn, "The Bloody Ould Sixth: A Social Analysis of a New York City Working-Class Community in the Mid-Nineteenth Century," Ph.D. diss., University of Rochester, 1973.

15. Raymond A. Mohl, *Poverty in New York, 1783-1825* (New York: Oxford University Press, 1971), pp. 105-107.

16. *Minutes of the Common Council*, 2: 496.

17. Pomerantz, *New York, an American City*, p. 203.

18. "To the Mayor, Aldermen, and the Commonality of the Said City . . . Respecting the Present State of the Almshouse," 8 February 1796, Broadside Collection, NYHS.

19. Mohl, *Poverty in New York*, pp. 68-70; Minutes of the Commissioners of the Almshouse and Bridewell, NYPL, pp. 63-64; *Minutes of the Common Council*, 1: 263, 287-288.

20. *Minutes of the Common Council*, 2: 568-569, 639; 3: 2; Mohl, *Poverty in New York*, p. 68.

21. *Minutes of the Common Council*, 2: 568; 3: 88, 314.

22. Ibid., 2: 666-672; Mohl, *Poverty in New York*, p. 69.

23. Schneider, *History of Public Welfare*, p. 134; Benjamin J. Klebaner, "State and Local Immigration Regulation in the United States Before 1882," *International Review of Social History* 3 (1958): 272-273, 291.

24. Charles Havens Hunt, *The Life of Edward Livingston* (New York: D. Appleton and Co., 1864), pp. 93-94, 95-96.

25. Mohl, *Poverty in New York*, pp. 226-237, passim; Rock, *Artisans of the New Republic*, pp. 65-66.

26. "Representation of the Superintendent of the Almshouse," 24 June 1805, Almshouse Folder, City Clerk's Files, NYMA.

27. "Representation of the Superintendent of the Almshouse," 30 October 1805, Almshouse Folder, City Clerk's Files, NYMA.

28. *Minutes of the Common Council,* 5: 714-726, passim; Mohl, *Poverty in New York,* pp. 74-78.

29. In regard to traditional and modern see Richard D. Brown, *Modernization: The Transformation of American Life, 1600-1865* (New York: Hill and Wang, 1976), pp. 8-9. The use of stocks could still be seen in rural society despite its demise in urban areas. See Schneider, *History of Public Welfare,* p. 149; Hicks, ed., *Records of North and South Hempstead,* 6: 438-439; *Bedford Historical Records* (5 vols.; Bedford Hills, N.Y.: Town of Bedford, 1966-1976), 5: 30.

30. John Jay, Original Manuscript of His Historical Account of the Town of Bedford, 15 December 1812, NYHS; William Strickland, *Journal of a Tour in the United States of America, 1794-1795,* ed. J. E. Strickland (New York: NYHS, 1971), p. 93; Diary of an Unknown Scot, 1821-1824, 3 vols., NYHS, 1: 383-391, passim.

31. Timothy Dwight, *Travels in New England and New York,* ed. Barbara M. Schoman (4 vols.; Cambridge, Mass.: Belknap Press of Harvard University Press, 1969), 3: 203, 212-213, 220-221. In 1801 the Town of Brookhaven still used arbitrators from among the citizenry rather than lawyers to decide such matters as slander, and they relied on public shaming to attain results. See Southold Town Records, Liber C (actual document is from Brookhaven), 7 April 1801, ICS, reel R.

32. Fernand Braudel, *Civilization and Capitalism, Fifteenth and Eighteenth Century,* vol. 2: *The Wheels of Commerce,* trans. Sian Reynolds (New York: Harper and Row, 1982), pp. 564-565. This point is also being made by American historians in different ways. See, for example, John Mack Faragher, *Sugar Creek and Life on the Illinois Prairie* (New Haven, Conn.: Yale University Press, 1986), pp. 130-136. Also consult George M. Frederickson, review of *The Countryside in the Age of Capitalist Transformation: Essays in the Social History of Rural America,* ed. Steven Hahn and Jonathan Prude, and Faragher's *Sugar Creek* in *New York Review of Books,* 23 April 1987, pp. 37-39.

33. Charles R. Street, ed., *Huntington Town Records* (3 vols.; Huntington, N.Y.: Town of Huntington, 1887-1889), 3: 200-201. For the existence of the pauper auction consult the Overseers of the Poor Book, 1805-1862, HHO. During the 1790s the town accounts suggest that a poorhouse was employed: poor relief costs are totaled rather than being listed next to the name of a pauper and a keeper. Still, one town account from 1792 shows a pauper being boarded out (Town Accounts Folder, HHO).

34. William S. Pelletreau, ed., *Records of the Town of Smithtown* (Smithtown, N.Y.: Town of Smithtown, 1898), pp. 135, 216-217; John Cox, ed., *Oyster Bay Town Records* (8 vols.; New York: Tobias Wright, 1931), 8: 27-28; Southold Town Records, ICS, reel S-141. North Hempstead also

NOTES TO CHAPTER IV

had a poorhouse that was sold during this period; see Hicks, ed., *Records of North and South Hempstead*, 6: 407.

35. *Historical Records of North Castle/New Castle*, 2: 84, 92-93, 96-97.

36. *Records of the Town of East Chester* (6 vols.; East Chester, N.Y.: East Chester Historical Society, 1964), 4: passim; Town of Islip, Town Board Minutes Resolutions, 1720-1850, Microfilm Collection, SUNY-Stony Brook, reel 33; Allan M. Butler, "Scarsdale," chap. 15 in J. Thomas Schaft, ed., *History of Westchester County* (2 vols.; Philadelphia: L. E. Preston and Co., 1886), 2: 659. In 1790 Scarsdale had 281, East Chester had 740, and Islip had 609 residents. See New York State Census of 1865, Microfilm Collection, SUNY-Stony Brook, for these figures.

37. John Lyons Gardiner, "Notes and Observations on the Town of Easthampton, 1798," *Collections of the NYHS*, 1869 (New York: NYHS, 1870), pp. 226-228, 259; Ralph H. Gabriel, *The Evolution of Long Island: A Story of Land and Sea* (New Haven, Conn.: Yale University Press, 1921), pp. 37-38; William S. Coffey, "General History," chap. 8 in Schaft, ed., *History of Westchester County*, 1: 473; Benjamin Strong to Selah Strong, 6 May 1790, 25 January 1792, 19 March 1792, New York City, Strong Family Papers, 1790-1839, NYHS (these letters were all directed to Selah at St. George Manor, Brookhaven); Gelston and Saltonstall, Merchants and Shippers, New York City, 1791-1800, Whaling and Sealing Manuscript, 21 May 1791, 23 May 1791, NYHS; Onderdonk Paper Mills, Letter Book, 1796-1810, NYHS, p. 22.

38. Benjamin J. Klebaner, "Pauper Auctions: New England Method of Poor Relief," *Essex Institute Historical Collections* 91 (April 1955): 195-210.

39. See Gordon Wood, *The Creation of the American Republic, 1776-1787* (Chapel Hill: Institute of Early American History and Culture, University of North Carolina Press, 1969), for a discussion of republican political values.

40. I develop this point about the pauper auction as a labor device at greater length at the end of the chapter.

41. Hempstead Town Records, MS vol. 5, 1709-1843, Town Clerk's Office, Hempstead, N.Y., pp. 234-235.

42. *New York Evening Post*, 24 November 1801.

43. *New York Evening Post*, 26 November 1801; *Minutes of the Common Council*, 4: 4; 5: 495, 577.

44. *New York Evening Post*, 26 November 1801; *Minutes of the Common Council*, 3: 393; 4: 1; 5: 266.

45. David J. Rothman, *The Discovery of the Asylum: Social Order and Disorder in the New Republic* (Boston: Little, Brown, and Co., 1971), pp. 171-172. This concern, however, was expressed well before the Age

of Jackson, contradicting Rothman's emphasis on this period as a crucial one.

46. John Lambert, *Travels Through Canada and the United States of North America in the Years 1806, 1807, 1808* (3 vols.; London: Richard Phillips, 1810), Microfilm Collection, SUNY-Stony Brook, 2: 157; Pomerantz, *New York, an American City*, p. 159.

47. Lambert, *Travels Through the United States*, 2: 157-158; Walter W. Jennings, *The American Embargo, 1807-1808, with Particular Reference to Its Effects on Industry* (Iowa City: Iowa University Press, 1921), remains the standard work.

48. Mohl, *Poverty in New York*, p. 91, table 4, p. 140; *Minutes of the Common Council*, 6: 3.

49. *Minutes of the Common Council*, 5: 495, 719.

50. Ezra Stiles Ely, *The Journal of the Stated Preacher to the Hospital and Almshouse in the City of New York, 1811* (New York: Whiting and Watson, 1812), p. 34.

51. "Almshouse Committee Report," 15 June 1812, City Clerk's Files, NYMA. The report also attacked "the aldermen and assistants of the various wards" for giving alms from the public purse to their various constituents. Quite possibly, as Raymond Mohl has suggested, this money was used by city officials as a means of buying votes. See Mohl, *Poverty in New York*, pp. 103-104.

52. Quoted in Rock, *Artisans of the New Republic*, p. 297; Mohl, *Poverty in New York*, p. 132; Rothman, *Discovery of the Asylum*, pp. 162-163. Also see William J. Rorabaugh, *The Alcoholic Republic: An American Tradition* (New York: Oxford University Press, 1979).

53. *Minutes of the Common Council*, 8: 661-662, 692. Mercein was a master baker who went on to hold an important position in the working-class community. See Sean Wilentz, *Chants Democratic*, pp. 38-39.

54. See John F. Kasson, *Civilizing the Machine: Technology and Republican Values, 1776-1900* (paperback ed.; London: Penguin Books, 1979).

55. Drew R. McCoy, *The Elusive Republic: Political Economy in Jeffersonian America* (Chapel Hill: Institute of Early American History and Culture, University of North Carolina Press, 1980), pp. 116-117, 174-176. Kasson notes that even Jefferson believed the employment of individuals in factories might be useful (*Civilizing the Machine*, pp. 22-27, passim).

56. Presumably, this fact alleviated some of the concern of the artisan community, while the War of 1812 may have kept their attention diverted.

57. Samuel ReznECK, "The Depression of 1819-1822: A Social History," *American Historical Review* 39 (October 1933): 31; R. S. Guernsey, *New York City and Vicinity During the War of 1812 to 1815* (2 vols.; New York: Charles L. Woodward, 1889), 2: 9-11; Thomas F. Devoe, *The Market Book* (2 vols.; New York: The Author, 1862), 1: 225-226.

58. "Report of the Sub-Committee to Enquire Into the Present State of Want Among the Poor of the City," 1 March 1819, and "Report of the Aldermen and Assistants," 26 July 1819, 8 November 1819, Almshouse Folder, City Clerk's Files, NYMA.

59. Minutes of the Commissioners of the Almshouse and Bridewell, 1808-1827, Almshouse Records, vol. 0190, 27 October 1821, NYMA; "Petition of Thomas Hayes," 2 April 1821, Almshouse Folder, City Clerk's Files, NYMA; "Report of the Superintendent of the Almshouse," 10 December 1821, Almshouse Folder, City Clerk's Files, NYMA; "Report of the Almshouse Commissioners," 26 May 1823, Almshouse Folder, City Clerk's Files, NYMA.

60. Mohl, *Poverty in New York*, p. 85.

61. John Stanford, "Annual Report, 1826, to the Honorable the Mayor and Common Council of the City of New York on the Subject of Religious Services Performed at the Almshouse, Penitentiary, Bellevue Hospital, Debtor's Prison, and the Bridewell," 1827, NYHS, p. 6.

62. Mohl, *Poverty in New York*, pp. 62-65; Branscombe, *Courts and the Poor Laws*, pp. 29-30, 33-34, 83-84.

63. The Report of the Commissioners of the Almshouse, Bridewell, and Penitentiary, 20 September 1830, NYHS.

64. Priscilla Ferguson Clement, *Welfare and the Poor in the Nineteenth-Century City: Philadelphia, 1800-1850* (Rutherford, N.J.: Fairleigh Dickinson University Press, 1985), pp. 51-52.

65. Quoted in Schneider, *History of Public Welfare*, pp. 167-168. For the Embargo's impact on Long Island's eastern coast see Harvey Strum, "Foreign Policy and Long Island Politics, 1808-1815," *Long Island Forum* 48 (November 1985): 224-230, passim.

66. Street, ed., *Huntington Town Records*, 3: 216, 230, 242; *Bedford Historical Records*, 5: 55-56; Pelletreau, ed., *Records of the Town of Smithtown*, pp. 138-139.

67. Transcript Minutes of the Town Board of Rye, 5 vols., Microfilm Collection, New York State Archives, Albany, 2: 156-158; Town Book of North Hempstead, Records of the Poor, 1785-1833, Microfilm Collection, New York State Archives, Albany, see entries for respective years; Town Board Minutes Resolutions, 1807-1808; Southold Town Records, ICS, Reel S-149-151.

68. C. Edward Skeen, "'The Year Without a Summer': A Historical View," *Journal of the Early American Republic* 1 (Spring 1981): 51-67.

69. Cox, ed., *Oyster Bay Town Records*, 8: 40, 79.

70. Hicks, ed., *Records of North and South Hempstead*, 6: 470, 476-477.

71. Transcript Minutes of the Town Board of Rye, 5: 4, 11, 14-15, 35; Schneider, *History of Public Welfare*, p. 221; Benjamin J. Klebaner, *Public Poor Relief in America, 1790-1860* (New York: Arno Press, 1976), p. 117.

72. New Rochelle may still have boarded out the poor without recourse to the pauper auction; we just cannot tell from the available sources. See Jeanne A. Forbes, ed., *Records of the Town of New Rochelle, 1699-1828* (New York: Paragraph Press, 1916), pp. 420-423.

73. *Bedford Historical Records*, 5: 74-75; *Historical Records of North Castle/New Castle*, 2: 154.

74. "Report of the Secretary of State, 1824," p. 1055. For the opening of the Westchester facility see Coffey, "General History," 1: 478.

75. Dwight, *Travels in New England and New York*, 3: 220-221.

76. Islip Town Board Minutes Resolutions, 1815-1819; Street, ed., *Huntington Town Records*, 3: 278-296; Pelletreau, ed., *Records of the Town of Smithtown*, pp. 144-147.

77. "Report of the Secretary of State, 1824," pp. 1228-1230.

78. Street, ed., *Huntington Town Records*, 3: 306; Overseers of the Poor Book, 1805-1862, entry for 1825; Pelletreau, ed., *Records of the Town of Smithtown*, pp. 150, 152, 156; "Report of the Secretary of State, 1824," pp. 448-449.

79. In Huntington the number of dependents rose from twenty-seven in 1810 to forty-nine in 1820, while the overall population increased by less than 12 percent during the period. See Overseers of the Poor Book, 1805-1862. See Appendix B for town population figures. Also consult the Overseers of the Poor Records, 1787-1828, Town Hall, Bedford, N.Y.

80. Samuel Chipman, *Report of an Examination of Poor Houses, Jails, etc. in the State of New York* (4th ed.; Albany: New York State Temperance Society, 1836), pp. 64-65. Also see Michael Zuckerman, *Peaceable Kingdoms: New England Towns in the Eighteenth Century* (New York: Alfred A. Knopf, 1970).

81. Horatio G. Spafford, *A Gazetteer of the State of New York* (Albany, N.Y.: B. D. Packard, 1824), pp. 43, 246.

82. Overseers of the Poor Records, 1787-1828, entries for 1806, 1807; *Bedford Historical Records*, 5: 66-70, passim.

83. *Bedford Historical Records*, 5: 75-76.

84. Ibid., pp. 76-78. Also see pp. 269-274 for the 1815 Tax List. Political offices for these people were found by consulting the index at the back of the book. For an account of William Jay's career see Bayard Tuckerman, *William Jay and the Constitutional Movement for the Abolition of Slavery* (New York: Dodd, Mead, and Co., 1893). Jay was an active member of the Episcopal Church, a member of the Westchester Bible Society and the American Bible Society, and a founder of the Bedford Society for the Suppression of Vice in 1815 (pp. 13-14).

85. *Bedford Historical Records*, 5: 81. Overseers of the Poor Records, 1787-1828, list the names of paupers and the cost of the upkeep but not their keepers during the late 1820s.

NOTES TO CHAPTER IV

86. Overseers of the Poor Book, 1805-1862.

87. Huntington *American Eagle*, 30 January 1823, 11 November 1824, Long Island Room, Smithtown Town Public Library, Smithtown, N.Y.; Overseers of the Poor Book, 1805-1862, entries for 1824 and 1825.

88. Huntington *Portico*, 18 May 1826, Huntington Public Library, Huntington, N.Y.; Peter Ross, *A History of Long Island* (3 vols.; New York: Lewis Publishing Co., 1902), 1: 92-99; 3: 370-371; Romanah Sammis, *Huntington-Babylon Town History* (Huntington, N.Y.: Huntington Historical Society, 1937), pp. 22, 62-63, 71-73, 130, 132. In regard to Hewlett's wealth see Tax List of 1793, Tax List Folder, HHO. Overseers of the Poor Book, 1805-1862, reveals Devine and Isaac Hewlett taking in paupers by means of the auction.

89. Huntington *Portico*, 18 May 1826, Huntington Public Library.

90. Ibid., 23 November 1826, Huntington Public Library.

91. Klebaner, "Pauper Auctions," pp. 195-210, passim. Some farmers clearly saw the auction as useful. John Carll of Huntington, a well-to-do farmer who had purchased a "grain cleaner" patent, also paid the town $10.50 for the labor of Joseph Price, a public dependent, in 1824. See Huntington *American Eagle*, 6 March 1823, Huntington Public Library; Overseers of the Poor Book, 1805-1862, 1824 entry. The book also shows the poor being taken in by their relatives via the auction; for example, Amy Baily went to Wilky Baily between 1806 and 1808.

92. "Report of the Secretary of State, 1824," pp. 1029, 1055. Benjamin F. Thompson, a nineteenth-century Long Island historian, objected to pauper auctions in the 1830s, describing them as "a most unfeeling and scandalous practice of selling the unfortunate poor, in the open market, to him who would undertake to save them from starving" (Thompson, *A History of Long Island* [3 vols., 3rd ed., reprint ed.; Port Washington, N.Y.: Ira J. Friedman, 1962], 2: 327).

93. Spafford, *Gazetteer of the State of New York*, p. 561.

94. "Report of the Secretary of State, 1824," p. 1056. For an insight into reformers and religion and their campaign to improve society see M. J. Heale, "Patterns of Benevolence: Charity and Morality in Rural and Urban New York, 1783-1830," *Societas* 3 (1973): 337-359. Also consult Paul E. Johnson, *A Shopkeeper's Millennium: Society and Revivals in Rochester, New York, 1815-1837* (New York: Hill and Wang, 1978).

95. Overseers of the Poor Book, 1805-1862, entries 1824, 1825; New York State Census of 1835, Microfilm Collection, SUNY-Stony Brook, reel A-267, shows very few paupers in individual towns. The dependent poor, however, could employ rural poorhouses for their own benefit, especially pregnant women, who used them as a lying-in facility in Pennsylvania; see Joan M. Jensen, *Loosening the Bonds: Mid-Atlantic Farm Women, 1750-1850* (New Haven, Conn.: Yale University Press, 1986), pp. 62-63,

66-68. The division between progressives and localists had been advanced by Jackson T. Main, *Political Parties Before the Constitution* (Chapel Hill: Institute of Early American History and Culture, University of North Carolina Press, 1974).
96. Chipman, *Report of an Examination of Poor Houses,* pp. 40-42, 54-55, 64-65, 73.

CHAPTER V

1. Deposition of Henry Thaler, 8 December 1819, Public Welfare Folder, HHO.
2. Deposition of Prince, 26 January 1821, HHO.
3. Fernand Braudel, *Civilization and Capitalism, Fifteenth and Eighteenth Century,* vol 2: *The Wheels of Commerce,* trans. Sian Reynold (New York: Harper and Row, 1982), p. 506. Also see pp. 507-512 for a detailed description of European poverty.
4. For a selected number of works dealing with the history of the inarticulate see Jesse Lemisch, "Jack Tar in the Streets: Merchant Seamen in the Politics of Revolutionary America," *William and Mary Quarterly* 25 (July 1968): 371-407; Jesse Lemisch "Listening to the Inarticulate: William Widger's Dream and the Loyalties of American Revolutionary Seamen in British Prisons," *Journal of Social History* 2 (1969-1970): 1-27; Alfred F. Young, "George Robert Twelves Hewes (1742-1840): A Boston Shoemaker and the Memory of the American Revolution," *William and Mary Quarterly* 38 (October 1981): 561-623; Douglas L. Jones, "The Strolling Poor: Transiency in Eighteenth-Century Massachusetts," *Journal of Social History* 8 (Spring 1975): 28-54; Billy G. Smith, "The Material Lives of Laboring Philadelphians, 1750-1800," *William and Mary Quarterly* 38 (April 1981): 163-202. For geographic mobility during the antebellum period see Stephen Thernstrom, *Poverty and Progress: Social Mobility in a Nineteenth-Century City* (Cambridge, Mass.: Harvard University Press, 1964); Peter Knights, *The Plain People of Boston, 1830-1860: A Study in City Growth* (New York: Oxford University Press, 1971). An even more detailed look at migration is James W. Oberly, "Westward Who: Estimates of Native White Interstate Migration After the War of 1812," *Journal of Economic History* 46 (June 1986): 431-440.
5. Mount Pleasant *Westchester Herald,* 18 December 1827; Samuel Thompson's Journal, 1800-1810, Manuscript Room, NYPL, 15 April 1800. Large-scale rural philanthropy was also not unknown. Samuel Jones established a $30,000 fund to support the poor of Oyster Bay and North Hempstead in 1836. See J. H. French, *Gazetteer of the State of New York, 1860* (Syracuse, N.Y.: R. Pearsall Smith, 1860), p. 550.

6. "Report of the Secretary of State on the Relief and Settlement of the Poor, 1824," in David J. Rothman, ed., *Poverty, U.S.A.* (New York: Arno Press, 1971), p. 1029; Samuel Chipman, *Report of an Examination of Poor Houses, Jails, Etc., in the State of New York* (4th ed.; Albany: New York State Temperance Society, 1836), p. 73.

7. Mount Pleasant *Westchester Herald*, 15 May 1827; Diary of Mary Guion, 1800-1852, NYHS, p. 26.

8. Information derived from the number of paupers listed in the "Report of the Secretary of State, 1824," and the population statistics from the state census of 1825 listed in *Journal of the Senate of the State of New York*, 49th Session (Albany, N.Y.: E. Craswell, 1826), Microfilm Collection, SUNY-Stony Brook, 3 January 1826.

9. This was also true for the eighteenth-century municipal almshouse in New York City. Civil officials may also have been more sympathetic to the plight of women and children.

10. There is a growing literature on the role of women in the household and the economy. See, for example, Nancy F. Cott, *The Bonds of Womanhood: "Woman's Sphere" in New England, 1780-1835* (New Haven, Conn.: Yale University Press, 1977); Mary P. Ryan, *Cradle of the Middle Class: The Family in Oneida County, New York, 1790-1860* (Cambridge, Eng.: Cambridge University Press, 1981); Alice Kessler-Harris, *Out to Work: A History of Wage-Earning Women in the United States* (New York: Oxford University Press, 1982); Christine Stansell, *City of Women: Sex and Class in New York, 1789-1860* (New York: Alfred A. Knopf, 1986).

11. James Fenimore Cooper, *Notions of the Americans* (2 vols.; London: Henry Colburn, 1828), 1: 266. Also see Chapter VI for additional information on the migration pattern of women into Manhattan.

12. David J. Rothman, *The Discovery of the Asylum: Social Order and Disorder in the New Republic* (Boston: Little, Brown, and Co., 1971), p. 34; Michael B. Katz, *In the Shadow of the Poorhouse: A Social History of Welfare* (New York: Basic Books, 1986), pp. 87-88.

13. Information derived by comparing the figures from "Report of the Secretary of State, 1824" with the state census of 1825.

14. See Chapter IV for a more detailed discussion of these ideas.

15. See Overseers of the Poor Book, 1805-1862, HHO, entries for 1823, 1824, 1825. It was often the policy to deny relief to all poor people who refused to enter the almshouse. Exceptions could occur in special instances, as was the case in Mount Pleasant. See "Report of the Secretary of State, 1824," p. 1055.

16. "Report of the Secretary of State, 1824," p. 1029. For a more quantitative look at poverty and public welfare see Joan Underhill Hannon, "The Generosity of Antebellum Poor Relief," *Journal of Economic History* 44 (September 1984): 810-821; Joan Underhill Hannon, "Poverty in

the Antebellum Northeast: The View from the New York State Poor Relief Rolls," *Journal of Economic History* 44 (December 1984): 1007-1032.

17. See Stuart Bruchey, *The Roots of American Economic Growth, 1607-1861: An Essay in Social Causation* (New York: Harper and Row, 1965), pp. 84-85, for a discussion of economic conditions and alterations in the structure of the marketplace.

18. David M. Schneider, *The History of Public Welfare in New York State, 1609-1866* (Chicago: University of Chicago Press, 1938), pp. 235-242.

19. Reverend William S. Coffey, "General History," chap. 8 in J. Thomas Schaft, ed., *The History of Westchester County* (2 vols.; Philadelphia: L. E. Preston & Co., 1886), 1: 477; Horatio G. Spafford, *A Gazetteer of the State of New York* (Albany, N.Y.: Southwick, 1813), p. 180; Romanah Sammis, *Huntington-Babylon Town History* (Huntington, N.Y.: Huntington Historical Society, 1937), pp. 44-57; Joshua Hartt, "Field Notes and Remarks on the Town Bounds of Huntington, Suffolk County, 1795," *Western Boundary Court of Appeals* (New York: Pondick Press, n.d.), p. 179; Huntington *American Eagle*, 12 May 1825. For a more analytical view detailing the transformation of rural life see Christopher Clark, "The Household Economy, Market Exchange, and the Rise of Capitalism in the Connecticut Valley, 1800-1860," *Journal of Social History* 13 (Winter 1979): 169-190.

20. Chapter III contains a discussion of these eighteenth-century codes. For the nineteenth century consult Charles R. Street, ed., *Huntington Town Records* (3 vols.; Huntington, N.Y.: Town of Huntington, 1887-1889), 3: 126, 279-280, 301; *Records of the Town of East Chester* (6 vols.; New York: East Chester Historical Society, 1964), 4: 192-194.

21. Quoted in Henry E. Waller, *The History of the Town of Flushing, Long Island, New York* (reprint ed.; Harrison, N.Y.: Harbor Hill Book, 1975), p. 57.

22. William Cobbett, *A Year's Residence in the United States* (reprint ed.; Carbondale: Southern Illinois University Press, 1964), pp. 120, 179. For a pictorial account of farm life on Long Island see the paintings of William Sidney Mount, Museums at Stony Brook, Stony Brook, N.Y.

23. John Harriot, *Struggles Through Life* (2 vols.; New York: Insheep and Bradford, 1809), 1: 152-155.

24. *Records of the Town of East Chester*, 4: 190-192, passim; Patrick Shirreff, *A Tour Through North America* (Edinburgh: Oliver and Boyd, 1835), Microfilm Collection, SUNY-Stony Brook, notes that Long Island laborers "occasionally absent themselves for a day or two without giving notice of their intentions" (p. 16). Also see the Farm Diary of Selah Strong, Brookhaven, 1817-1833, NYHS, passim, for the length of time laborers remained on a farm.

25. Cobbett, *A Year's Residence*, p. 23; Braudel, *Civilization and Capi-*

talism, *Fifteenth-Eighteenth Century*, vol. 1: *The Structures of Everyday Life: The Limits of the Possible*, suggests that four acres was the minimum needed to support a single individual, p. 61. This, of course, is an arbitrary figure. Poor land required more acreage to support an individual. A farmer and his family might need a minimum of forty acres, some in woodland for fuel. See Jackson T. Main, "Standards of Living and the Life Cycle in Colonial Connecticut," *Journal of Economic History* 43 (March 1983): 159-165.

26. Harriot, *Struggles Through Life*, 1: 58-59; Daniel M. Tredwell, *Personal Reminiscences of Men and Things on Long Island* (2 vols.; Brooklyn: Charles A. Ditmas, 1912), 1: 230-231, 254; Richard M. Bayles, *Historic and Descriptive Sketches of Suffolk County* (Port Jefferson, N.Y.: The Author, 1874), p. 112. Nathan Jackson, for example, was a south shore resident and later public dependent who robbed a beached ship of a rope, coffee mill, and rug in 1792. See Suffolk County Court of Session Records, ICS, reel F-283.

27. Tredwell, *Personal Reminiscences*, 1: 145.

28. Cooper, *Notions of the Americans*, 2: 371-373; Nathaniel S. Prime, *A History of Long Island from Its First Settlement by Europeans to the Year 1845* (New York: Robert Carter, 1845), pp. 100-101.

29. Silva, Inventory of Household Furniture, 19 April 1809, Smithtown, PRP, folder 74. Silva was a Brookhaven resident who settled in Smithtown, hence the inventory of her goods by Smithtown officials.

30. We still lack a detailed sketch of Indian life on Long Island for the nineteenth century. Useful material, however, can be found in Prime, *History of Long Island*, pp. 101, 118-120.

31. See my article on "White Welfare and Black Strategies: The Dynamics of Race and Poor Relief in Early New York, 1700-1825," *Slavery and Abolition* 7 (December 1986): 273-289, passim.

32. Deposition of Peter Fleet, 25 July 1828, Public Welfare Folder, HHO; Deposition of Ceasar, 26 February 1820, Public Welfare Folder, HHO; Deposition of Elijah Cooks, 27 November 1819, Public Welfare Folder, HHO. Also see Arthur Zilversmit, *The First Emancipation: The Abolition of Slavery in the North* (Chicago: University of Chicago Press, 1967), pp. 180-184.

33. Deposition of Elijah Ferris, 27 November 1819, Town Accounts Folder, HHO; Deposition of Elijah Cooks, 27 November 1819; Deposition of Peter Prince, 9 November 1820, Town Accounts Folder, HHO; Agreement of Roderic Townsend and Peter Prince, East Chester, 28 February 1818, Town Accounts Folder, HHO. The fact that some blacks had difficulty in acquiring freedom legally is attested to in court records. See Suffolk County Court of Sessions Records, reel F-284, 285, 290, 291.

34. Leon Litwack, *North of Slavery: The Negro in the Free States*,

1790-1860 (Chicago: University of Chicago Press, 1961); Zilversmit, *First Emancipation;* Ira Berlin, "The Structure of the Free Negro Caste in the Antebellum United States," *Journal of Social History* 9 (Spring 1976): 297-318; Winthrop Jordon, *White Over Black: American Attitudes Toward the Negro, 1550-1812* (Chapel Hill: Institute of Early American History and Culture, University of North Carolina Press, 1968); Leonard P. Curry, *The Free Black in Urban America, 1800-1850: The Shadow of the Dream* (Chicago: University of Chicago Press, 1981); Gary Nash, "Forging Freedom: The Emancipation Experience in Northern Seaport Cities, 1775-1820," in Ira Berlin and Ronald Hoffman, eds., *Slavery and Freedom in the Age of the American Revolution* (Charlottesville: United States Capitol Historical Society, University Press of Virginia, 1983), pp. 3-48.

35. No one to my knowldege has examined this point about households in analyzing black autonomy in rural communities. Given the dearth of source material on rural black life I consider it a useful, if crude, tool.

36. Information drawn from *Heads of Families of the First Census of the United States Taken in 1790, New York* (Washington, D.C.: Government Printing Office, 1908), pp. 163-165. It is possible that some of the people listed as "non-whites" were indeed Indians, mulattoes, or mustees, since people of the period were not always precise in their racial definitions. Whenever possible, I have adopted their usage. There is no way to be absolutely certain about whom they are referring to.

37. Deposition of Benjamin Hammond, 25 January 1821, Public Welfare Folder, HHO; Deposition of Steven Ogden, 29 November 1824, Black Slave Folder, HHO. For Jonah Mott consult the 1820 Census Population Schedules, New York, Suffolk County, Microfilm Collection, SUNY-Stony Brook.

38. See the 1820 and 1830 Census Population Schedules, New York, Suffolk County, Microfilm Collection, SUNY-Stony Brook. For a glance at the geographic distribution of the black population see Coastal Survey Map of Long Island, 1836, HHO.

39. For James Benson see Nathaniel Potter's Store Ledger, 1 April 1825, Huntington Historical Society, Huntington, N.Y.: Deposition of Lydia, 5 July 1824, Public Welfare Folder, HHO; Deposition of Elias Hearden, 27 November 1819, Public Welfare Folder, HHO.

40. Deposition of Charles Potter, 9 February 1821, Public Welfare Folder, HHO. Consult Chapter IV for information on Devine Hewlett.

41. *Heads of Families of the First Census,* p. 165; 1820 and 1830 Census Population Schedules, Suffolk and Queens; W. W. Munsell, *History of Queens County* (New York: W. W. Munsell and Co., 1882), pp. 161-162.

42. Jamaica Town Records, vol. 600, entry for 1814, ICS, reel LK, pp. 18-25, passim; Munsell, *History of Queens County,* pp. 90-91; Waller, *History of the Town of Flushing,* pp. 176-177.

NOTES TO CHAPTER V

43. Cray, "White Welfare and Black Strategies," p. 284.
44. Ibid., pp. 284–285.
45. John Cox, ed., *Oyster Bay Town Records* (8 vols.; New York: Tobias Wright, 1931), 7: 100; Munsell, *History of Queens County*, p. 489; Tredwell, *Personal Reminiscences*, 1: 12; James Riker, Jr., *The Annals of Newtown in Queens County* (New York: D. Fanshaw, 1852), p. 264 n.
46. Cray, "White Welfare and Black Strategies," p. 284; PRP folders 74 and 75.
47. Nathaniel Potter's Store Ledger, 1827, p. 448.
48. Deposition of Benjamin Johnson, 4 July 1839, Town Accounts Folder, HHO; Deposition of Cornelius Hendrickson, 15 August 1835, Town Accounts Folder, HHO; Deposition of John Van Nort, 26 November 1819, Public Welfare Folder, HHO; Deposition of Nathaniel Ketcham, Public Welfare Folder, HHO; Deposition of Guy William Augustine Hait, 26 November 1819, Public Welfare Folder, HHO; Deposition of Charles Cuthing, 18 April 1820, Public Welfare Folder, HHO; Examination of Jeremiah Terry, 24 April 1824, PRP, folder 74; Examination of Alexander Raynor, 24 February 1826, PRP, folder 75; Examination of Henry Nicols, 4 April 1843, PRP, folder 75.
49. Deposition of Stephen Nicolls, 18 June 1823, Public Welfare Folder, HHO; Deposition of Samuel Conkling, 1823, Public Welfare Folder, HHO; Deposition of Stephen Stratten, 16 October 1819, Town Accounts Folder, HHO.
50. Overseers of the Poor Book, 1805–1862, HHO, entries for 1823 and 1824.
51. Deposition of John Stiverson, 12 January 1832, 9 May 1834, Public Welfare Folder, HHO.
52. Thomas Dublin, *Women at Work: The Formation of Work and Community in Lowell, Massachusetts, 1826–1860* (New York: Columbia University Press, 1979); Kessler-Harris, *Out to Work*. For a good overview of where the field of women's history is headed see Nancy Wolock, *Women and the American Experience* (New York: Alfred A. Knopf, 1984).
53. Deposition of Sabrina Worth, 28 August 1835, Town Accounts Folder, HHO; Deposition of Fanny Frost, 12 October 1830, Town Accounts Folder, HHO.
54. Justice Order for the Support of Margaret Ludlow, 13 April 1811, PRP, folder 74; Order of Removal of Jane Butler, 9 June 1820, Southampton, PRP, folder 74.
55. Deposition of Nancy Hallek, 12 January 1823, Public Welfare Folder, HHO; Examination of Phebe Davis, 16 August 1806, PRP, folder 74.
56. Deposition of Catherine L'Homedine, 7 July 1823, Public Welfare Folder, HHO.
57. Deposition of Hannah Whitman, 15 March 1821, Public Welfare

Folder, HHO. Useful works on illegitimacy and pre-marital pregnancies include Robert Gross, *The Minutemen and Their World* (New York: Hill and Wang, 1976), pp. 100, 106, 181-182, 184-185; Michael Hindus and Daniel Scott-Smith, "Premarital Pregnancy in America, 1640-1971: An Overview and Interpretation," *Journal of Interdisciplinary History* 4 (Spring 1975): 537-570. Some of the best work on bastardy comes from England; see Peter Laslett, "The Bastardy Prone Sub-Society," in Peter Laslett, Karla Oosterveen, and Richard M. Smith, eds., *Bastardy and Its Comparative History* (Cambridge, Mass.: Harvard University Press, 1980), pp. 217-246.

58. Deposition of Lydia, 5 July 1824, Public Welfare Folder, HHO. Other data are also drawn from the Public Welfare Folder, HHO. For a look at black attitudes toward illegitimacy see Herbert G. Gutman, *Black Family in Slavery and Freedom, 1750-1925* (New York: Pantheon, 1976), pp. 73-75, 117-118.

59. See Peter Clark, "The Migrant in Kentish Towns, 1580-1640," in Peter Clark and Paul Slack, eds., *Crisis and Order in English Towns, 1500-1700* (Toronto: University of Toronto Press, 1972), pp. 117-163, passim, for a discussion of betterment and subsistence forms of migration.

60. Timothy Dwight, *Travels in New England and New York* (4 vols.; New Haven, Conn.: The Author, 1822), 3: 283-286, passim. On Westchester towns consult Robert Bolton, Jr., *A History of the Several Towns, Manors, and Patents of the County of Westchester from Its First Settlement to the Present Time* (2 vols.; New York: A. S. Gould, 1848).

61. Reverend Jenny to Secretary, SPG, 27 June 1728, Hempstead, N.Y., SPG Letter Books, Letter ser. A, vol. 21, Microfilm Collection, SUNY-Stony Brook, p. 346.

62. Prime, *History of Long Island*, p. 52.

63. Sojourner Truth, *The Narrative of Sojournor Truth: A Northern Slave* (Boston: The Author, 1850), Microprint Collection, SUNY-Stony Brook, pp. 100-104.

64. Deposition of John Thuilby, 25 June 1825, Public Welfare Folder, HHO; Deposition of Joseph Still, 19 November 1834, Town Accounts Folder, HHO.

65. Deposition of George Tigney, 8 October 1831, Town Accounts Folder, HHO; Deposition of Jeremiah Haff, 14 October 1823, Public Welfare Folder, HHO; Deposition of Richard Jones, 3 November 1823, Public Welfare Folder, HHO; Deposition of Platt Jones, 10 February 1820, Public Welfare Folder, HHO; Deposition of Ceasar, 26 February 1820; Deposition of David Helms, 24 November 1820, Public Welfare Folder, HHO.

66. Data drawn from PRP, folder 74.

67. See A. Gordon Darrock, "Migrants in the Nineteenth Century: Fugitives or Families in Motion," *Journal of Family History* 6 (Fall 1981):

257-277. Local migration was also typical of eighteenth-century migrants in New England; see Jones, "The Strolling Poor," pp. 39-40.

68. Deposition of Eneas Cook, 26 November 1819, Public Welfare Folder, HHO; Deposition of Elijah Smith, 26 November 1819, Public Welfare Folder, HHO; Deposition of Samuel Conkling, 1823; Deposition of Conkling Wicks, 20 May 1823, Public Welfare Folder, HHO; Examination of Catherine Nicolls and her child, 3 October 1821, New York City, PRP, folder 75; Order of Removal of Catherine Nicolls 28 August 1824, PRP, folder 75. Dwight claims that migrants from Long Island formed a "considerable proportion" of those who headed to Manhattan (*Travels in New England and New York*, 3: 469).

69. Deposition of John Thuilby, 25 June 1825.

70. Examination of James Martin, 9 March 1825, PRP, folder 75.

71. For social and economic conditions in northern New York State see Philip L. White, *Beekmantown, New York: Forest Frontier to Farm Community* (Austin: University of Texas Press, 1979). Also see Eric H. Monkkonen, ed., *Walking to Work: Tramps in America, 1790-1935* (Lincoln: University of Nebraska 1984), for a discussion of different kinds of strolling poor.

72. Deposition of Richard Haply, 30 November 1838, Town Accounts Folder, HHO; Deposition of Jarvis Smith, 9 October 1837, Public Welfare Folder, HHO; Deposition of Stephen Nicolls, 18 June 1823. It is perhaps significant that Nicolls purchased his Islip property from his father-in-law. He may have returned purposely to Long Island to marry.

73. Deposition of Jarvis Smith, 9 October 1837.

74. Deposition of James Riggs, 9 January 1835, Town Accounts Folder, HHO.

75. No account describes the transformation of the rural economy on Long Island adequately. One of the best sources for New York, however, is Stuart Blumin, *The Urban Threshold: Growth and Change in a Nineteenth-Century American Community* (Chicago: University of Chicago Press, 1976).

76. Farm Diary of Selah Strong, NYHS, reveals that farm laborers often moved on after a few weeks or months.

77. Information derived from poor relief records in Huntington and Brookhaven.

78. We have no decent study of Long Island's black community for this period. For information on this topic see Prime, *History of Long Island*, pp. 118-119, 416-417.

CHAPTER VI

1. Ezra Stiles Ely, *The Journal of the Stated Preacher to the Hospital and Almshouse in the City of New York, 1811* (New York: Whiting and Watson, 1812), p. 87.

2. Samuel L. Mitchell, *The Picture of New York, or the Traveler's Guide Through the Commercial Metropolis of the United States* (New York: I. Ripley and Co., 1807), p. 122.

3. Raymond A. Mohl, *Poverty in New York, 1783-1825* (New York: Oxford University Press, 1971), mentions the existence of the foreign poor but does not go into detail in regard to their growth or decline over time in the almshouse.

4. Almshouse Censuses, Almshouse Folder, 1805, 1813, 1814, 1815, 1818, 1826, 1828, 1830, City Clerk's Files, NYMA, for the number of foreign poor during these years.

5. Samuel Griscomb Diary, 1824, Microfilm Collection, NYHS, p. 27; Ely, *Journal of the Stated Preacher,* p. 86; John Stanford, "Annual Report, 1826, to the Honorable the Mayor and Common Council of the City of New York on the Subject of Religious Services Performed at the Almshouse, Penitentiary, Bellevue Hospital, Debtors' Prison, and the Bridewell," 1827, NYHS, p. 6.

6. Information derived from censuses located in Almshouse Folders, City Clerk's Files, NYMA

7. *Minutes of the Common Council of the City of New York, 1784-1831* (21 vols.; New York: City of New York, 1917), 8: 765; Robert G. Albion, *The Rise of the Port of New York, 1815-1860* (New York: Charles Scribner's Sons, 1939), remains the classic account of the period in this regard.

8. James Stuart, *Three Years in America* (Edinburgh: Robert Cadell, 1833), Microfilm Collection, SUNY-Stony Brook, p. 25; John Palmer, *Journals of the Travels of the United States and Lower Canada* (London: Sherwood, Neely, and Jones, 1818), Microfilm Collection, SUNY-Stony Brook, p. 175; Diary of an Unknown Scot, 1821-1824, 3 vols., NYHS, 1: 104-105.

9. It is perhaps significant that wards with large foreign elements also had proportionately more mechanics than merchants residing in them. This would be an indication of a less well-to-do neighborhood. See Horatio G. Spafford, *Gazetteer of the State of New York* (Albany, N.Y.: B. D. Packard, 1824), p. 312.

10. See Carol Gronemen Pernicorn, "The Bloody Ould Sixth: A Social Analysis of a New York City Working-Class Community in the Mid-Nineteenth Century," Ph.D. diss., University of Rochester, 1973.

11. Discharge, Admission, and Deaths, 1826-1829, vol. 146, Almshouse Records, NYMA, entry for December 1826.

12. Ibid. The percentage of people labeled as foreign would have risen from 28 percent to 33 percent if the offspring had been included with the parents in the December 1826 tally ("Report of the Committee Visiting the Almshouse," 9 November 1819, Almshouse Folder, City Clerk's Files, NYMA).

13. William Cobbett, *A Year's Residence in the United States* (reprint ed.; Carbondale: Southern Illinois University Press, 1964), p. 204. For the elimination of overseas removal see Mohl, *Poverty in New York*, pp. 60-61. Also consult Benjamin J. Klebaner, "State and Local Immigration Regulation in the United States Before 1882," *International Review of Social History* 3 (1958): 272-273.

14. Information derived from the Almshouse Censuses, 1805, 1813, 1814, 1815, 1818, 1824, 1826, 1828, 1830. All of these can be found in the Almshouse Folder, City Clerk's Files, NYMA, with the exception of the 1824 census located in *Minutes of the Common Council*, 13: 739.

15. Ibid.

16. Ely, *Journal of the Stated Preacher*, pp. 95, 239. For an understanding of Ely's missionary philosophy toward the poor in general see Caroll Smith-Rosenberg, *Religion and the Rise of the City: The New York City Mission Movement, 1812-1870* (Ithaca, N.Y.: Cornell University Press, 1971), p. 53.

17. Kirby A. Miller, *Emigrants and Exiles: Ireland and the Irish Exodus to North America* (New York: Oxford University Press, 1985), pp. 193-279, passim; Lynn Hollen Lees, *Exiles of Erin: Irish Migrants in Victorian London* (Ithaca, N.Y.: Cornell University Press, 1979), pp. 22-38. Also see Karl S. Bottigheimer, *Ireland and the Irish: A Short History* (New York: Columbia University Press, 1982).

18. Robert Ernst, *Immigrant Life in New York City, 1825-1863* (reprint ed.; Port Washington, N.Y.: Ira J. Friedman, 1965), app. 2, table 8, p. 187; H. J. M. Johnson, *British Emigration Policy, 1815-1830: Shovelling Out Paupers* (New York: Oxford University Press, 1972), p. 25; David M. Schneider, *The History of Public Welfare in New York State, 1609-1866* (Chicago: University of Chicago Press, 1938), pp. 132-133; *Minutes of the Common Council*, 13: 304-306; Klebaner, "State and Local Immigration," p. 273 n. 2. Also see William Forbes Adams, *Ireland and the Irish Emigration to the New World from 1815 to the Famine* (reprint ed.; New York: Russell and Russell, 1967).

19. Sidney I. Pomerantz, *New York, an American City, 1783-1803: A Study of Urban Life* (New York: Columbia University Press, 1938), pp. 203-204; F. S. Eastman, *History of the State of New York* (New York: Augustus K. White, 1832), pp. 382-384, supplied a biographical account of Thomas Addis Emmet.

20. Diary of Unknown Scot, 1: 105; Adams, *Ireland and Irish Emigration*, pp. 37-41, 54, 114; Miller, *Emigrants and Exiles*, pp. 194-198; Karl Bern-

hard, Duke of Saxe Keimor Eisenach, *Travels Through North America During the Years 1825-1826* (2 vols.; Philadelphia: Carey, Lea, and Carey, 1828), Microfilm Collection, SUNY-Stony Brook, 1: 126; E. S. Abdy, *Journal of a Residence and Tour in the United States of North America from April 1833 to October 1834* (3 vols.; London: John Murray, 1835), Microfilm Collection, SUNY-Stony Brook, 1: 66-69.

21. Howard Rock, *Artisans of the New Republic: The Tradesmen of New York City in the Age of Jefferson* (New York: New York University Press, 1979), pp. 224-226; John W. Pratt, *Religion, Politics, and Diversity: The Church-State Theme in New York History* (Ithaca, N.Y.: Cornell University Press, 1967), pp. 122-129; James Richardson, *New York City Police Force from Colonial Times to 1901* (New York: Oxford University Press, 1970), p. 14.

22. Mohl, *Poverty in New York*, pp. 154-157; Edmund Blunt, *The Stranger's Guide to the City of New York* (London: Samuel Laight, 1818), Microfilm Collection SUNY-Stony Brook, p. 186. For information on the pre-famine Irish community of Manhattan see John J. Lenehan, "The Society of the Friendly Sons of St. Patrick for the City of New York," *Journal of the American Irish Historical Society* 8 (1909): 183-194; William V. Shannon, *The American Irish* (New York: Macmillan Co., 1963). Maldwin A. Jones, "Ulster Emigration, 1783-1815," in E. R. R. Green, ed., *Essays in Scotch Irish History* (London: Routledge and Kegan Paul, 1969), pp. 46-68, notes that "group consciousness" existed between Catholics and Protestants until the Catholic Emancipation issue of the 1820s in England revived old animosities between the two in the New World.

23. Jay Dolan, *The Immigrant Church: New York's Irish and German Catholics, 1815-1865* (Baltimore: Johns Hopkins University Press, 1975), pp. 36-37, 69, 89-92. Dolan also claims that the Irish American community was not self-sufficient in terms of social organizations until the 1830s (p. 21). Also see Mohl, *Poverty in New York*, pp. 156-157; Seamus P. Metress, "The History of Irish American Care of the Aged," *Social Service Review* 59 (March 1985): 18-31.

24. Schneider, *History of Public Welfare*, p. 137; Mohl, *Poverty in New York*, p. 154.

25. Charlotte Erickson, *Invisible Immigrants: The Adaption of English and Scottish Immigrants in Nineteenth-Century America* (Coral Gables, Fla.: University of Miami Press, 1972); Ernst, *Immigrant Life in New York City*, p. 66.

26. Mohl, *Poverty in New York*, p. 151; "Committee of the Society for the Relief of the Unfortunate French Refugees," 12 July 1813, Charity Folder, City Clerk's Files, NYMA; "Committee of French Benevolent Society of the City of New York," 22 December 1814, Charity Folder, City Clerk's Files,

NYMA. Also see Almshouse Censuses, 1813, 1814, Almshouse Folder, City Clerk's Files, NYMA.

27. Mohl, *Poverty in New York*, p. 151; "Petition of the Committee of the Administration of the Frenchmen's Benevolent Society of the City of New York," 22 May 1829, Almshouse Folder, City Clerk's Files, NYMA. Also see Frances S. Childs, *French Refugee Life in the United States* (Baltimore: Johns Hopkins University Press, 1940), p. 67.

28. Hyman B. Grinstein, *The Rise of the Jewish Community of New York, 1654-1860* (reprint ed.; Philadelphia: Porcupine Press, 1976), pp. 133-136, 139, 142-145, 150 n. 1.

29. Poverty also prevented many Irish immigrants from leaving the city, unlike some of the Germans; see Everett S. Lee and Michael Lalli, "Population," in David T. Gilchrist, ed., *The Growth of Seaport Cities* (Charlottesville: University Press of Virginia, 1967), p. 49.

30. Mitchell, *Picture of New York*, p. 122.

31. See James T. Lemon, *The Best Poor Man's Country: A Geographic Study of Early Southeastern Pennsylvania* (Baltimore: Johns Hopkins University Press, 1972); Allen R. Pred, *Urban Growth and the Circulation of Information: The United States System of Cities, 1790-1840* (Cambridge, Mass.: Harvard University Press, 1973), for a discussion of city and countryside and the impact of urban centers on population growth in the countryside. For the population figures of New York City and its nearby countryside consult the *Fifth Census of the United States, 1830* (Washington, D.C.: Duff Green, 1832).

32. For examples of destitute mothers from the countryside giving birth in the almshouse consult Almshouse Records, vol. 146, NYMA; Ely, *Journal of the Stated Preacher*, pp. 85-86; Almshouse Folder, 1806, City Clerk's Files, NYMA.

33. Schneider, *History of Public Welfare*, pp. 235-240. For the number of people transported consult Table 6.

34. *Minutes of the Common Council*, 8: 765; Cobbett, *A Year's Residence*, p. 61.

35. Figures derived from Queens County Records, vol. 517, ICS, reel ME. Also see David Montgomery, "The Working Classes of the Pre-Industrial City, 1780-1830," *Labor History* 9 (Winter 1968): 3-32, passim, on the mobility of the working class.

36. Albion, *Rise of the Port of New York*, contains information about the development of the city and its transportation system to the countryside.

37. Rock, *Artisans of the New Republic*, p. 243; Citizenship Folder, 1812, 1813, City Clerk's Files, NYMA; Timothy Dwight, *Travels in New England and New York* (4 vols.; New Haven, Conn.: The Author, 1822), 3: 469.

38. Information derived from Register of Persons Transported or Re-

NOTES TO CHAPTER VI

moved, 1808-1811, Vessel Book, vol. 089, Almshouse Records, NYMA.

39. Ibid.

40. Ibid.

41. Taverns probably furnished safe quarters for many non-residents, as did some of the poorer and more notorious neighborhoods of the city.

42. There were 282 families and individuals sent out of state compared to 149 who were removed to in-state locations. See Register of Persons Transported or Removed, NYMA.

43. Douglas L. Jones, *Village and Seaport: Migration and Society in Eighteenth-Century Massachusetts* (Hanover, N.H., and New London, Conn.: University Press of New England, 1981); Everett S. Lee, "A Theory of Migration," *Demography* 3 (1966): 47-57. In terms of men being removed compared to women out of state there were fifty-four single men as compared to thirty single women sent to Philadelphia.

44. Benjamin Strong to Thomas Strong, 21 March 1804, Strong Family Papers, 1790-1839, NYHS. For insight into the geographic mobility of rural women consult Diary of Mary Guion, 1800-1852, NYHS. The social visits of urban women are treated by Nancy Tomes, "The Quaker Connection: Visiting Patterns Among Women in the Philadelphia Society of Friends, 1730-1800," in Michael Zuckerman, ed., *Friends and Neighbors: Group Life in America's First Plural Society* (Philadelphia: Temple University Press, 1982), pp. 174-195.

45. A. Gordon Darrock, "Migrants in the Nineteenth Century: Fugitives or Families in Motion," *Journal of Family History* 6 (Fall 1981): 257-277, passim, notes that most migration took place in a family setting, with female servants often being exchanged among relatives and friends. Also see Register of Persons Transported or Removed, NYMA.

46. Abdy, *Journal of a Residence*, p. 66; Mahlan Day, *New York Street Cries in Rhyme* (reprint ed.; New York: Dover Press, 1977), p. 18.

47. Leonard P. Curry, *The Free Black in Urban America, 1800-1850: The Shadow of the Dream* (Chicago: University of Chicago Press, 1981), pp. 18-19; Leo Hirsh, "The Negro and New York, 1783-1865," *Journal of Negro History* 16 (October 1931): 384-436; Abdy, *Journal of a Residence*, pp. 46-47; Ernst, *Immigrant Life in New York City*, p. 71.

48. Among the remaining slaves black females outnumbered black males in all ten wards; see New York City Census, 1813, Census Folder, City Clerk's Files, NYMA.

49. *Minutes of the Common Council*, 4: 577; figures drawn from Register of Persons Transported or Removed, NYMA.

50. Curry, *Free Black*, pp. 113-115; Abdy, *Journal of a Residence*, pp. 46-47. It is difficult to determine correctly how many blacks entered the city until the Federal Census of 1850. Ira Rosenwaite, *The Population History of New York City* (Syracuse, N.Y.: Syracuse University Press, 1972), p. 32,

NOTES TO CHAPTER VI

contends that blacks from Long Island and Staten Island did migrate into the city quite regularly during the 1820s. By contrast the city of Boston did not have a noticeable group of incoming black migrants until 1830. See Peter Knights, *The Plain People of Boston, 1830-1860; A Study in City Growth* (New York: Oxford University Press, 1971), pp. 28-30.

51. Edgar J. McManus, *A History of Negro Slavery in New York*, with a foreword by Richard B. Morris (Syracuse, N.Y.: Syracuse University Press, 1966), pp. 187-188; Curry, *Free Black* p. 83.

52. *Minutes of the Common Council*, 11: 440; Curry, *Free Black*, notes that one-fifth of the black population of Bancker Street lived in cellars (pp. 50-51).

53. Figures derived from 1756 colonial census in McManus, *History of Negro Slavery*, p. 198; Hirsh, "The Negro and New York," p. 415; Curry, *Free Black*, p. 137.

54. Cobbett, *A Year's Residence*, p. 204; Diary of an Unknown Scot, 1:156-157; *Minutes of the Common Council*, 4: 368, 5: 192, 10: 52-53.

55. Percentages drawn from Almshouse Census, Almshouse Folder, 1806, City Clerk's Files, NYMA.

56. New York City Census, 1813, Census Folder, 1813, City Clerk's Files, NYMA. The Census of 1821 can be found in Spafford, *Gazetteer of the State of New York*, p. 352; Curry, *Free Black*, p. 4.

57. Curry, *Free Black*, p. 124.

58. Ibid., p. 200; Daniel Perman, "Organizations of the Free Negroes in New York City, 1800-1820," *Journal of Negro History* 56 (July 1971): 181-197.

59. Almshouse Censuses, Almshouse Folders, 1814, 1815, City Clerk's Files, NYMA.

60. The almshouse also segregated blacks from whites, which may have been another reason why blacks avoided the structure, especially since they were put in the basement. See Mohl, *Poverty in New York*, p. 93.

61. Ibid., pp. 132-143, 155, passim; Smith-Rosenberg, *Religion and the Rise of the American City*, pp. 97-124, passim; M. J. Heale, "From City Fathers to Social Critics: Humanitarianism and Government in New York, 1790-1860," *Journal of American History* 63 (June 1976): 21-41.

62. "Petition of Elizabeth Burnes, 1803, Charity Folder, City Clerk's Files, NYMA, Petition of Jonathan Seamen, 22 May 1815, Charity Folder, City Clerk's Files, NYMA. For an added insight into poor women and the almshouse see Christine Stansell, *City of Women: Sex and Class in New York, 1789-1860* (New York: Alfred A. Knopf, 1986).

63. *Minutes of the Common Council*, 4: 701.

64. Mohl, *Poverty in New York*, pp. 103-104; Dwight, *Travels in New England and New York*, 3: 458. Compare the entries from the Account Book of Cash Distributed to the Poor, 1809-1816, Almshouse Records, vol.

0383, NYMA, with the Records of Admissions, Discharges, and Death, vol. 160. Both list aged and sick people. Evidence that some of the poor may have avoided being incarcerated is revealed in an official's comment next to the name of Hugh Cannon, 25 June 1810: "Not home to come to the House." Perhaps Cannon stayed away from home to avoid being put into the almshouse. See Account Book of Cash Distributed to the Poor, 25 June 1810.

Selected Bibliography

PRIMARY SOURCES

Unpublished Documents

Various source materials proved useful for this study. Any student interested in public welfare should first consult the holdings of the Municipal Archives of the City of New York. Here can be found official accounts and reports on the poor, many of them in the city clerk's files of the Common Council. There is also a separate section of records pertaining directly to the almshouse. This had admission, discharge, and death records for the inmates of the almshouse as well as cash amounts of assistance given to them. Removal records for the poor during the early nineteenth century can be found here, too. The Manuscript Room of the New York Public Library has valuable records, in particular, the Minutes of the Commissioners of the Almshouse and Bridewell, 1791-1797, and the Minutes of the Justices, Churchwardens, and Vestrymen, 1694-1747. The New York Historical Society has useful material dealing with the rules and regulations of the almshouse and official reports in its broadside collection. The Society's holdings, moreover, prove useful for detailing the social and economic characteristics of the city and the countryside.

Smaller but no less valuable collections away from the city helped in the writing of this manuscript. I benefited from the records of the Bedford Town Clerk's Office, the Brookhaven Town Clerk's Office, Patchogue, and the Hempstead Town Clerk's Office; each of them has fairly complete collections of welfare records for either the eighteenth or nineteenth century. The Huntington Town Historian's Office possesses a very full set of welfare-related records. The legal depositions of the poor for the early nineteenth century aided significantly in sketching a portrait of the poor in the countryside. Useful material can also be found in the Long Island Room of the Smithtown Public Library and the East Hampton Free Library. No less important is the material in the Institute of Colonial Studies

248 SELECTED BIBLIOGRAPHY

at the Ward Melville Library of the State University of New York at Stony Brook. This microfilm collection, which includes unpublished town records, tax lists, and court records, remains a treasure trove for the discerning researcher on Long Island history.

Published Documents

Bedford Historical Records. 5 vols. Bedford Hills, N.Y.: Town of Bedford, 1966-1976.
The Colonial Laws of the State of New York from the Year 1664 to the Revolution. 5 vols. Albany, N.Y.: J. B. Lyon, 1894.
Corwin, Edward T., ed. *Ecclesiastical Records of the State of New York.* 7 vols. Albany, N.Y.: J. B. Lyon, 1901-1916.
Cox, John, ed. *Oyster Bay Town Records.* 8 vols. New York: Tobias Wright, 1931.
Downs, Arthur C., ed. *Riverhead Town Records, 1792-1886.* Huntington, N.Y.: Long Islander, 1967.
East Hampton Trustees Journal. 7 vols. East Hampton, N.Y.: No publ., 1926-1927.
Forbes, Jeanne A., ed. *Records of the Town of New Rochelle, 1699-1828.* New York: Paragraph Press, 1916.
Force, Peter, ed. *American Archives: A Documentary History.* 9 vols. Washington, D.C.: M. St. Clair and Peter Force, 1837-1854.
Hicks, Benjamin D., ed. *The Records of North and South Hempstead.* 8 vols. Jamaica, N.Y.: Long Island Farmer Print, 1896-1904.
Historical Records, North Castle/New Castle: Colonial History and Minutes of the Town Meetings. 2 vols. Armonk and Chappaqua, N.Y.: Towns of North Castle and New Castle, 1975, 1977.
Jameson, J. Franklin, ed. *Narratives of New Netherland.* New York: Charles Scribner's Sons, 1909.
Jaray, Cornell, ed. *Historical Chronicles of New Amsterdam, Colonial New York, and Early Long Island.* 2 vols. 2nd ser. Port Washington, N.Y.: Ira J. Friedman, 1968.
Journal of the Provincial Congress, Provincial Convention, Committee of Safety, and Council of Safety of the State of New York. 2 vols. Albany, N.Y.: T. Weed, 1847.
Minutes of the Common Council of the City of New York, 1784-1831. 21 vols. New York: City of New York, 1917.
New York in the Revolution as Colony and State. 2 vols. Albany, N.Y.: J. B. Lyon, 1904.
O'Callaghan, E. B., ed. *Documentary History of the State of New York.* 4 vols. Albany, N.Y.: Weed, Parson, and Co., 1850-1851.
O'Callaghan, E. B., and Berthold Fernow, eds., and John Brodhead, comp.

SELECTED BIBLIOGRAPHY 249

Documents Relative to the Colonial History of the State of New York. 15 vols. Albany, N.Y.: Weed, Parson, and Co., 1856-1887.
Osgood, Herbert, et al., eds. *Minutes of the Common Council of the City of New York.* 8 vols. New York: Dodd, Mead, and Co., 1905.
Pelletreau, William S., ed. *Records of the Town of Smithtown.* Smithtown, N.Y.: Town of Smithtown, 1898.
Records of the Town of Brookhaven, bk. C: *1687-1789.* New York: Derrydale Press, 1931.
Records of the Town of Brookhaven, 1798-1856. Port Jefferson, N.Y.: Steam Job Print., 1888.
Records of the Town of Brookhaven Up to 1800. Patchogue, N.Y.: Office of the Advance, 1880.
Records of the Town of East Chester. 6 vols. East Chester, N.Y.: East Chester Historical Society, 1964.
Records of the Town of East Hampton. 5 vols. Sag Harbor, N.Y.: John R. Hunt, 1887-1905.
Street, Charles R., ed. *Huntington Town Records.* 3 vols. Huntington, N.Y.: Town of Huntington, 1887-1889.
Southold Town Records, vol. 3: *1683-1856.* Southold, N.Y.: Town of Southold, 1983.

Newspapers

Huntington, *American Eagle*
Huntington, *Portico*
Mount Pleasant, *Westchester Herald*
New York Gazette
New York Mercury
New York Evening Post

Journals, Diaries, Travel Accounts, Reports

Abdy, E. S. *Journal of a Residence and Tour in the United States of North America from April 1833 to October 1834.* 3 vols. London: John Murray, 1835.
Bernhard, Karl, Duke of Saxe Weimer Eisenach. *Travels Through North America During the Years 1825-1826.* 2 vols. Philadelphia: Carey, Lea, and Carey, 1828.
Blunt, Edmund. *The Stranger's Guide to the City of New York.* London: Samuel Laight, 1818.
Burnaby, Reverend Andrew. *Travels Through the Middle Settlements of North America, 1759-1760.* 3rd ed. London: T. Payne, 1798.
Chipman, Samuel, *Report of an Examination of Poor Houses, Jails, etc.,*

in the State of New York. 4th ed. Albany: New York State Temperance Society, 1836.
Cobbett, William. *A Year's Residence in the United States.* Reprint ed. Carbondale: Southern Illinois University Press, 1964.
Cooper, James Fenimore, *Notions of the Americans.* 2 vols. London: Henry Colburn, 1828.
Crevecoeur, Michael G. St. John. *Letters from an American Farmer.* Gloucester, Mass.: Peter Smith, 1968.
Denton, Daniel. *A Brief Description of New York, 1670.* Ann Arbor, Mich.: University Microfilms, 1966.
Dwight, Timothy. *Travels in New England and New York.* 4 vols. New Haven, Conn.: The Author, 1822.
―――. *Travels in New England and New York,* ed. Barbara M. Schoman. 4 vols. Cambridge, Mass.: Belknap Press of Harvard University Press, 1969.
Ely, Ezra Stiles. *The Journal of the Stated Preacher to the Hospital and Almshouse in the City of New York, 1811.* New York: Whiting and Watson, 1812.
French, J. H. *Gazetteer of the State of New York, 1860.* Syracuse, N.Y.: R. Pearsall Smith, 1860.
Hamilton, Dr. Alexander. *The Itinerarium of Doctor Alexander Hamilton, 1744,* ed. Carl T. Bridenbaugh. Chapel Hill: Institute of Early American History, University of North Carolina Press, 1948.
Harriot, James. *Struggles Through Life.* 2 vols. New York: Insheep and Bradford, 1809.
Hempstead, Joshua. *Diary of Joshua Hempstead, September 1711 to November 1758.* New London, Conn.: New London Historical Society, 1901.
Jeremy, David J., ed. *Henry Wansey and His American Journal, 1794.* Philadelphia: American Philosophical Society, 1971.
Kalm, Peter. *Peter Kalm's Travels in North America,* ed. Adolph B. Benson. 2 vols. New York: Dover Press, 1966.
Knight, Sarah Kemble. *Private Journal of Sarah Kemble Knight, 1704.* Reprint ed. Norwich, Conn.: Academy Press, 1901.
Lambert, John. *Travels Through Canada and the United States of North America in the Years 1806, 1807, 1808.* 3 vols. London: Richard Phillips, 1810.
Livingston, William, et al. *The Independent Reflector, or Weekly Essays on Sundry Important Subjects More Particularly Adapted to the Province of New York, by William Livingston and Others,* ed. Milton M. Klein. Cambridge, Mass.: Belknap Press of Harvard University Press, 1963.
Miller, John. *New York Considered and Improved, 1695,* with an intro. by Hugo Paltsits. New York: Burt Franklin, 1970.

Mitchell, Samuel L. *The Picture of New York, or the Traveler's Guide Through the Commercial Metropolis of the United States.* New York: I. Ripley and Co., 1807.
M'Roberts, Patrick. *Tour Through Part of the Northern Province of America, 1774-1775,* ed. Carl T. Bridenbaugh. Reprint ed. New York: Arno Press, 1965.
Palmer, John. *Journals of the Travels of the United States and Lower Canada.* London: Sherwood, Neely, and Jones, 1818.
Shirreff, Patrick. *A Tour Through North America.* Edinburgh: Oliver and Boyd, 1835.
Spafford, Horatio G. *A Gazetteer of the State of New York.* Albany, N.Y.: B. D. Packard, 1824.
Strickland, William. *Journal of a Tour in the United States of America, 1794-1795,* ed. J. E. Strickland. New York: New York Historical Society, 1971.
Stuart, James. *Three Years in America.* Edinburgh: Robert Cadell, 1833.
Truth, Sojournor. *The Narrative of Sojournor Truth: A Northern Slave.* Boston: The Author, 1850.

SECONDARY SOURCES

Abbot, Carl. "The Neighborhoods of New York." *New York History* 55 (January 1974): 33-54.
Abramovitz, Mimi. "The Family Ethic: The Female Pauper and Public Aid, pre-1900." *Social Service Review* 59 (March 1985): 121-135.
Adams, William Forbes. *Ireland and Irish Emigration to the New World from 1815 to the Famine.* Reprint ed. New York: Russell and Russell, 1967.
Albion, Robert G. *The Rise of the Port of New York, 1815-1860.* New York: Charles Scribner's Sons, 1939.
Alexander, John K. *Render Them Submissive: Responses to Poverty in Philadelphia, 1760-1800.* Amherst: University of Massachusetts Press, 1980.
Andrews, Wayne, ed. "A Glance at New York in 1697: The Travel Diary of Dr. Benjamin Bullivant." *New York Historical Society Quarterly* 40 (January 1956): 55-73.
Archdeacon, Thomas J. *New York City, 1664-1710: Conquest and Change.* Ithaca, N.Y.: Cornell University Press, 1976.
Bailey, Paul, ed. *Long Island: A History of Two Great Counties.* 2 vols. New York: Lewis Historical Publishing Co., 1949.
Baird, Charles W. *The History of Rye: Chronicle of a Border Town.* New York: Anson D. F. Randolph and Co., 1871.

SELECTED BIBLIOGRAPHY

Barck, Oscar Theodore. *New York City During the War for Independence.* New York: Columbia University Press, 1931.
Bayles, Richard M. *Historical and Descriptive Sketches of Suffolk County.* Port Jefferson, N.Y.: The Author, 1874.
Becker, E. Marie. "The 801 Westchester County Freeholders of 1763." *New York Historical Society Quarterly* 25 (July 1951): 283-321.
Bernhard, Virginia. "Poverty and the Social Order in Seventeenth-Century Virginia." *Virginia Magazine of History and Biography* 85 (April 1977): 141-155.
Berrian, Reverend William. *An Historical Sketch of Trinity Church, New York.* New York: Stanford and Swords, 1847.
Bidwell, Percy W., and John I. Falconer. *The History of Agriculture in the Northern United States, 1620-1860.* New York: Peter Smith, 1941.
Blumin, Stuart. *The Urban Threshold: Growth and Change in a Nineteenth-Century American Community.* Chicago: University of Chicago Press, 1976.
Bolton, Robert, Jr. *A History of the Protestant Episcopal Church in the County of Westchester.* New York: Stanford and Swords, 1855.
——. *A History of the Several Towns, Manors, and Patents of the County of Westchester from Its First Settlement to the Present Time.* 2 vols. New York: A. S. Gould, 1848.
Bonomi, Patricia U. *A Factious People: Politics and Society in Colonial New York.* New York: Columbia University Press, 1971.
Booth, Mary L. *History of the City of New York.* New York: W. R. C. Clark, 1867.
Bottigheimer, Karl S. *Ireland and the Irish: A Short History.* New York: Columbia University Press, 1982.
Branscombe, Martha. *The Courts and the Poor Laws in New York State, 1784-1929.* Chicago: University of Chicago Press, 1943.
Braudel, Fernand. *Civilization and Capitalism, Fifteenth-Eighteenth Century,* vol. 1: *The Structures of Everyday Life: The Limits of the Possible,* trans. Sian Reynolds. New York: Harper and Row, 1982.
——. *Civilization and Capitalism, Fifteenth and Eighteenth Century,* vol. 2: *The Wheels of Commerce,* trans. Sian Reynolds. New York: Harper and Row, 1982.
Bridenbaugh, Carl T. *Cities in the Wilderness: The First Century of Urban Life in America, 1625-1742.* New York: Oxford University Press, 1938.
——. *Cities in Revolt: Urban Life in America, 1743-1775.* New York: Alfred A. Knopf, 1955.
Bristol, Theresa H. "Westchester County, New York, Miscellanea." *New York Historical and Genealogical Record* 49 (January 1928): 66-88.
Brown, Richard D. *Modernization: The Transformation of American Life, 1600-1865.* New York: Hill and Wang, 1976.

Bruchey, Stuart. *The Roots of American Economic Growth, 1607-1861: An Essay in Social Causation.* New York: Harper and Row, 1965.
Butler, Jon. *The Huguenots in America: A Refugee People in New World Society.* Cambridge, Mass.: Harvard University Press, 1983.
Chambers, Clark A. "Toward a Redefinition of Welfare History." *Journal of American History* 73 (September 1986): 407-433.
Chase, Arthur. *History of Ware, Massachusetts.* Cambridge, Eng.: Cambridge University Press, 1911.
Childs, Frances S. *French Refugee Life in the United States.* Baltimore: Johns Hopkins University Press, 1940.
Clark, Christopher. "The Household Economy, Market Exchange, and the Rise of Capitalism in the Connecticut Valley, 1800-1860." *Journal of Social History* 13 (Winter 1979): 169-190.
Clark, Peter. "The Migrant in Kentish Towns, 1580-1640." In Peter Clark and Paul Slack, eds., *Crisis and Order in English Towns, 1500-1700*, pp. 117-163. Toronto: University of Toronto Press, 1972.
Clement, Priscilla Ferguson. *Welfare and the Poor in the Nineteenth-Century City: Philadelphia, 1800-1850.* Rutherford, N.J.: Fairleigh Dickinson University Press, 1985.
Cole, Arthur H., and Walter B. Smith. *Fluctuations in American Business, 1790-1860.* Cambridge, Mass.: Harvard University Press, 1935.
Cott, Nancy F. *The Bonds of Womanhood: "Woman's Sphere" in New England, 1780-1835.* New Haven, Conn.: Yale University Press, 1977.
Countryman, Edward. *A People in Revolution: The American Revolution and Political Society in New York, 1760-1790.* Baltimore: Johns Hopkins University Press, 1981.
Cox, John. *Quakerism in the City of New York, 1657-1930.* New York: Privately printed, 1930.
Cray, Robert E., Jr. "White Welfare and Black Strategies: The Dynamics of Race and Poor Relief in Early New York, 1700-1825." *Slavery and Abolition* 7 (December 1986): 273-289.
Curry, Leonard P. *The Free Black in Urban America, 1800-1850: The Shadow of the Dream.* Chicago: University of Chicago Press, 1981.
Daniels, Bruce C. *The Connecticut Town: Growth and Development, 1635-1790.* Middletown, Conn.: Wesleyan University Press, 1979.
Darrock, A. Gordon. "Migrants in the Nineteenth Century: Fugitives or Families in Motion." *Journal of Family History* 6 (Fall 1981): 257-277.
De Jong, Gerald F. *The Dutch in America, 1609-1974.* Boston: Twayne Publishers, 1975.
Deutsche, Albert. "The Sick Poor in Colonial Times." *American Historical Review* 44 (April 1941): 560-579.
Devoe, Thomas F. *The Market Book.* 2 vols. New York: The Author, 1862.
Diamond, Beatrice. *An Episode in American Journalism: A History of*

SELECTED BIBLIOGRAPHY

David Frothingham and His Long Island Herald. Port Washington, N.Y.: Kennikat Press, 1964.

Dickinson, H. T. "The Poor Palatines and the Parties." *English Historical Review* 82 (July 1967): 464-485.

Disoway, Gabriel P. *The Earliest Churches of New York.* New York: J. G. Gregory, 1865.

Dolan, Jay. *The Immigrant Church: New York's Irish and German Catholics, 1815-1865.* Baltimore: Johns Hopkins University Press, 1975.

Dublin, Thomas. *Women at Work: The Formation of Work and Community in Lowell, Massachusetts, 1826-1860.* New York: Columbia University Press, 1979.

Erickson, Charlotte. *Invisible Immigrants: The Adaption of English and Scottish Immigrants in Nineteenth-Century America.* Coral Gables, Fla.: University of Miami Press, 1972.

Ernst, Robert. *Immigrant Life in New York City, 1825-1863.* New York: Columbia University Press, 1949.

Fairlie, John A. *Local Government in Counties, Towns, and Villages.* New York: Century Co., 1909.

Faragher, John Mack. *Sugar Creek and Life on the Illinois Prairie.* New Haven, Conn.: Yale University Press, 1986.

Flint, Martha B. *Long Island Before the Revolution.* Reprint ed. Port Washington, N.Y.: Ira J. Friedman, 1967.

Foster, Stephen. *Their Solitary Way: The Puritan Social Ethic in the First Century of Settlement in New England.* New Haven, Conn.: Yale University Press, 1971.

French, Alvah P., ed. *History of Westchester County.* 2 vols. New York: Lewis Historical Publishing Co., 1925.

Gabriel, Ralph H. *The Evolution of Long Island: A Study of Land and Sea.* New Haven, Conn.: Yale University Press, 1921.

Gardiner, David L. *Chronicles of the Town of Easthampton.* New York: Brown and Co., 1871.

Goodfriend, Joyce D. "Too Great a Mixture of Nations: The Development of New York City Society in the Seventeenth Century." Ph.D. diss., UCLA, 1975.

Greene, Evarts B., and Virginia D. Harrington. *American Population Before the Federal Census of 1790.* New York: Columbia University Press, 1932.

Grinstein, Hyman B. *The Rise of the Jewish Community of New York, 1654-1860.* Reprint ed. Philadelphia: Porcupine Press, 1976.

Gross, Robert. *The Minutemen and Their World.* New York: Hill and Wang, 1976.

Guernsey, R. S. *New York City and Vicinity During the War of 1812 to 1815.* 2 vols. New York: Charles L. Woodward, 1889.

SELECTED BIBLIOGRAPHY

Gutman, Herbert G. *Black Family in Slavery and Freedom, 1750-1925.* New York: Pantheon, 1976.

Hannon, Joan Underhill. "The Generosity of Antebellum Poor Relief." *Journal of Economic History* 44 (September 1984): 810-821.

———. "Poverty in the Antebellum Northeast: The View from the New York State Poor Relief Rolls." *Journal of Economic History* 44 (December 1984): 1007-1032.

Hansen, Marcus Lee. *The Atlantic Migration, 1607-1860.* Reprint ed. New York: Harper and Row, 1961.

Harlow, Alvin. *Old Bowery Days: The Chronicles of a Famous Street.* New York: D. Appleton and Co., 1941.

Heale, M. J. "From City Fathers to Social Critics: Humanitarianism and Government in New York, 1790-1860." *Journal of American History* 63 (June 1976): 21-41.

———. "Patterns of Benevolence: Charity and Morality in Rural and Urban New York, 1783-1830." *Societas* 3 (1973): 337-359.

Henretta, James A. "Economic Development and Social Structure in Colonial Boston." *William and Mary Quarterly* 22 (January 1965): 75-92.

———. "Families and Farms: Mentalité in Pre-Industrial America." *William and Mary Quarterly* 35 (January 1978): 3-32.

Christine L. Heyrman. "A Model of Christian Charity: The Rich and the Poor in New England, 1630-1730." Ph.D. diss, Yale University, 1977.

Hindus, Michael, and Scott-Smith, Daniel. "Premarital Pregnancy in America, 1640-1971: An Overview and Interpretation." *Journal of Interdisciplinary History* 4 (Spring 1975): 537-570.

Hirsh, Leo. "The Negro and New York, 1783-1865." *Journal of Negro History* 16 (October 1931): 384-436.

Hunt, Charles Havens. *The Life of Edward Livingston.* New York: D. Appleton and Co., 1864.

Jennings, Walter W. *The American Embargo, 1807-1808, with Particular Reference to Its Effects on Industry.* Iowa City: Iowa University Press, 1921.

Jensen, Joan M. *Loosening the Bonds: Mid-Atlantic Farm Women, 1750-1850.* New Haven, Conn.: Yale University Press, 1986.

Jeregan, Marcus W. *Laboring and Dependent Classes in Colonial America, 1607-1783.* Chicago: University of Chicago Press, 1931.

Johnson, H. J. M. *British Emigration Policy, 1815-1830: Shovelling Out Paupers.* New York: Oxford University Press, 1972.

Johnson, Paul E. *A Shopkeeper's Millennium: Society and Revivals in Rochester, New York, 1815-1837.* New York: Hill and Wang, 1978.

Jones, Douglas L. "The Strolling Poor: Transiency in Eighteenth-Century Massachusetts." *Journal of Social History* 8 (Spring 1975): 28-54.

———. *Village and Seaport: Migration and Society in Eighteenth-Century*

Massachusetts. Hanover, N.H., and New London, Conn.: University Press of New England, 1981.
Jordon, Winthrop. *White Over Black: American Attitudes Toward the Negro, 1550-1812.* Chapel Hill: Institute of Early American History and Culture, University of North Carolina Press, 1968.
Kammen, Michael. *Colonial New York: A History.* New York: Charles Scribner's Sons, 1975.
Kasson, John F. *Civilizing the Machine: Technology and Republican Values, 1776-1900.* Paperback ed. London: Penguin Books, 1979.
Katz, Michael B. *In the Shadow of the Poorhouse: A Social History of Welfare.* New York: Basic Books, 1986.
——— . *Poverty and Policy in American History.* New York: Academic Press, 1983.
Kemp, William W. *The Support of Schools in Colonial New York by the Society for the Propagation of the Gospel in Foreign Parts.* New York: Teacher's College, Columbia University Press, 1913.
Kerber, Linda K. *Women of the Republic: Intellect and Ideology in Revolutionary America.* Chapel Hill: Institute of Early American History and Culture, University of North Carolina Press, 1980.
Kessler-Harris, Alice. *Out to Work: A History of Wage-Earning Women in the United States.* New York: Oxford University Press, 1982.
Keyssar, Alexander. "Widowhood in Eighteenth-Century Massachusetts: A Problem in the History of the Family." *Perspectives in American History* 8 (1974): 83-117.
Kim, Sung Bok. *Landlord and Tenant in Colonial New York: Manorial Society, 1664-1775.* Chapel Hill: Institute of Early American History and Culture, University of North Carolina Press, 1978.
Klebaner, Benjamin J. "The Myth of Foreign Pauper Dumping." *Social Science Review* 35 (September 1961): 302-309.
——— . "Pauper Auctions: The New England Method of Poor Relief." *Essex Institute Historical Collections* 91 (April 1955): 195-210.
——— . *Public Poor Relief in America, 1790-1860.* New York: Arno Press, 1976.
——— . "State and Local Immigration Regulation in the United States Before 1882." *International Review of Social History* 3 (1958): 269-295.
Knights, Peter. *The Plain People of Boston, 1830-1860: A Study in City Growth.* New York: Oxford University Press, 1971.
Knittle, Walter Allen. *Early Eighteenth-Century Palatine Emigration.* Reprint ed. Baltimore: Genealogical Publishing Co., 1965.
Kross, Jessica. *The Evolution of an American Town: Newtown, New York, 1642-1775.* Philadelphia: Temple University Press, 1983.
Laslett, Peter. "The Bastardy Prone Sub-Society." In Peter Laslett, Karla

Oosterveen, and Richard M. Smith, eds., *Bastardy and Its Comparative History*, pp. 217-246. Cambridge, Mass.: Harvard University Press, 1980.

Lauber, Alman W. *Indian Slavery in Colonial Times Within the Present Limits of the United States*. New York: Columbia University Press, 1913.

Lee, Charles R. "Public Poor Relief and the Massachusetts Community, 1620-1715." *New England Quarterly* 55 (December 1982): 564-585.

Lee, Everett S. "A Theory of Migration." *Demography* 3 (1966): 47-57.

Lees, Lynn Hollen. *Exiles of Erin: Irish Migrants in Victorian London*. Ithaca, N.Y.: Cornell University Press, 1979.

Lemisch, Jesse. "Jack Tar in the Streets: Merchant Seamen in the Politics of Revolutionary America." *William and Mary Quarterly* 25 (July 1968): 371-407.

——. "Listening to the Inarticulate: William Widger's Dream and the Loyalties of American Revolutionary Seamen in British Prisons." *Journal of Social History* 2 (1969-1970): 1-27.

Lemon, James T. *The Best Poor Man's Country: A Geographic Study of Early Southeastern Pennsylvania*. Baltimore: Johns Hopkins University Press, 1972.

Lenehan, John J. "The Society of the Friendly Sons of St. Patrick for the City of New York." *Journal of the American Irish Historical Society* 8 (1909): 183-194.

Leonard, Eugenie Andress. *The Dear Bought Heritage*. Philadelphia: University of Pennsylvania Press, 1965.

Leonard, E. M. *The Early History of English Poor Relief*. Cambridge, Eng.: Cambridge University Press, 1900.

Litwack, Leon. *North of Slavery: The Negro in the Free States, 1790-1860*. Chicago: University of Chicago Press, 1961.

Lockridge, Kenneth. "Land, Population, and the Evolution of New England Society." *Past and Present* 39 (April 1968): 62-80.

Lustig, Mary Lou. *Robert Hunter, 1664-1734: New York Augustan Statesman*. Syracuse, N.Y.: Syracuse University Press, 1983.

Lydon, James G. *Pirates, Privateers, and Profits*, with an intro. by Richard B. Morris. Upper Saddle River, N.J.: Gregg Press, 1970.

Main, Jackson T. *Political Parties Before the Constitution*. Chapel Hill: Institute of Early American History and Culture, University of North Carolina Press, 1974.

——. *The Social Structure of Revolutionary America*. Princeton, N.J.: Princeton University Press, 1965.

——. *Society and Economy in Colonial Connecticut*. Princeton, N.J.: Princeton University Press, 1985.

——. "Standards of Living and the Life Cycle in Colonial Connecticut." *Journal of Economic History* 43 (March 1983): 159-165.

Marshall, Bernice. *Colonial Hempstead: Long Island Life Under the Dutch and English.* 2nd ed. Reprint ed. Port Washington, N.Y.: Ira J. Friedman, 1962.

McCoy, Drew R. *The Elusive Republic: Political Economy in Jeffersonian America.* Chapel Hill: Institute of Early American History and Culture, University of North Carolina Press, 1980.

McEntegart, Bryan J. "How Seventeenth-Century New York Cared for Its Poor." *Thought* 1 (March 1927): 588-612 and 2 (1927): 404-429.

McKee, Samuel. *Labor in Colonial New York.* Reprint ed. Port Washington, N.Y.: Ira J. Friedman, 1963.

McManis, Douglas A. *Colonial New England: A Historical Geography.* New York: Oxford University Press, 1966.

McManus, Edgar J. *A History of Negro Slavery in New York,* with a foreword by Richard B. Morris. Syracuse, N.Y.: Syracuse University Press, 1966.

Miller, Kirby A. *Emigrants and Exiles: Ireland and the Irish Exodus to North America.* New York: Oxford University Press, 1985.

Mohl, Raymond A. *Poverty in New York, 1783-1825.* New York: Oxford University Press, 1971.

Monkkonen, Eric H., ed. *Walking to Work: Tramps in America, 1790-1935.* Lincoln: University of Nebraska Press, 1984.

Montgomery, David. "The Working Classes of the Pre-Industrial City, 1780-1830." *Labor History* 9 (Winter 1968): 3-22.

Munsell, W. W. *History of Queens County,* New York: W. W. Munsell and Co., 1882.

Narrett, David E. "Preparation for Death and Provision for the Living: Notes on New York Wills (1665-1760). *New York History* 57 (October 1976): 417-437.

Nash, Gary. "Forging Freedom: The Emanicipation Experience in Northern Seaport Cities, 1775-1820. In Ira Berlin and Ronald Hoffman, eds., *Slavery and Freedom in the Age of the American Revolution,* pp. 3-48. Charlottesville: United States Capitol Historical Society, University Press of Virginia, 1983.

——. *The Urban Crucible: Social Change, Political Consciousness, and the Origins of the American Revolution.* Cambridge, Mass.: Harvard University Press, 1979.

——. "Urban Wealth and Poverty in Pre-Revolutionary America." *Journal of Interdisciplinary History* 6 (Spring 1976): 545-584.

Norton, Mary Beth. *Liberty's Daughters: The Revolutionary Experience of American Women, 1750-1800.* Boston: Little, Brown, and Co., 1980.

Oberly, James W. "Westward Who: Estimates of Native White Interstate Migration After the War of 1812." *Journal of Economic History* 46 (June 1986): 431-440.

Onderdonk, Henry, Jr. *The History of the First Reformed Dutch Church of Jamaica, Long Island.* Jamaica, N.Y.: The Consistory, 1884.

Perman, Daniel. "Organizations of the Free Negros in New York City, 1800-1820." *Journal of Negro History* 56 (July 1971): 181-197.

Pernicorn, Carol Gronemen. "The Bloody Ould Sixth: A Social Analysis of a New York City Working-Class Community in the Mid-Nineteenth Century." Ph.D. diss., University of Rochester, 1973.

Pessen, Edward. *Riches, Class, and Power Before the Civil War.* Lexington, Mass.: D. C. Heath, 1973.

Peterson, Arthur Everett. *New York as an Eighteenth-Century Municipality Prior to 1731.* New York: Longmans, Green, and Co., 1917.

Peyer, Jean B. "Jamaica, Long Island, 1656-1776: A Study of the Roots of American Urbanism." Ph.D. diss., CUNY, 1974.

Pomerantz, Sidney I. *New York, an American City, 1783-1803: A Study of Urban Life.* New York: Columbia University Press, 1938.

Poynter, J. R. *Society and Pauperism: English Ideas of Poor Relief, 1795-1834.* London: Routledge and Kegan Paul, 1969.

Pratt, John W. *Religion, Politics, and Diversity: The Church-State Theme in New York History.* Ithaca, N.Y.: Cornell University Press, 1967.

Price, Jacob M. "Economic Functions in the Growth of American Port Towns in the Eighteenth Century." *Perspectives in American History* 8 (1974): 123-188.

Prime, Nathaniel S. *A History of Long Island from Its First Settlement by Europeans to the Year 1845.* New York: Robert Carter, 1845.

Pruitt, Bettye Hobbs. "Self-Sufficiency and the Agricultural Economy of Eighteenth-Century Massachusetts." *William and Mary Quarterly* 41 (July 1984): 333-364.

Rezneck, Samuel. "The Depression of 1819-1822: A Social History." *American Historical Review* 39 (October 1933): 28-47.

Riker, James, Jr. *The Annals of Newtown in Queens County.* New York: D. Fanshaw, 1852.

Ritchie, Robert C. *The Duke's Province: A Study of New York Politics and Society, 1664-1691.* Chapel Hill: University of North Carolina Press, 1977.

Rock, Howard. *Artisans of the New Republic: The Tradesmen of New York City in the Age of Jefferson.* New York: New York University Press, 1979.

Rorabaugh, William J. *The Alcoholic Republic: An American Tradition.* New York: Oxford University Press, 1979.

—————. *The Craft Apprentice: From Franklin to the Machine Age in America.* New York: Oxford University Press, 1986.

Rosenwaite, Ira. *The Population History of New York City.* Syracuse, N.Y.: Syracuse University Press, 1972.

Ross, Peter. *A History of Long Island.* 3 vols. New York: Lewis Publishing Co., 1902.

Ross, Steven J. "Objects of Charity: Poor Relief, Poverty, and the Rise of the Almshouse in Early Eighteenth-Century New York City," pp. 1-56. Paper to be published in Conrad Wright and William Pencak, eds., *New Approaches to Colonial and Revolutionary New York.* Charlottesville: University Press of Virginia, 1988.

Rothman, David J. *The Discovery of the Asylum: Social Order and Disorder in the New Republic.* Boston: Little, Brown, and Co., 1971.

———, ed. *Poverty, U.S.A.* New York: Arno Press, 1971.

Rude, George. *The Crowd in History: A Study in Popular Disturbances in France and England, 1730-1848.* New York: John Wiley and Sons, 1964.

Ryan, Mary P. *Cradle of the Middle Class: The Family in Oneida County, New York, 1790-1860.* Cambridge, Eng.: Cambridge University Press, 1981.

Salinger, Sharon V. "Artisans, Journeymen, and the Transformation of Labor in Late Eighteenth-Century Philadelphia." *William and Mary Quarterly* 40 (January 1983): 62-84.

Sammis, Romanah. *Huntington-Babylon Town History.* Huntington, N.Y.: Huntington Historical Society, 1937.

Schaft, J. Thomas, ed. *The History of Westchester County.* 2 vols. Philadelphia: L. E. Preston and Co., 1886.

Schneider, David M. *The History of Public Welfare in New York State, 1609-1866.* Chicago: University of Chicago Press, 1938.

———. "The Patchwork of Relief in Provincial New York, 1664-1775." *Social Service Review* 12 (December 1938): 469-494.

Schumacher, Max. *The Northern Farmer and His Market During the Colonial Period.* New York: Arno Press, 1975.

Scott, Kenneth. "The Churchwardens and the Poor in New York City, 1693-1747." *New York Genealogical and Biographical Record* 99-102 (1968-1971): 157-164, 18-26, 141-147, 33-40, 164-173, 50-56, 150-156.

———. "The New York Slave Insurrection of 1712." *New York Historical Society Quarterly* 45 (January 1961): 43-74.

Scott, Kenneth, and Susan E. Klaffry. *A History of the Joseph Lloyd Manor House.* Setauket, N.Y.: Society for the Preservation of Long Island Antiquities, 1976.

Seybolt, Robert E. *Apprenticeship and Apprenticeship Education in Colonial New England and New York.* New York: Teacher's College, Columbia University Press, 1917.

Skeen, C. Edward. "'The Year Without a Summer': A Historical View." *Journal of the Early American Republic* 1 (Spring 1981): 51-67.

Smith, Billy G. "The Material Lives of Laboring Philadelphians, 1750-1800." *William and Mary Quarterly* 38 (April 1981): 163-202.

SELECTED BIBLIOGRAPHY   261

Smith, Thomas E. V. *The City of New York in the Year of Washington's Inauguration, 1789.* New York: Anson D. F. Randolph and Co., 1889.
Smith-Rosenberg, Caroll. *Religion and the Rise of the City: The New York City Mission Movement, 1812-1870.* Ithaca, N.Y.: Cornell University Press, 1971.
Stansell, Christine. *City of Women: Sex and Class in New York, 1789-1860.* New York: Alfred A. Knopf, 1986.
Strum, Harvey. "Foreign Policy and Long Island Politics, 1808-1815." *Long Island Forum* 48 (November 1985): 224-230.
Thernstrom, Stephen. *Poverty and Progress: Social Mobility in a Nineteenth-Century City.* Cambridge, Mass.: Harvard University Press, 1964.
Thompson, Benjamin F. *A History of Long Island.* 3 vols. 3rd ed. Reprint ed. Port Washington, N.Y.: Ira J. Friedman, 1962.
Thompson, E. P. "The Moral Economy of the English Crowd in the Eighteenth Century." *Past and Present* 50 (February 1971): 76-135.
Thompson, John H., ed. *Geography of New York State.* Syracuse, N.Y.: Syracuse University Press, 1966.
Trattner, Walter I. *From Poor Law to Welfare State: A History of Social Welfare in America.* New York: Free Press, 1974.
Tredwell, Daniel M. *Personal Reminiscences of Men and Things on Long Island.* 2 vols. Brooklyn, N.Y.: Charles A. Ditmas, 1912.
Turner, Charles W. *Annals of St. John's Church, Huntington.* Huntington, N.Y.: Stiles Printing House, 1895.
Valentine, David T. *History of the City of New York.* New York: G. P. Putnam and Co., 1853.
Watson, Alan D. "Public Poor Relief in Colonial North Carolina." *North Carolina Historical Review* 54 (October 1977): 347-366.
Webb, Anne Baxter. "On the Eve of Revolution: Northampton, Massachusetts, 1750-1775." Ph.D. diss., University of Minnesota, 1976.
White, Philip L. *Beekmantown, New York: Forest Frontier to Farm Community.* Austin: University of Texas Press, 1979.
Wiberly, Stephen E. "Four Cities: Public Poor Relief in Urban America." Ph.D. diss., Yale University, 1975.
Wilentz, Sean. *Chants Democratic: New York City and the Rise of the American Working Class, 1788-1850.* New York: Oxford University Press, 1984.
Wilkenfeld, Bruce M. "New York City Neighborhoods, 1730." *New York History* 57 (January 1976): 165-182.
———. "The Social and Economic Structure of the City of New York, 1695-1796." Ph.D. diss., Columbia University, 1973.
Withey, Lynne. *Urban Growth in Colonial Rhode Island: Newport and Providence in the Eighteenth Century.* Albany: SUNY Press, 1984.

Wolf, Stephanie G. *Urban Village: Population, Community, and Family Structure in Germantown, Pennsylvania, 1683-1800*. Princeton, N.J.: Princeton University Press, 1976.

Wolock, Nancy. *Women and the American Experience*. New York: Alfred A. Knopf, 1984.

Wood, Gordon. *The Creation of the American Republic, 1776-1787*. Chapel Hill: Institute of Early American History and Culture, University of North Carolina Press, 1969.

Woolsey, C. M. *The History of the Town of Marlborough, Ulster County*. Albany, N.Y.: J. B. Lyon, 1908.

Wright, Langdon G. "In Search of Peace and Harmony: New York Communities in the Seventeenth Century." *New York History* 61 (January 1980): 5-21.

Zilversmit, Arthur. *The First Emancipation: The Abolition of Slavery in the North*. Chicago: University of Chicago Press, 1967.

Zuckerman, Michael. *Peaceable Kingdoms: New England Towns in the Eighteenth Century*. New York: Alfred A. Knopf, 1970.

Index

Acadians, 89
Adrian, Robert, 176
Albany, 27, 154
Alexander, John K., 5
Allegheny County, 164
Allyn, 60
Almshouse, 36, 40-41, 45, 46, 47, 71-72, 79-80, 100-101, 102-103, 108; Bellevue Almshouse, 115, 117, 119-122. *See also* Bridewell; House of correction; Poorhouse
Almshouse Census, 79, 170, 173 Table 12, 174 Table 13, 178 Table 14, 181 Table 15
Almshouse Commissioners, 78-79, 81-83, 100
American Eagle, 130
American Revolution, 68, 75-76, 77, 97
Amos, Richard, 82
Anderson, Mary, 82
Andros, Edmund, 22
Angle, Anna Maria, 43
Angle, Christine, 43
Anglicans, 18, 54, 56-57, 77, 86, 91, 92, 144
Apprenticeship, 43, 71, 81-82, 89
Archdeacon, Thomas, 21, 29, 30
Arcularius, Philip, 108-109, 116
Armstrong, John, 80
Arthur, Widow, 61
Assistance Society, 117

Baker, William, 39
Baltimore, 122
Bancker Street, 190
Baptists, 18, 144
Barn Island, 29
Barrett, Richard, 55
Bartow, Rev. Mr., 54
Bedford, 16, 18, 50, 56, 63, 76-77, 97-98, 101, 113, 123, 126, 128-130, 132, 138

Bedlow Street, 116, 184
Bellomont, Lord, 24, 28, 33-34, 35
Benevolent Societies. *See names of individual societies*
Benson, James, 151
Blacks, 21, 61, 90, 95, 148, 166; black community, rural, 148-154; black community, urban, 188-192, 235 n. 36
Blake, Benjamin, 82
Bogard, Alexander, 185
Bonnis, William, 65
Boston, 22, 26, 30, 84, 116, 122, 187
Bradford, William, 43
Braudel, Fernand, 137
Bridewell, 74, 78, 100, 189
Bridge, Charles, 33
Brook, Betts, 58
Brookhaven, 13, 33, 53, 55, 58, 60, 62, 63, 84, 91, 97, 126, 138, 142, 147, 148, 149, 155, 157, 158, 162, 163
Brooklyn. *See* Kings County
Brown, Isaac, 91
Brush, Platt, 158
Bullivant, Benjamin, 30
Bunce, Thomas, 53
Burtis, James, 63
Butler, Jon, 29, 39

Canada, 163, 164
Carleton, Guy, 77
Carll, Annias, 149
Carll, Jesse, 149
Carll, John, 165
Caryn, Sarah, 52
Catholic Church, 177
Catholic Orphans Society, 177
Ceasar, 149
Chambers, Phebe, 63
Chappel, James, 54
Charity Committee, 193
Chichester, James, 59

263

INDEX

Chichester, Sarah, 59
Chipman, Samuel, 138
Church of England. *See* Anglicans
Clement, Priscilla E., 122
Climatic conditions, 125
Cobbett, William, 145, 173, 183
Coleman, William, 109
Coles, Peter, 107
Common Council, 19-20, 42, 44, 72, 79, 100, 105, 106, 116-117, 118, 188, 193
Contract system, 102, 127, 141-142
Coram, 97
Closback, John, 121
Conkling, Samuel, 156, 162
Connecticut, 32, 86, 98, 162, 164, 176, 183, 185, 186
Cook, Elijah, 149
Cooks, Eneas, 162
Cooper, James Fenimore, 147
Cornish, George, 165
Councel, Daniel, 58
Crevecoeur, Michael G. St. John, 3-4
Crown Hill, 153
Curry, Leonard, 149
Cuthing, Charles, 155

Davis, Phebe, 158
Davis, Thomas, 39
De Lancy, Stephen, 129
Delavall, Thomas, 29
Delavall, William, 29
Denton, Daniel, 9, 26
De Peyster, Abraham, 28, 40
Deschamp, Isaac, 29
Dewose, Thomas, 62
Discovery of the Asylum, 4
Dodge, Samuel, 107
Dongan, Thomas, 15, 20, 35
Drake, Benjamin, 61
Dublin, Thomas, 157
Duke's Laws, 36
Dunlop, William, 116
Dutch, 11, 20, 21, 28, 29, 30, 46
Dutch East Indies Company, 11
Dutchess County, 76, 90

Dutch Reformed Church, 18, 22, 36, 37, 38, 54, 91
Dutch West Indies Company, 11
Dwight, Timothy, 110, 126, 184
Dyer, Alexander, 185

East Chester, 9, 10, 16, 18, 32, 51, 55, 61, 63, 112, 142, 144, 145, 148, 153, 154
East George Street, 116
East Hampton, 13, 26, 27, 31, 50, 53, 55, 83, 84, 85, 94, 140
Economy: rural, 25-27, 83-85, 112-113; urban, 22-25, 44, 69, 74, 116-117, 170
Edows, David, 53
Elemes, James, 43
Ely, Ezra Stiles, 118, 168, 170, 182
Emancipation Act, 148
Embargo Act, 115, 117, 123, 193
Emmet, Thomas Addis, 176
English, 46, 75, 169, 174, 175, 177, 178
Erie Canal, 183
Europe, 88

Female Reform Society, 192
Ferris, Elijah, 149
Finch, John, 50
Flatbush, 12, 50
Fleet, Augustine, 149
Fleet, Gilbert, 148
Fleet, Peter, 148
Fleet, Samuel, 131
Fletcher, Benjamin, 15, 20, 23, 24, 37
Flowolling, Thomas, 56
Floyd, Richard, 33, 60
Flushing, 13, 16, 17, 29, 33, 125, 153, 156, 162
Forbes, Alexander, 72
Fowler, Widow, 153
Francis, William, 58
Free Peg, 91
French, 21, 28, 30, 169, 175, 178
Frenchmen's Benevolent Society, 178-179

INDEX

Friendly Sons of St. Patrick, 177
Frost, Fanny, 157
Furman, Richard, 109

General Society of Mechanics and Tradesmen, 108, 193
Germans, 169, 175, 177-178; Palatines, 42-43
Germantown, 98
Germany, 136
Gimberton, 62
Goodfriend, Joyce, 21
Gravesend, 12
Gray, Joseph, 62
Gray, Sarah, 62
Green, Jane, 81-82
Greenport, 155

Haff, Jeremiah, 162
Haight, Jonathan, 61
Hait, Guy William Augustine, 155
Hallek, Nancy, 157
Hammond, Benjamin, 150, 154
Hancock, Betsy, 184, 185
Hand, Silas, 61
Haply, Richard, 164
Harriot, James, 145-146
Harrison, 125, 160
Harrison, Widow, 151
Hearden, Elias, 151
Heathcote, Caleb, 19
Heathcote, George, 29
Hempstead, 13, 16, 17, 18, 26, 29, 50, 51, 56, 58, 60, 61, 63, 64, 86, 87, 89, 90, 91, 93, 94, 95, 101, 138, 147, 152, 154
Hempstead Plains, 26, 146, 160
Henretta, James, 4
Henry, John, 106
Hewlett, Divine, 131, 134, 152
Hewlett, Isaac, 156
Hewlett, Townsend, 152
Hilt, Samuel, 51
Hoit, Samuel, 55
Home relief. *See* Outdoor relief
Horton, Captain, 58
House of correction, 45, 72, 74

Huguenots, 16, 18, 20, 22, 29, 39
Hulse, Richard, 58
Humane Society, 118, 179
Humbleton, William, 39
Hunter, Robert, 43
Huntington, 13, 26, 35, 50, 53, 54, 61, 64, 65, 67, 86, 87, 91, 92, 93, 94, 111, 113, 123, 126, 127, 128, 130-133, 136, 140, 141, 142, 144, 148, 149, 150-152, 153, 155, 156-157, 162, 164, 165
Hurst, Widow, 63
Hutton, Johanna, 98
Hyde, Edward, Lord Cornbury, 27

Illegitimacy, 157-159, 182
Immigrants, 73-74, 88-89, 105, 159; poor immigrants, 170-180
Independent Reflector, 69, 73
Independents, 13
Indians, 13, 27, 90-91, 147-148
Institutional relief. *See* Almshouse; Poorhouse
Insinghart, Christopher, 52, 63
Irish, 105, 167, 169, 171-172, 174, 194
Islip, 98, 112, 123, 152, 162

Jackson, Johannah, 153
Jamaica, 13, 16, 17, 32, 54, 55, 56, 140
James, Duke of York, 14
Jay, John, 110, 129
Jay, William, 129-130, 134
Jefferson County, 163
Jews, 21, 28, 29, 30, 37, 38, 179-180
Jogues, Isaac, 11
Johnson, Benjamin, 155
Johnson, Ize, 147
Jones, Douglas L., 5, 65
Jones, John, 136
Jones, Platt, 162
Jones, Richard, 162
Jones, Tom, 63
Jones, William, 156

Kalm, Peter, 69

INDEX

Katz, Michael, 6, 79
Keepers, 57-63, 215 n. 60; rural, 60-62, 94-95; urban, 72-73
Kessler-Harris, Alice, 157
Ketcham, Nathaniel, 155
Kiersteed, Jacobus, 73
Kings County, 15, 154, 162, 182
Kissam, Justice, 58
Kit, Ruth, 154
Klebaner, Benjamin, 114
Knight, Sarah, 9-10, 23, 30
Knights, Peter, 137
Knowlton, Catherine, 52

Lambert, John, 117, 123
Lees, Lynn, 175
Leisler, Jacob, 8
Leisler's Rebellion, 9, 21
L'Homedine, Catherine, 158
Liberty Street, 153
Litwack, Leon, 149
Livingston, William, 73
Lloyd, Benjamin, 154
Lloyd Manor, 15
Lloyds, 26, 92, 151
Lloyd's Neck, 164, 165
Lodwick, Charles, 8, 9, 21
Lodwick, Francis, 9
London, 29
Longbottom, Joseph, 33
Long Island, 7, 9, 10, 13-14, 16, 32-33, 39, 50, 144, 147, 160, 165, 175
Lotts, Colonel, 76
Ludlow, Margaret, 157
Lutherans, 18, 22, 37
Lydia, 151, 159

McBride, Walter, 81
McCloon, Widow, 59
Mackie, James, 172
McKinn, William, 158
McNevins, William, 176
Main, Jackson T., 32
Mamaroneck, 9, 10, 16, 50
Manhattan. *See* New York City
Manors, 15

Marine Society, 193
Marlborough, 98
Martin, James, 155, 163-164, 166
Masey, Squaw, 91
Massachusetts, 5, 25, 65, 98
Mercein, Thomas, 119
Miller, David, 129
Miller, John, 17-18, 23, 30
Miller, Kirby, 175
Mills, Eanack, 146
Mills, Timothy, 158
Ministry Act, 37
Moger, Widow, 62
Mohl, Raymond A., 78, 106, 109, 192, 193, 227 n. 51
Mooney, William, 109
Moore, Benjamin, 58
Morrisson, David, 81
Mott, Jonah, 151
Mount Pleasant, 125, 126, 132, 138, 140
Mulatto. *See* Blacks
Mulatto, Phebe, 62

Napoleonic Wars, 117
Nash, Gary, 4, 5, 31, 44, 74, 150
Nero, 153
Newburgh, 98
New Castle, 101, 111, 126, 138, 140
New Jersey, 16, 39, 149, 162, 164, 176, 183, 186, 187
New London, 187
New Rochelle, 9, 10, 16, 17, 87, 126, 154
New York City, 6, 7, 8-9, 10-12, 15, 20, 21, 36, 64, 68, 70, 84, 100, 116, 154
New York Evening Post, 109, 116
New York Gazetteer, 75, 133
New York Mercury, 75
New York Society for the Prevention of Pauperism, 120
Nicolls, Catherine, 162
Nicolls, Richard, 15
Nicolls, Stephen, 164-165, 166
Nicols, Henry, 155
North Carolina, 64

Northampton, 98
North Castle, 50, 55, 101
North Hempstead, 101, 125, 140, 142, 149, 154, 162
North Kingston, 98
Nova Scotia, 175
Nutten Island, 42

Ogden, Stephen, 151
Ogdenbury, 163
Old Richard, 55
Orange County, 16
Outdoor relief, 36, 79, 102, 112, 118-119, 122, 192-194
Outsiders, 87-88
Overseers of the poor, 85
Oyster Bay, 13, 16, 50, 65, 98, 111, 125, 136, 137, 149, 151, 152, 154, 156, 157, 162

Panic of 1819, 115, 120, 124-125, 127, 142
Panic of 1837, 142
Parker, Francis, 60
Parks, Major, 76
Pauper auctions, 95-98, 102, 111, 113-114, 130, 230 n. 92
Peleg, 159
Pelham, 15
Pell, Thomas, 14
Pelletreau, John, 29
Pennsylvania, 39, 98, 164, 183, 186
Perth Amboy, 176
Pessen, Edward, 4
Philadelphia, 22, 39, 44, 116, 122, 185, 186, 187
Philipsburgh Manor, 17, 18, 54
Philipse, Frederick, 26
Pilots Charitable Society, 193
Pirates, 24
Plattsburgh, 163
Poor: badging of, 41-42; domestic, 180-187; foreign, 73-74, 105, 170-180; geographic mobility of, 159-166, 186-187, 230 n. 95; rural, 63-65, 134, 136-140, 143; urban, 47-50, 64, 69-70, 73-82

Poorhouse, 85, 94-98, 102, 111, 115, 125-127, 130-132, 142
Poor laws, 36-37, 39, 78, 90, 92-93, 121-122
Poor rates, 40, 44, 51, 74-75, 93-94, 123-125
Poor relief: rural, 50-65, 83, 85-98, 110-115, 123-134; urban, 37-46, 49-50, 70-72, 103, 107-109, 119-122. *See also* Almshouse; Bridewell; House of correction; Outdoor relief; Pauper auctions; Poorhouse; Private charity
Poor removal, 39-40, 54-56, 76, 144, 184-185
Population, 16-17, 20-21, 103-104, 143 Table 10, 148, 150-151, 172 Table 11, 190, 201, 202
Portico, 131-132
Presbyterians, 13, 91, 92
Prince, 136-137
Prince, Peter, 149
Private charity, 37-40, 53-54, 75, 117, 154, 177-179, 191-192
Provoost, Robert, 73
Pruitt, Bettye, 25
Public lottery, 103
Purdy, Captain Joshua, 95
Purdy, Samuel, 60
Purdy, Sarah, 61

Quakers, 13, 18, 38, 91, 144, 163
Queens, 6, 16, 17, 18, 25, 36, 50, 56, 63, 68, 76, 83, 87, 88, 100, 138, 182, 183

Raynor, Alexander, 155
Rebellion of 1798, 175, 176
Religion. *See names of individual denominations*
Rhode Island, 43, 98
Riggs, James, 165
Ritchie, Robert, 32, 33
Riverhead, 98, 155, 162
Robinson, Mary, 43
Robinson, Robert, 62
Rodriques, Isaac, 30

INDEX

Rogers, Elkhanah, 155
Rogers, James, 54
Rogers, John, 52, 55, 63
Rogers, Ned, 57
Rolph, Moses, 136
Romers, Peter, 42
Ross, Steven, 45, 47, 57, 97
Rothman, David J., 4, 5, 49, 59, 64, 98, 214 n. 53
Rotten Egg Club, 153
Rump, Hannah, 91
Rural laborers, 145-147, 155, 233 n. 24
Rural reformers, 128-134
Rural social change, 86-87, 144, 208 n. 41, 225 n. 32
Rye, 16, 17, 18, 27, 51, 55, 56, 58, 60, 61, 62, 63, 64, 83, 86, 87, 90, 91, 94, 95, 123, 125-126, 160

Sag Harbor, 83, 84, 123
St. Andrew Society, 75, 172
St. George Society, 75
St. John's Parish, 64
St. Lawrence County, 163
St. Paul's Parish, 64
Salem, 130
Samons, Jane, 62
Sampson, Enos, 154
Sanford, Bartlet, 164
Santon, Jerry, 154
Saratoga County, 163
Scarsdale, 15, 19, 56, 112, 160
Schellinx, Jacob, 53
Schnectady, 163
Scots. *See* English
Scott, Kenneth, 39
Scudder, Joseph, 165
Seaman, Jonathan, 193
Sebring, Frederick, 73
Sebring, John, 72-73
Shearith Israel, 38, 179
Shellfisheries, 87-88
Shute, Gilbert, 146
Silva, 147
Sixth ward, 104
Slattery, Mary, 62

Sloo, William, 78
Smith, Dorothy, 60
Smith, Elijah, 162
Smith, Jarvis, 164-165
Smith, Mary, 60
Smith-Rosenberg, Caroll, 192
Smithtown, 15, 33, 91, 98, 111, 123, 126, 127, 140, 154, 162, 164
Social structure: rural, 31-33, 109-110; urban, 28-31, 103-104
Soper, Thankful, 134
Southampton, 13, 16, 27, 33, 54, 84, 157, 162
South Carolina, 165
Southold, 13, 52, 55, 58, 63, 84, 85, 94, 111, 113, 124, 162
South Salem, 110, 126
Spafford, Horatio, 133
Squaw Deborah, 91
Standard, Thomas, 25
Stanerd, Martha, 50
Stanford, John, 121, 170, 191
Starr, Samuel, 154
Staten Island, 12
Still, Joseph, 161
Stiverson, John, 156-157, 159
Stratten, Stephen, 156
Strickland, William, 110
Stringham, Margaret, 51, 58
Strong, Benjamin, 187
Strong, Silas, 165
Stuyvesant, Peter, 12
Suffolk, 6, 16, 17, 25, 36, 37, 56, 68, 83, 88, 100, 110, 126-127, 138
Sword, Mary, 81, 82

Telford, Archibald, 163
Terry, Jeremiah, 155
Thaler, Henry, 136
Thernstrom, Stephen, 137
Thomas, John, 91
Thomas, Thomas, 82
Thompson, Samuel, 138
Thompson, William, 138
Thorn, Judge, 60
Thuilby, John, 161, 163, 166
Thurston, Widow, 61, 90

INDEX

Tice, 58
Tigney, George, 161
Tomkins, Susannah, 61
Tondor Jack, 90
Toney, 153
Tooker, John, 33
Tottin, Nathan, 165
Treaty of Hartford, 14
Trinity Church, 22, 26
Troy, 163
Truth, Sojournor, 161
Tubs, James, 146
Tuthill, Henry, 52
Tuthill, Thomas, 52

Udle, Doctor, 165
Ulster County, 76, 81, 98
Underwood, Henry, 60

Vail, Harvey, 165
Van Cortland, Jacobus, 28
Van Dyck, Isaac, 81
Van Nort, John, 155
Van Wyck, Abraham, 136
Van Zandt, Tobias, 72
Varnell, John, 59
Veal, Thomas, 63
Veil, Israel, 154
Vermont, 163
Vestrymen, 37, 49

Wall Street, 19
Ware, 98
War of 1812, 115, 120
Washington, George, 75-76
Watson, Allan, 64

Westchester County, 6, 7, 10, 13, 15, 17, 18, 25, 26, 28, 32, 36, 51, 56, 68, 76, 83, 88, 93, 100, 132, 138, 142, 144, 147, 182
Westchester Town, 18, 32, 33, 87
West Greenwich, 98
West Indies, 178
Wetmore, James, 27
Whaling, 27
White, Rebecca, 55-56
Whitehair, Sarah, 50
Whitehair, William, 58
White Plains, 16
Whitman, Isaiah, 149
Whitman, Jarvis, 149
Wiberly, Stephen, 47, 49
Wicks, Conkling, 162
Wicks, Dig, 154
Wilberforce Philanthropic Society, 191
Wilkes, John, 39
Wilkes, Widow, 61
Women, 54, 59, 61-64, 138-140, 153, 157-159, 185-188, 244 n. 62
Wood, Stephen, 82
Woodhull, Henry, 62
Workhouses, 34, 35, 86, 97-98
Working-class poor, 107-108
Worth, Sabrina, 157

Yates Report, 138-140
Yellow fever, 104-105
Young, Mary, 58

Zenger, John Peter, 43
Zilversmit, Michael, 86
Zuckerman, Michael, 86